Praise for *Ultimate Insiders*

The president's "bully pulpit" at the White House is commanded as much by the visual as the verbal. This new book significantly captures this truth in a wonderful collection of images that have shaped our nation's history, along with the personal stories of the artists who "did the snaps." A must for every student of White House history.

Mike McCurry, *White House Press Secretary to President Bill Clinton*

Ken Walsh has become one of America's great chroniclers of all things presidential. *Ultimate Insiders* is a marvelous look at the role White House photographers play in setting the tone and tenor of our times. Highly recommended!

Douglas Brinkley, *Rice University*

Remember the picture of Kennedy sheepishly walking away from Marilyn Monroe. Or of Reagan meeting Gorbachev. Or iconic shots of Obama's anguish in defeat and Trump's frustration with the swamp. The only people in the world close enough to touch the people in these photos are the presidential photographers, but we only see the back of their heads. In this book the consummate historian of the modern presidency, Ken Walsh, has given them all faces. Walsh's book describes and tells the stories of the characters, charmers, egos, and true believers who photograph the lives of our presidents. It's a great read.

Marlin Fitzwater, *White House Press Secretary to Presidents Ronald Reagan and George H.W. Bush*

Ken Walsh, veteran White House reporter, gives us a fascinating and well-written account of the presidential photographers who have chronicled our presidents. The book looks at the untold story of who these people have been and, in doing so, explicates the power and politics of images that have shaped every presidency in the modern era.

Julian E. Zelizer, *Princeton University*

More often than not, a single photograph can tell a story with more detail than a news article ever could. Ken Walsh expertly conveys this message, taking readers behind the curtain of the White House and into the most intimate moments of a president's time in office. He shows readers the important role of White House photographers and how our history is lost without them.

Dana Perino, *White House Press Secretary to President George W. Bush*

Ken Walsh captures the extraordinary "snapshots" that provide context and texture to a full view of our presidents. Well done!

Kenneth M. Duberstein, *White House Chief of Staff to President Ronald Reagan*

In *Ultimate Insiders*, Ken Walsh tells the story of one of the most exclusive clubs in photojournalism: personal photographers to the President of the United States. Behind-the-scenes stories and intimate portraits of the brilliant men and women in this club are preserved forever here . . . Ken Walsh's book is an affecting portrait of this work and the special people who have practiced it.

Neil Leifer, *Time, Inc.; Photographer and documentary filmmaker*

ULTIMATE INSIDERS

Virtually unknown to the public or historians, White House photographers have developed amazing access to the presidents of the United States over the past half-century. In this book, long-time White House correspondent Kenneth T. Walsh tells their stories, emphasizing observations about the presidents the photographers got to know so well along with other key figures close to those presidents—including the first ladies, members of Congress, and important world leaders.

This book shows how official White House photographers have morphed into ultimate insiders within the American presidency, allowed to observe and take pictures of nearly everything Chief Executives do related to their job. The "photogs" have often become close friends with the presidents they have served. Using these bonds of trust and their own powers of observation, they created fundamental impressions and public images of the presidents through the art of photography. Acting not only as image makers but as visual historians, they have built pictorial chronicles of the presidency—intimate narratives of America's leaders in public and private, showing how they dealt with everyday life as well as moments of great crisis and opportunity. From children playing in the Oval Office to decisions to send troops into harm's way, images created by White House photographers can make or break a presidential administration as well as define an era.

Kenneth T. Walsh has been White House correspondent for *U.S. News & World Report* since 1986. He writes a weekly column, "The Presidency," and a daily blog, "Ken Walsh's Washington," both for *U.S. News & World Report*. He is one of the longest-serving White House correspondents in history and is the former president of The White House Correspondents' Association.

ALSO BY KENNETH T. WALSH

Feeding the Beast: The White House Versus the Press

Ronald Reagan: Biography

Air Force One: A History of the Presidents and Their Planes

From Mount Vernon to Crawford: A History of the Presidents and Their Retreats

Family of Freedom: Presidents and African Americans in the White House

Prisoners of the White House: The Isolation of America's Presidents and the Crisis of Leadership

Celebrity in Chief: A History of the Presidents and the Culture of Stardom

ULTIMATE INSIDERS

WHITE HOUSE PHOTOGRAPHERS
AND HOW THEY SHAPE HISTORY

BY KENNETH T. WALSH

Nov. 8, 2017

To Jerry,

Great to meet you at the FDR library.

With all best wishes,

Ken Walsh

Routledge
Taylor & Francis Group

NEW YORK AND LONDON

Published 2018
by Routledge
711 Third Avenue, New York, NY 10017

and by Routledge
2 Park Square, Milton Park, Abingdon, Oxon, OX14 4RN

Routledge is an imprint of the Taylor & Francis Group, an informa business

© 2018 Taylor & Francis

Library of Congress Cataloging-in-Publication Data
A catalog record for this book has been requested

ISBN: 978-1-138-73760-0 (hbk)
ISBN: 978-1-315-10627-4 (ebk)

Typeset in ITC Galliard
by Apex CoVantage, LLC

Printed and bound in the United States of America by Sheridan

For Barclay and Gloria

CONTENTS

ABOUT THE AUTHOR

Kenneth T. Walsh has been White House correspondent for *U.S. News & World Report* since 1986. He writes a weekly column, "The Presidency," for usnews.com and is the author of a daily blog, "Ken Walsh's Washington," also for *U.S. News & World Report*. He is one of the longest-serving White House correspondents in history. This is his eighth book. Walsh is the former president of the White House Correspondents' Association, and he has won the most prestigious awards for White House coverage. Walsh also has served as an adjunct professorial lecturer at American University's School of Communication in Washington, D.C. He appears frequently on television and radio, and gives many speeches around the country and abroad. He and his wife Barclay live in Bethesda, Maryland, and Shady Side, Maryland. They have two children, Jean and Chris.

NOTE TO READERS

Many of the photographs in this book have been rarely if ever seen by the public. One of my goals was to offer fresh visual insights into the presidents as real human beings, not just more glimpses of the cardboard cutouts so often presented to the public by their media handlers. I have found that the best White House staff photographers and the best photojournalists often captured the essence of the presidents, but most of their pictures are stored unseen by the public in the presidential libraries and the National Archives, or kept in their personal collections. I looked at thousands of photographs in researching this book, and it is the fresh images that I wanted to show above all.

Readers are certainly more familiar with some pictures of the presidents than others, such as the images of Lyndon B. Johnson's famous swearing-in ceremony aboard *Air Force One* after John F. Kennedy was assassinated on November 22, 1963. This photo sent a message to the world that the U.S. Constitution endured and that Johnson would continue Kennedy's legacy. I have included it because of its historic nature.

But most of the photographs in this book will be unfamiliar to the reader. My hope is that they reveal something new and different about the presidents and their times.

Kenneth T. Walsh
Bethesda, Maryland

ACKNOWLEDGEMENTS

First of all, my profound thanks go to Barclay Walsh, my wife and life partner. Barclay researched key parts of this book and was a strong advocate of the project from the beginning. Her wise counsel, editing skills, and creativity and her help in finding the photographs used in this volume were invaluable.

My gratitude goes to the many people who provided insights and shaped my thinking about this project, including White House staff photographers Ralph Alswang, Susan Biddle, Eric Draper, Sharon Farmer, David Kennerly, Bob McNeely, and David Valdez, all of whom I interviewed for *Ultimate Insiders*. Thanks also to Charlie Archambault, Doug Brinkley, Don Carleton, Bob Dallek, Frank Donatelli, Ken Duberstein, Al Felzenberg, Marlin Fitzwater, Geoff Garin, Jim Gerstenzang, Stan Greenberg, Frank Luntz, Mike McCurry, Sean Spicer, and Doug Wead.

A special note of thanks goes to Doug Mills, the excellent White House photographer for the *New York Times*. Over the years, he has been a strong advocate for the news photographers in dealing with the White House and he provided many insights to me regarding the relationship between the "stills" and the West Wing.

The staff and resources at the presidential libraries were indispensable, as was the Briscoe Center for American History at the University of Texas in Austin, which has become an important repository for presidential photography. And there have been many insightful articles, interviews, and books that enlightened me while writing *Ultimate Insiders*. They are listed in the "Selected Reading."

I wish I'd had the opportunity to talk to some of the other past icons of White House photography such as the late Yoichi Okamoto, Jacques Lowe, George Tames, Stanley Tretick, and Mike Evans. But their passing has not deprived us of their personal observations as recorded in interviews, oral histories, panel discussions and in some cases books they have written. And of course, their pictures live on.

I also found that my 31 years of covering the White House for *U.S. News & World Report* gave me many insights into the life and work of the White House photographers, both those who serve the president on his staff and those who are photojournalists independent of the White House. They are a very special cadre of talented people, and I'm privileged to have known them. I'd like to acknowledge in particular the professional excellence and personal friendship provided by the photographers at *U.S. News & World Report* over the years, such as Charlie Archambault, Chick Harrity, and Jim LoScalzo.

Thanks to Jennifer Knerr, my editor at Routledge, who provided constant encouragement and guidance along the way. She is simply the best.

Kenneth T. Walsh
Bethesda, Maryland

INTRODUCTION
INSIDER VIEWS AND INSIDER INSIGHTS

For more than half a century, presidential photographers have been vital fixtures inside the White House. Virtually unknown to the public, they developed amazing access to America's presidents, using it to carefully observe the nation's leaders and get to know them better than virtually anyone else outside of the first families. Just as important, they played a key role in shaping the images of the presidents and visually chronicling their lives. Veteran photojournalist Cornell Capra said being a presidential photographer is "like sitting on God's left arm."[1] He was right.

This book tells the photographers' extraordinary story. It is fascinating in its own right, and also provides portraits of America's presidents as seen through the eyes and the lenses of these ultimate insiders at the White House. In fundamental ways, official photographers have morphed into presidential anthropologists who are allowed to watch, listen, and document visually nearly everything that chief executives do related to their jobs. Sometimes the photographers are privy to the most profound personal moments, the emotional highs and lows, and the key decisions involving war and peace. Most of the official photographers' pictures—millions of them—were never released to the public and are stored in the presidential libraries. Many are now being published in this book as part of a very special insiders' history of the presidency.

"The White House photographer, more than almost anyone else on the president's staff, has virtually unfettered access to the Oval Office and to the president's every activity, from his travels abroad to his most sensitive meetings in the Situation Room," said Howard Baker, Ronald Reagan's former White House chief of staff (and an amateur photographer who would frequently tote his own camera and snap pictures at presidential events). "The presidential photographic archives, then, are a far more thorough record of presidential activity than any other source."[2]

This book brings together the story of the White House staff photographers for the first time. It offers a new and insightful look at the presidents and the history of the past half century starting in 1961 when John F. Kennedy created the position of official presidential photographer by assigning military cameraman Cecil Stoughton to the job. Kennedy also worked with and hired some of the best private photographers of his era to supplement Stoughton's work.

The president's official photographer has two jobs: First, to record the president at official events such as the seemingly endless series of greetings, receptions, and meetings with foreign leaders, members of Congress and other officials and guests at the White House and wherever the chief executive might be. This might not be exciting or elevating, but effective presidents and their staffs know it is essential to a successful White House operation. Such photos are often treasured by the people who receive them (free of charge), and they are placed in prominent positions in countless homes and offices around the country. (As a White House correspondent for more than 30 years, I have many of these photos framed and on the walls of my study at home.)

Second, to document for history the presidency as an institution and presidents as individuals. This is the task that White House photographers value the most and what animates them day after day. As eyewitnesses to history—captured with their ever-present cameras—they are the consummate storytellers about life and work at the White House.[3]

Even Richard Nixon, no friend of photographers for most of his presidency and reluctant to give them much access, still recognized that his own chief photographer Ollie Atkins had a distinct role to play. Nixon has noted that Atkins' "eye and his camera lens penetrated the superficial 'news value' of an event, and captured its deeper human dimension. That is why I asked Ollie to head the White House photographic office. As a friend, he has been with us in the good times and the bad times. As a craftsman, he did more than just take pictures of events and individuals;

in effect, he wrote with photographs the intimate, inside story of the Presidential years."[4] This is what every presidential photographer aims to do.

Ari Fleischer, former White House press secretary for President George W. Bush, observed: "There's a political element to make the President look strong, decisive, in charge. Unless it's for humor, you'll never see any White House release pictures that make the President look bad."[5]

Certainly the White House won't intentionally release negative pictures, but it does happen. Bush endured harsh criticism when the White House released a photo of him looking out the window of *Air Force One*, the presidential jet, at the disaster caused by Hurricane Katrina along the Gulf Coast in 2005 (after Fleischer had left the administration). White House officials thought the image would be positive, showing Bush displaying empathy for the victims. But the photo had the opposite effect, impressing on people that Bush viewed the human tragedy and weak government response from the sky and didn't get an on-the-ground view until later. He seemed out of touch, too distant from the suffering below.

But Fleischer's overall point about what can amount to visual public relations is correct. Don Carleton, director of the Briscoe Center for American History at the University of Texas in Austin, says the photographers essentially are PR people. "These are official photographers and they're serving at the discretion of the president," Carleton told me. "Their whole raison d'etre is making the president look good. The ones who are honest will admit that's what they do." Nevertheless, Carleton recognizes the historical importance of their work. And the center is accumulating the archives of both White House staff photographers and news photographers—collectively known as "shooters"—over many years.[6]

Even if a presidential photographer is mostly a PR man, the work still has enormous value. "It shows us how the president wants to look; it shows the administration and the culture and how they ran the presidency," Carleton said.[7]

During my three decades covering the White House for *U.S. News & World Report*, I developed enormous respect for the White House staff photographers and, although their access has been much less, for the news photographers. One thing I've learned is that the best photographers are by nature keen observers. They have the president in their viewfinders and framed by their cameras as much as they can: That's their job. Their close-up lenses reveal the presidents' moods, whether they are out of sorts or feeling upbeat and whether they are weary or sick. They are experts on the individuals who have occupied the nation's highest office.

"The men [and, more recently, women] in the photographic press corps have strong feelings about the President they cover," wrote Ollie Atkins, a news photographer for Curtis Publishing Co., in a 1967 magazine article before he started working for President Nixon in 1969. "Best loved of all the Presidents in my lifetime was President Harry Truman. President Truman genuinely liked news photographers. He was most obliging in obeying their commands and even ordered balky visitors to cooperate in setting up the scene when they ignored the photographers' requests."

"Least liked of the Presidents," Atkins wrote contemporaneously, "is Lyndon Baines Johnson. Like most other people, the photographers do not really understand President Johnson. They rebel at his many restrictions which prevent photographs from being taken at all, or made only from the [left] side of his face, or not clicked from behind him, or not made while he is eating, or seldom allowed when he is speaking—and nearly always improperly lighted."

"President John F. Kennedy was vain about his image, almost as much as Mr. Johnson is, and he allowed the great advantage of exclusive photographic coverage to favored photographers. But, most press photographers liked him. Mr. Kennedy had his unreasonable restrictions, too—the photographers' vehicles in motorcades were always back several cars in the Presidential motorcades and advance arrangements were often forgotten. When the photographers' motorcade vehicle was a dozen cars back in the motorcade, that prevented the photographers from seeing or photographing the President at all times. It is the reason that no professional pictures were made of President Kennedy's assassination. However, Mr. Kennedy was completely casual in the presence of cameras of all types. He disliked posed and set-up pictures. This suited the photographers for they preferred the un-posed action too."[8]

Atkins also wrote that the news photographers were sometimes unruly and disheveled but were very serious about their work and some were "true artists" seeking to make prize-winning photos. These observations are still true today, more than 50 years later.

*   *   *

HISTORIANS DEBATE the issue of which president was the first to be photographed, and they make the distinction between the first to be photographed at all and the first to be photographed while in office.

Some of the images have been lost over the years, making the debate even more difficult to resolve. It's certainly true that one of the first photos of a president in office was taken in 1846 of President James Polk and his cabinet. It was suggested by First Lady Sarah Polk, who was interested in what was at that time the novelty of photography.[9] This shows how long there has been a White House focus on creating images of the nation's top leader.

Seven of the 44 individuals who were president of the United States were never photographed—George Washington, John Adams, Thomas Jefferson, James Madison, James Monroe, Martin Van Buren, and John Tyler. At least two were photographed using an early technique called the daguerreotype, but it happened after they left office: Andrew Jackson and John Quincy Adams.[10]

"Before the advent of photography, presidents were obliged to sit for long hours over many days to have their portraits painted in oil by the likes of Gilbert Stuart, renowned for his likenesses of George Washington, Thomas Jefferson and James Madison," writes historian Douglas Brinkley. "However, no matter how skilled the artist, photographer Ansel Adams had a point when he said, 'Not everybody trusts paintings but people believe photographs.' The [perceived] truthfulness of moments captured on film is all the more compelling when the subjects are historical figures, as in the well-known daguerreotype of Polk with Dolley Madison, widow of the fourth president. Taken [in the late 1840s] by [photographer Mathew] Brady, the stark image remains a national treasure as a visual link across time between the War of 1812 and the just-ended Mexican American War."[11]

As Brinkley notes, "the formal, stiffly posed presidential portraits of the 19th century became less compelling to the public as the novelty of photography wore off. By the 1880s, the appearance of photographs in newspapers and magazines was commonplace; to command notice an image now had to *look* interesting. This became easier to accomplish after 1888, when the Eastman Company of Rochester, N.Y., introduced photographic roll film that allowed for shots in quicker succession and the handheld Kodak camera that freed subjects from the formal studio."[12]

*   *   *

AMONG THE PRESIDENTS who were photographed, there are many examples of how they tried to manipulate their images through visuals, which will be described throughout this book.

Presidential historian Robert Dallek told me that "in this age of visual attention," presidents have been eager to make themselves look as good as possible for the public and use the media to promote themselves and their agendas. Modern-day presidents believe that projecting favorable images can mean votes in the next election, Dallek adds, so they are constantly trying to enhance themselves through photography.[13]

In conducting my research and reviewing thousands of photos of presidents, it struck me how smart some of them were to give photographers close access, and then release photos of interesting or compelling scenes. It clearly enhanced their images.

Theodore Roosevelt was a pioneer in visual self-promotion. Prior to his becoming president in 1901, he received enormous publicity by distributing photos to the newspapers of him in a flashy uniform, posing with his troops as commander of a cavalry unit known as the Rough Riders during the Spanish American War. This strengthened his reputation as a war hero because people could visualize it through the pictures.

As president, he would play to the cameras with dramatic hand and arm gestures and dynamic, theatrical poses when he gave speeches, such as addressing crowds from the back of trains. He was nicknamed "a steam engine in trousers."[14]

* * *

THREE DECADES LATER, there was another key moment for presidential photography. It came when Abbie Rowe, a federal employee working on a public road project in the Washington, D.C., area, saw First Lady Eleanor Roosevelt riding a horse nearby and took her picture. She saw the resulting image and arranged for Rowe to take pictures full-time for the National Park Service. In 1941, he was assigned to photograph President Franklin D. Roosevelt, Eleanor's husband, although his access was far more limited than what White House photographers have had in recent years.[15]

Rowe was the first photographer to document a president's official life, emphasizing major speeches and announcements, ceremonies, and visits from foreign leaders and ambassadors. Rowe welcomed the White House rule not to take pictures of the president in a wheelchair or being carried from one place to another, such as into and out of vehicles. Rowe was disabled from polio, as Roosevelt was, although in a relatively mild way, and he sympathized with his boss's desire not to appear vulnerable.[16] Rowe kept his photo job for many years, although his talents were largely wasted. During the Kennedy administration, his role was mostly to take official pictures and add them to scrapbooks, which also included news clippings. The scrapbooks were given to the president periodically as a private memento of White House life.[17]

John F. Kennedy and Franklin Roosevelt shared a keen sensitivity to public perceptions. "They were intensely mindful of their image and their appearance," says historian Dallek.[18] Kennedy allowed the widespread distribution of behind-the-scenes pictures of him with his lovely wife and endearing children to create the image of a family man, and Roosevelt liked to pose grinning with his cigarette holder gripped in his teeth in what became a widely familiar image of him as an optimistic and jaunty leader. "The whole image was to be robust and healthy," even though toward the end of Roosevelt's life the image was false, Dallek says. FDR suffered from severe heart disease, which eventually killed him in 1945.

In contrast, Richard Nixon disliked still photography and distrusted the people who ran network television, branding them liberal elitists who were smitten by Kennedy and would never give Nixon fair treatment. Jimmy Carter also neglected personal photography, considering it frivolous and not valuable in running the presidency. As a result, Carter and Nixon were far behind the flow. It is difficult to find many charming, historic or behind-the-scenes photographs of them that might have softened their images.

* * *

CECIL STOUGHTON is a wonderful case study of the important role of the chief White House photographer. Stoughton took many of the iconic pictures of Kennedy with his wife and children that built JFK's reputation as a family man, which was vital to his image, even though Kennedy was a womanizer. Stoughton also took the famous photo of LBJ being sworn in as president aboard *Air Force One* after Kennedy was assassinated in Dallas in November 1963.

* * *

BARACK OBAMA's emphasis on photography was strengthened by the arrival of easy-to-use digital cameras and greatly facilitated by other forms of modern technology, especially social media such as Flickr and Facebook and the White House website. These have allowed the dissemination of presidential images to millions more people than ever. Pete Souza, Obama's chief photographer, has been a pioneer in promoting

Obama's image as a strong leader and likeable family man, and he circulated his photos farther and wider than ever before. Souza also added the extensive use of video to the White House public-relations repertoire. He hired former college film instructor Arun Chaudhary as the White House videographer, rather than using only still photography.

Obama was an eager participant in Souza's aggressive promotion, and was proud of his own celebrity. He said in May 2016, as his presidency was winding down: "One thing you have to keep in mind is that I'm probably the most recorded, filmed and photographed person in history up to now, because I'm the first president who came along in the digital age."[19]

The eleven chief White House staff photographers over the years, in addition to Stoughton and Souza, were Yoichi Okamoto, who worked for Lyndon Johnson and is considered one of the absolute best, a man who helped to define the mission of presidential photography in terms of illustrating the life of the person in power; Ollie Atkins, the White House photographer for Richard Nixon; David Kennerly, who worked for Gerald Ford; Michael Evans, for Ronald Reagan; David Valdez, for George H.W. Bush; Bob McNeely and Sharon Farmer, for Bill Clinton, and Eric Draper for George W. Bush, and, most recently, Shealah Craighead for Donald Trump.

This book will tell their stories, with the larger goal of shedding light on the presidents themselves.

*   *   *

WHAT MAKES a good White House photographer? Access is all-important. And those who have held the position often managed to develop enough trust to gain admission to the most important and the most private moments of a presidency, such as when a chief executive was dealing with defeat or a crisis. In some cases the best and most revealing photographs were taken in the inner sanctums of the White House, such as the Oval Office, the Situation Room, the East Wing residence, or aboard *Air Force One*, the president's iconic plane, or on the road in the United States and abroad. And getting into those places at the right moment is key.

"This job is all about access and trust and if you have both of those you're going to make interesting, historic pictures, and I think I have both of those," Souza said.[20] In a 2011 interview, Souza explained: "My forte is being able to develop relationships where my subjects trust me. My continuing coverage of the Reagans long after I was an official White

House photographer [for President Reagan] is an example of my ability to build lasting relationships that earn me trust and access."[21]

"All photojournalists have the same dream: to be the only photographer with complete access at a historically significant event," said Bob McNeely, President Bill Clinton's official White House photographer and former director of White House photographic operations. "I had the opportunity to live that dream every day for five-and-a-half years." McNeely sought "to make a photographic record of the Clinton presidency—within the White House and beyond. I worked to make a record that would enable historians of the future to gain a deeper understanding of the office and the man who occupied it at the end of the 20th century."

"My basic approach was to photograph everything that I could from every angle possible. After years of photographing political figures, the White House and the presidency, I learned that an on-the-spot judgment about an image's importance doesn't necessarily hold true over time. If you are thinking too hard about the meaning of each picture in the heat of moment, you probably missed the shot. I often only discovered a photograph's importance many months later, when I went back and looked at it with a fresh eye and historical perspective. So I just tried to get it all."[22]

David Kennerly, who worked for President Ford, said it's vital to connect with the first lady. He noted that he and Okamoto before him had access "upstairs and downstairs" at the White House. "Upstairs [a reference to the White House residence in the East Wing] is the first lady's domain," Kennerly said. "You know, if you don't get along with both of them [the president and first lady], you can't go into the family quarters because that's the first lady's empire. And a lot of these White House photographers haven't been able to just do that with impunity. I was one of them who could."[23]

But White House shooters quickly realize that they also must form bonds of trust and alliances with key presidential aides. The most valuable are the gate keepers who are closest to the president and know the boss's schedule minute to minute and can most accurately assess his mood and how willing he might be to allow photography. These include Secret Service agents, who understand the logistics as well as anyone in the government. And the information flow works both ways. Sometimes a photographer will make his or her unused pictures available to the service so agents can scour crowds, rope lines, or receptions for people they suspect might be a threat or to identify situations that might turn dangerous and should be avoided.

Other people who are indispensable to the photographers are the White House chief of staff, the White House director of operations, the president's personal assistant known in recent years as the "body man," the president's scheduler, the White House press secretary, and the White House trip director.

Souza became an expert on the folkways of the Obama presidency. He understood Obama as an individual, knowing when to slip into a meeting or capture the president during private time, and when to leave him alone. Obama described him as "part of the family."[24]

"The only restrictions are really trying to let him have some privacy," Souza said during Obama's second term. "So if he's in a holding room and there's not really much going on, I'll probably step out. Last week, he was in a holding room and there was a nice picture of him with Senator Brown from Ohio. You know, that was sort of a nice situation, so I stay in for those kinds of things. But if he's just hanging out, or is eating lunch, you know, I just step outside the room."[25]

The best White House photographers develop a keen sense about when to absent themselves. After taking a few pictures to record a meeting, a good shooter will sometimes realize that the president wants to be left alone with the guest or guests and the photographer will slip out of the room. It's uncomfortable for everyone if the president has to ask the shooter to leave, so the photographers are very sensitive to the times their presence isn't wanted.

Clearly, a big part of the job is discretion, and it's vital that the photographers don't reveal what they see and hear unless the president wants them to, at least while a president is still in office.

"It's amazing how much you can be involved in a situation without affecting it," says McNeely, the Clinton photographer "You know, you think, oh, I gotta stay back here against the wall of the room because otherwise I'm going to be in the middle of the picture. Well, it's not true. You can get out there and get close, and make good pictures and it's such an intense moment in what they're dealing with that they'll pretty much ignore you."[26]

"Most of our work isn't seen immediately," McNeely says. "A lot of our imagery is made for history" and kept in the National Archives and the presidential libraries for historians to explore later. And of course the photographers do release some of their most compelling images immediately if the events or decisions that are illustrated are import-ant or interesting enough. To generate maximum interest in his work, McNeely shot mostly in black-and-white because he considered those images more dramatic and interesting than color shots.[27]

One of the reasons for Okamoto's amazing access was his ability to remain unobtrusive. Johnson insisted on full control over the images that Oke and his photo staff released to the media and the public. And LBJ, eager to look as good as his predecessor John F. Kennedy, wanted to sign off on the release of each photograph. But LBJ did give Oke remarkable entrée.

Since Okamoto, it hasn't been the president but mostly key aides, such as his White House chief of staff, press secretary, or communica-tions director, who have filtered the photos and decided which ones should be released.

What the best staff photographers want is to be ignored while they are doing their jobs. They want to record history as it occurs, and don't want to be snapping pictures only of staged moments. So they attempt to develop a sort of invisibility, born of trust. They become so much a part of the White House scene that, like the desk in the Oval Office or the portrait of Theodore Roosevelt in the Roosevelt Room, no one even notices their presence. That's the best approach for any White House photographer.

But the routine can be tedious. Most of the work is not historic or exciting but service-oriented. "Actually the meat and potatoes of what we do is hand out pictures," said Alice Gabriner, the official White House photo editor and deputy director of the photo office under President Obama. "Each time the president shakes a hand, that picture gets sent to the person he's meeting with and that happens every single day, and there are a lot of pictures." The office reviewed an average of 400 to 1,000 greeting shots out of a total of 8,000 to 20,000 photos a week, and sometimes many more with the year-end holidays. Christmas always is an especially busy time because the president and first lady attend so many parties and receptions at which they shake hundreds, sometimes thousands, of hands per day.[28]

*　*　*

IT'S VERY HELPFUL for the camera people to have a member of the first family as an amateur photographer. They become natural allies. Frances Cleveland, Grace Coolidge, and Jackie Kennedy were among several first ladies who liked to take pictures, creating an affinity with the professionals.

Sometimes presidential children such as Susan Ford shared the same interest. She learned about picture-taking from David Kennerly, her father's personal photographer, and studied photography at the University of Kansas. Margaret Truman was a shutterbug, prompting her father Harry to joke, "It's not enough that my homely countenance is at the mercy of the press—I have to have a photographer in the family?"[29]

*   *   *

THE VISUAL HISTORIANS at the White House generally agree with the conclusion I reached as a correspondent who has closely observed presidents for 31 years: it takes a high degree of emotional maturity and flexibility to do the best job as president because the range of activities is so vast. Arun Chaudhary, who served as President Obama's White House videographer during his first term, wrote: "One of the most underappreciated parts . . . is the vast emotional intelligence required to shift between different frequencies for different events, day out and day in, as the schedule veers wildly from a press conference to a major national disaster to a state dinner. When, after the transition, I joined the White House photo department as the official videographer, I grew accustomed to capturing all the dramatic transitions of a president's day. One minute, I'd be filming a tearful embrace between POTUS [President of the United States] and a shooting victim's family member in the oval office; the next I'd be helping Samantha Tubman, deputy Social Secretary, pep up a drooping sports team unused to standing for hours in suits. When my footage of the Obama Presidency becomes public by law, as all film and photos of the president do, I believe people will be surprised by the sheer volume of these shifts in the president's schedule."[30]

Chaudhary, a former college film instructor, added: "Our leaders need to keep up an authentic core. This is not something Lee Strasberg can teach you. Our very best actors, to say nothing of politicians, would be unable to sustain that much false emotion. Americans seem to, again and again, send individuals to the White House who are capable of projecting authentic personalities."

*   *   *

A DISTINCT IMAGE emerges of each president as revealed through the lenses of the chief photographers and in the shooters' personal observations.

John F. Kennedy came across as a charming and suave aristocrat who understood the importance of image. He did everything he could to build his public persona as a modern leader of vigor and intelligence and a family man who was close to his children and to portray his wife Jacqueline as a lovely and accomplished patron of the arts and a devoted wife and mother. These perceptions turned out to be true, although in his private life Kennedy was a womanizer and had many physical ailments that he hid from the public.

Lyndon B. Johnson emerged as the paradigm of the politician with a towering ego, willing to berate and belittle even his closest aides to get his way. He was eager to use his dominant personality to win congressional approval for his massive agenda and keep support for his hated commitment to the Vietnam war. He went too far and couldn't rein himself in.

Richard Nixon was a loner who was insecure in many ways and was plagued by his own distrust even of people around him at the White House, including his photographers. He was brilliant and worked very hard. But he was limited in his relationships and his ability to connect with the public by his insular and resentful personality.

Gerald Ford was another self-effacing Midwesterner who came to the presidency under very unusual circumstances when Nixon resigned amid the Watergate scandal. Ford, then vice president, succeeded him in office and was never elected in his own right. Ford was a talented legislator, having spent a career in the House of Representatives, and was devoted to openness after the cloistered Nixon approach. But he couldn't shake off the connection to his despised predecessor and lost his bid for election in 1976.

Jimmy Carter, former governor of Georgia, was idealistic, which impressed many Americans, but also very stubborn, which was a big vulnerability because he alienated so many people with his inflexibility and self-righteousness.

Ronald Reagan was a celebrity president, having been a movie and television star. He was difficult to get to know because he held back parts of himself and revealed them only to his wife Nancy. But he was a brilliant communicator and pioneered many methods of White House public relations that are still used today.

George H.W. Bush was bred to wield power. He was the son of Senator Prescott Bush (R-Conn.) and imbued with the tradition of noblesse oblige. He had served as a U.S. representative from Texas, U.S. ambassador to the United Nations, chairman of the Republican National

Committee, U.S. envoy to the People's Republic of China, director of central intelligence, and vice-president. He was an expert on foreign policy but was unable to come up with economic and domestic policies that Americans would accept. In person, he was a considerate and engaging individual who couldn't convey his best qualities to the country. He lost his bid for reelection to Bill Clinton in 1992.

Clinton was energized by people and loved attention. He could connect easily with virtually anyone and became a political celebrity through the force of his personality and his willingness and ability to dominate the media. He endured widespread ridicule when he was impeached for lying under oath about his improper relationship with a former White House intern. But the Senate declined to remove him from office and his celebrity-driven popularity rebounded.

George W. Bush was very engaging in person but was not a good communicator and had difficulty explaining his policies, especially the need for war against Iraq and the U.S. occupation of that country. He said dictator Saddam Hussein possessed weapons of mass destruction, using this allegation as a prime reason for going to war, but WMDs were never found. Bush served two terms as he waged a global war on terrorism, but his popularity plummeted toward the end of his presidency amid opposition to his war policies and a severe economic downturn.

Barack Obama was another true celebrity president, able to dominate mainstream media and the rising social media. He was an eager participant in popular culture, and his photographers led the way in image-making by releasing more photos and videos to more places than any of his predecessors, ranging from the White House website to Twitter, Facebook and Flickr, a website for sharing photographs. Obama took seriously the fact that he was the first African American president and he tried to be a role model for everyone.

Donald Trump, like LBJ before him, wants to control everything. As a billionaire businessman who never held public office before winning the White House in 2016, he is obsessed with perfecting his personal brand as the ultimate dealmaker and success story, partly by making frequent use of Twitter. For many years he has sought to control even the smallest details of his image. He prefers to be known as the scowling, angry leader who rarely shows a kinder, gentler side. The effectiveness of his approach will be tested severely as he settles into the presidency.

All this and much more will be discussed in later chapters of this book.

Notes

1. Geraldine Baum, "Eyewitness to History," *Los Angeles Times*, Sept. 9, 1990, p. E1. Cornell Capra covered President John F. Kennedy for *Life* magazine and later became director of the International Center of Photography.

2. Pete Souza, *Images of Greatness: An Intimate Look at the Presidency of Ronald Reagan*, Chicago: Triumph Books, 2004, p. vi.

3. See "White House Photographers," panel discussion at the Lyndon Baines Johnson Presidential Library, Austin, Texas, Jan 20, 2010, www.c-span.org/video/? 291502-1/white-house-photographers.

4. Ollie Atkins, *The White House Years: Triumph and Tragedy*, Chicago: Playboy Press, 1977, p. v.

5. Olivier Laurent, "What We can Learn from Behind-the-Scenes Photos of Dick Cheney on 9/11," *Time*, July 28, 2015, www.time.com/3975126/dick-cheney-9-11-photos.

6. Don Carleton, interview with author, Apr. 25, 2016.

7. Ibid.

8. Ollie Atkins, "Photographing the President," *U.S. Camera World Annual 1968*, New York: U.S. Camera Publishing Corp., 1967, pp. 7–8.

9. John Bredar, *The President's Photographer: Fifty Years Inside the Oval Office*. Washington, D.C.: National Geographic Society, 2010, pp. 37, 39; see also Megan Garber, "The Oldest Known Photographs of a U.S. President," *The Atlantic*, Feb. 5, 2013.

10. Bredar, *The President's Photographer*, pp. 43, 40–41.

11. Robert McNeely, *The Clinton Years: The Photographs of Robert McNeely*. New York: Callaway, 2000, pp. 22–23.

12. Ibid., p. 23.

13. Robert Dallek, interview with author, July 17, 2016.

14. NcNeely, *The Clinton Years*, p. 23.

15. Sarah Laskow, "How One Photographer Finally Convinced a President to Give Him Full Access," *Atlas Obscura Newsletter*, May 4, 2016, p. 1.

16. Ibid.

17. Barbara J. Coleman, oral history interview JFK #2, Oct. 24, 1969, pp. 40–41, John F. Kennedy Library Oral History Program, www.jfklibrary.org/Asset-Viewer/ Archives/JFKOH-BJC-02.aspx.

18. Dallek, interview with author, Mar. 31, 2016.

19. Philip Galanes, "The Role of a Lifetime," *New York Times: Sunday Styles*, May 8, 2016, p. 1.

20. Bredar, *The President's Photographer*, p. 120.

21. "Time for Your Closeup, Mr. President: Pete Souza Gains Access by Building Trust," *Imaging Info*, Jan. 12, 2011, www.imaginginfo.com/online/printer.jsp?id=2781.

This interview took place after Souza worked for Reagan but prior to his joining the Obama White House as chief photographer in January 2009.

22. McNeely, *The Clinton Years*, p. 243.

23. James Estrin, "Photographing the White House from the Inside," *New York Times*, Dec. 10, 2013, https://lens.blogs.nytimes.com/2013/12/10/photographing-the-white-house-from-the-inside/?_r=2.

24. Bredar, *The President's Photographer*, p. 82.

25. Ibid., p. 76.

26. Ibid., p. 86.

27. Comments by Bob McNeely, "White House Photographers."

28. Bredar, *The President's Photographer*, p. 103.

29. Carl Sferrazza Anthony, *America's First Families: An Inside View of 200 Years of Private Life in the White House*, New York: Touchstone, 2000, pp. 339–340.

30. Arun Chaudhary, "I was with President Obama when He First Visited George W. Bush," *New Republic*, Nov. 22, 2013, p. 1.

CHAPTER ONE
HOW LINCOLN AND FDR SET THE PACE, AND HOW THEIR SUCCESSORS WROTE THEIR OWN RULES

Abraham Lincoln understood the importance of image, and he was the first president to use photography to enhance his reputation. An important moment came when he gave a speech at New York's Cooper Union, an academy in Manhattan, on February 27, 1860. Lincoln scholar Harold Holzer writes that it transformed Lincoln "from a relatively obscure Illinois favorite son into a viable national contender for his party's presidential nomination."[1] He won that nomination three months later and was elected president six months after that.

Lincoln realized that his speech to this influential audience could affect his chances to win the presidency, so he prepared it carefully, as a summary of his stand against slavery and his defense of the Union.[2] He would use this address as the basis for many other speeches across the country.[3]

"As if to illustrate his metamorphosis," Holzer adds, "the Cooper Union appearance also inspired the most important single visual record of Lincoln's, or perhaps any, American presidential campaign: an image-transforming Mathew Brady photograph. Its later proliferation and reproduction in prints, medallions, broadsides, and banners said perhaps as much to create a 'new' Abraham Lincoln as did the Cooper Union address itself."[4]

Lincoln had allowed photographs to be taken before, but he wanted this one to be special because it would be what amounted to his official presidential campaign image. So he went to Brady, the most celebrated photographer of his day, and sat for a picture at Brady's Bleecker Street gallery in New York on February 27, a few hours before his Cooper Union speech. He hoped both the speech and the photograph would add to his celebrity. They did, but getting the right photograph was a challenge.

Lincoln, 51, arrived looking haggard, and his clothes seemed too small. A friend conceded that his appearance was less than appealing because he had "a large mole on his right cheek and an uncommonly prominent Adam's apple on his throat."[5]

Assessing his subject, Brady hit upon a brilliant idea. He would photograph this homely man standing up, at a distance, rather than doing the customary head shot, to emphasize his impressive height of six-foot-four. Brady posed him with a false pillar in the background, a table piled with books and Lincoln lightly touching the top volume with his left hand, to suggest erudition. This technique diverted attention away from Lincoln's rough-hewn facial features and his ill-fitting clothes.[6] Brady also pulled up Lincoln's collar to make Lincoln's neck look shorter and to give him a more dignified appearance.[7] This prompted a mild rebuke from his subject. "I see you want to shorten my neck," Lincoln said, but he went along with the adjustment.[8]

Afterward, Brady retouched the photo, removing the dark circles around Lincoln's eyes and blurring the deep lines in his face. He came up with an image of someone who appeared to be a strong, serious, determined leader.

In May, after Lincoln won the Republican presidential nomination, Brady decided to distribute the photograph as widely as he could. He was hoping to add to his own notoriety as well as Lincoln's.

The photo was circulated very widely, and it introduced the man known as "the rail-splitter" to the electorate not as the country bumpkin portrayed by his critics but as a sophisticated and confident individual. At one point, Brady produced and sold a large number of 3-by-4-inch cards containing his original photograph in order to meet public demand for images of the Republican candidate. Such "cartes de visite" were becoming popular at this time, bearing images not only of political figures but of other famous people and celebrities, akin to the baseball cards of the twentieth century. Lincoln later credited the distribution of the photo along with texts of his Cooper Union speech as having won the election for him.[9]

The photo showed Lincoln clean-shaven, but he grew a beard shortly before his election in November. The president posed in Brady's Washington studio for another portrait, this time featuring his whiskers, taken by Brady associate Alexander Gardner, who would later take other pictures of the president.[10] Enterprising printmakers doctored Brady's original photograph, adding facial hair, so the first image lived on for years.[11]

Lincoln went on to pioneer the use of photography by political figures.

"During his lifetime, Lincoln was the subject of more than 130 photographs, more than virtually any other person of his generation," writes author Richard Lowry. "About half of these were taken during the four and a half years between his nomination as the Republican presidential candidate and his death. Clearly Lincoln understood the new medium—photography had become commercially viable only in the early 1840s—as an emerging force in politics, capable of bringing the face of the president to the electorate with unprecedented objectivity and variety."[12] Many of these photographs were taken by Gardner, who brilliantly documented the Civil War and the overall Lincoln presidency. Eventually, Lincoln's visage became "the most recognizable face in the country, but also the face of the nation," Lowry writes.[13]

* * *

GARDNER AND LINCOLN first met at the gallery and studio of Mathew Brady in Washington, D.C., on Sunday, February 24, 1861. Gardner at this point had worked for Brady for nearly five years, first in Brady's New York galley and then, for three years, as manager of Brady's Washington operation. When Brady was commissioned to supply a photo of Lincoln for *Harper's Weekly*, he accepted the job, got Lincoln's agreement, and assigned Gardner to take the pictures. Brady was at his main office in New York when the photo session occurred, so Gardner, a burly immigrant from Scotland, was on his own.

The photos were not among Lincoln's best. The president-elect was understandably preoccupied during the session. The southern states had begun to secede from the Union and war was looming. Lincoln said little and seemed disinterested in the whole process. Gardner took 14 images, whereupon Lincoln abruptly left the studio to manage the crisis at hand. The pictures were undistinguished and captured Lincoln looking at the floor, stolid and bored. The artist who rendered the engraving for

Harper's Weekly did some primitive photo-shopping to define Lincoln's cheeks and add roundness to his face, giving him more of a contemplative look than the unretouched photos.[14]

But Lincoln's attitude about official photographs gradually changed. He returned to his belief, manifested at Cooper Union, that image was important and he needed to have more impressive pictures taken than the lackluster ones from February 1861.

During the next four years, Lincoln posed for nearly 70 photographs, most of them in studios but on some occasions at important venues, such as battlefields. "He would come to understand photography as one of the crucial media of office—not in the way presidents today understand media as an arena for controlling a 'message' . . . but as that space that humanized him for the public," Lowry wrote. "He would present himself variously as commander in chief, as a citizen, as the leader of a democratic republic, and as a 'careworn' face of the Union, embodying the harrowing grief and resolve he shared with those who elected him. In the end, photographs were for Lincoln in all senses of the word political. They proved effective tools in the rough-and-tumble of partisanship, sectional loyalty, and power-mongering. But they also offered the president's craggy face and long, gangly body as a symbolic image of the body politic and the ideals of democracy and equality on which it was founded."[15]

Sometimes photographers find entrée to presidents through their families—a tactic that also goes back to Lincoln. Henry F. Warren, a photographer from Waltham, Massachusetts, got several pictures of the president on March 6, 1865, two days after his second inauguration, by cozying up to a family member. These were among the last photos taken of Lincoln before he was fatally shot on April 14, 1865. Warren learned that Tad Lincoln, the president's young son, rode his pony, accompanied by a military orderly, nearly every afternoon at 3:00. Warren sought out Tad at his riding spot outside the White House one afternoon, took several photos of him, and gave Tad the prints the next day. Tad was delighted, and Warren immediately made a bold suggestion. "Now, bring out your father and I will make a picture of him for you," Warren said. Tad ran inside and came out with the president, who brought a chair to sit in for a portrait. Warren made three photographs. After Lincoln's assassination, thousands of copies of one of them, a close-up, were sold to grieving Americans across the country.[16]

One other photograph stands out: Gardner's image of Lincoln in the spring of 1865, just before his assassination. Lincoln is a frail, gaunt figure staring into the distance, smiling faintly as if a passing thought had brightened the moment but exhausted by the burdens of leading the Union through four years of carnage and suffering.

*   *   *

IT TOOK many years for other presidents to effectively advance from the first political use of photography by Lincoln. The process was incremental. The story of the presidents was told by the working press, and to some extent by official government photographers from the U.S. Army Signal Corps, the National Park Service, and the U.S. Navy.

As the technology of photography improved and began to replace engraving as a form of public portraiture, several star photographer-promoters led the way. One of these was a German immigrant named Gotthelf Pach who, with his brothers, started out after the Civil War as itinerant portrait photographers in New York and New Jersey. While working their way through Tom's River, New Jersey, in 1868 with a mobile dark room on a horse-drawn wagon, the brothers encountered soon-to-be President Ulysses Grant sitting on a porch with two friends. Impressed with the pictures they saw, Grant began a long friendship with Pach and often posed for him, sometimes with his family, for the remainder of his life. Pach was the Annie Leibowitz of his time, photographing many posed celebrities and other personalities, as well as Presidents Grover Cleveland, James Garfield, Theodore Roosevelt (starting as a child), and Calvin Coolidge. Pach's firm initiated the dry-plate method of image developing, and also made advances in "flashlight picture taking," a dangerous enterprise with frequently explosive results.[17]

By 1888, during the era of Cleveland and his fascinating young wife Frankie, cameras had become widely available, and photography was being taken up as a hobby by many Americans. Early etiquette rules on picture taking had not been established, and one brazen cameraman was thrown off the White House grounds by a presidential aide; his box camera and tripod were confiscated. The man was warned that shooting pictures of public buildings, and especially the White House, was a serious offense. "My dear boy," the aide said, "if we took no steps to prevent it, there would be a double file of amateur photographers encircling the White House from morning until night, every one of them ready to take a snap shot at Mrs. Cleveland should she venture to show her head. We really can't allow it, you know."[18]

The aide had a point. Grover and Frankie Folsom Cleveland were a celebrity couple, married in the White House, and Grover, 49, was old enough to be the father of his 21-year-old bride, causing a sensation. People lined the streets to get a glimpse of the lovely and talented first lady, and many presumably wanted to take her picture, as did the newspapers of the time. Allowing photographers to wait for her on the White House grounds would have been a real problem for her privacy and security.

In contrast, some presidents were interested in calling attention to themselves through photography. Several allowed their picture to be taken in memorable scenes to soften their images, such as Calvin Coolidge posing in a Native American feather headdress, and Theodore Roosevelt standing proudly in what became Yosemite National Park in California to underscore his commitment to preserving federal lands for posterity.

TR had an up-and-down relationship with the media, as has become common for presidents over the years, and he was eager to control his image and his family's image as much as possible—another common trait in presidents.

During TR's administration, Kodak "Brownie" cameras added to the photography craze. Designed for young boys and girls, the cameras cost one dollar each, and sometimes were available on sale as cheaply as 80 cents. Teddy Roosevelt encountered one of these "Kodakers" on the steps of church one Sunday in 1901, and gave the teenage boy a thorough scolding, after ordering a policeman to block the shot. "You shall not take pictures on the steps of a church if I can help it," he fumed. Furthermore, the newspapers reported: "The police hereafter will arrest anyone attempting to take a picture of the President at short range or in such a way as to annoy him."[19] Indeed, in a rare candid Kodak shot of Roosevelt from 1903, he looked quite annoyed at the intrusion

A local newspaper photographer once snapped pictures of Alice Roosevelt, TR's daughter, as she placed bets at a race track outside Washington, D.C., in 1904, the year TR was running for a full term as president. The photographer offered the pictures for sale to various major newspapers. White House officials found out about it and asked the newspapers not to publish the photos because they "might be embarrassing to the president." These officials also complained to the photographer who owned the negatives. The pressure worked—the photographer retracted his sales offer and kept the negatives to himself. And Alice was sent by her father to the family home in New York until the racing season ended.[20]

But TR could also be very accessible personally, using his gregariousness to his advantage in cultivating the media. During a nationwide tour in the spring of 1903, the president allowed many newspaper reporters and photographers to travel with him on a special train. He frequently let them dine with him at his table, and this created a camaraderie between them that helped TR win favorable coverage.[21]

It was under Teddy Roosevelt that an enterprising studio photographer named Barnett McFee Clinedinst first saw commercial possibilities in the photogenic chief executive. Clinedinst was the son of an early photographic innovator, once the proprietor of a circus, and a popular portrait photographer for social Washington. His adoption of cutting-edge stop-motion camera equipment allowed him to capture TR jumping his Kentucky saddle-horse over fences, walls, and hedges, a project with which the ebullient Roosevelt enthusiastically cooperated.

Clinedinst recorded many White House interiors, including Alice's bedroom, and pioneered photo-shopping by assembling composite portraits of Roosevelt with members of his cabinet on horseback, or in other groupings which may never have taken place. By some accounts, Clinedinst was also a portrait photographer for Presidents William McKinley, William Howard Taft, and Woodrow Wilson.[22]

It would have been in a studio like Clinedinst's that passers-by could first pose with a lifesize cardboard cutout of the president—something that still occurs today.

*   *   *

FRANKLIN D. ROOSEVELT, TR's distant cousin, was a pacesetter in using imagery to promote himself even before he became president.

In 1928, Roosevelt was elected governor of New York, despite being unable to use his legs, which had been paralyzed from polio since he was in his late thirties. He earlier had served as assistant secretary of the Navy and generated favorable publicity in that role. By the time he became president, he had vast experience in manipulating the media for his own purposes.

"Roosevelt's relationship with the press began long before March 4, 1933 [when he took office as president]," writes journalism professor Betty Houchin Winfield. "His media roots were deep, based on his own personal interest in the media and his press interactions during a twenty-two-year political history. These pre-inaugural press experiences laid the groundwork for his early days in the presidency and set the tone for his subsequent media relationship."

"Franklin Delano Roosevelt, born into an aristocratic well-to-do, upstate New York family, had the benefits of an education at Groton, Harvard, and Columbia Law School and travel in Europe," Winfield adds. "He was not to be intimidated by corporate opulence or wealthy media owners. Much like many turn-of-the-century progressives . . . FDR had a sense of responsibility—a noblesse oblige, inherited from his parents, developed by Endicott Peabody at Groton, and influenced by his cousin, President Theodore Roosevelt."[23]

Running for governor of New York, he admitted that he had contracted polio years earlier but said the paralysis in his legs wouldn't slow him down as a leader, and people believed him. "When Roosevelt focused attention on the state's problems, the audience forgot his legs," Winfield says. "His energetic stumping throughout the state served to convince journalists and audiences alike that he was in magnificent health. Although it sometimes took him as long as five minutes to walk painfully to a platform and once he had to be carried up a fire escape and in through a back window, he appeared unruffled. His spectacular display of physical endurance endowed him with media celebrity status. However, he would have to keep proving his physical ability again and again."[24]

FDR tried to limit pictures showing his disability, which he felt made him look weak and vulnerable. He was largely successful in his media management. On November 6, 1928, arriving at his hometown Hyde Park, New York town hall to vote for himself as governor, several newspaper and newsreel photographers were prepared to take his picture emerging from the car. He waved them off, insisting that there be no pictures of him struggling to get out of the vehicle and adjusting the braces on his legs. The photographers agreed, as they would later agree not to take pictures of President Roosevelt in situations that showed his handicap.[25]

At this time, photography was growing in importance in American journalism. The first illustrated rotogravure sections began to appear in newspapers in 1914. Presidents were increasingly the focus of the newspapers' and magazines' photographic attention, and these publications used more and more pictures through the 1920s and 1930s. The importance of White House photography was illustrated by the formation of the White House Photographers Association in 1921 as the lensmen banded together to obtain greater access. The illustration-filled *Life* and *Look* magazines were established, emphasizing their weekly pictorials. The Associated Press pioneered use of a wire photo service which gave newspapers the option of using pictures much more quickly and easily than ever.

"Roosevelt took great care to control his pictorial image," Winfield writes. "With new flash attachments, new miniature cameras with wide-angle lenses and fast shutters, and prepackaged daylight-loading 35 mm. cartridges, photographers had a greater ability to take candid snapshots. At the same time, newspapers began printing more pictures. With the introduction of the Associated Press Wirephoto Service in late 1934, any AP-affiliated newspaper could immediately receive and publish pictures from across the country."

"The White House News Photographers Association had existed for a decade, but it took on a new life during the Roosevelt era. Because Roosevelt loved the dramatic and the unusual, he gave the photographers something newsworthy to shoot. FDR's informality and ever-changing facial expressions sharply contrasted to the stoic and deadpan Herbert Hoover [FDR's predecessor]. Photographers, both still and newsreel, went on his inspection tours, his many trips to Hyde Park and Warm Springs, and his travels to the Pacific and the Panama Canal. Franklin D. Roosevelt's image sometimes dominated the Sunday rotogravure section of the newspapers as well as the front pages."[26]

At the White House, Press Secretary Steve Early, following FDR's wishes, refused to allow photographs to be taken without permission, and there was a prohibition against any pictures showing the president's physical handicap. Early allowed pictures only for ceremonial occasions, speeches, group portraits, and other carefully staged events.[27]

Occasionally, the system broke down. President Roosevelt became probably the first president to be photographed unaware at work. In 1935, a young *Time* magazine photographer named Thomas D. McAvoy, toting a tiny and innovative new camera, caught an unsuspecting FDR at his desk, while other news photographers were setting up and taking down their ponderous equipment. Thirteen of these "candids" appeared in *Time* shortly thereafter, with the observation: "Although informal photographs of Franklin D. Roosevelt are common, un-posed shots showing the natural play of his expression are rare."[28] But this break with protocol was very unusual.

Despite McAvoy's intrusion and an occasional mini-rebellion, nearly all the rules imposed by FDR and his staff were accepted by the photographers, and the camera operators for the newsreels agreed, too. One was a ban on photos showing the president in pain or discomfort. Un-posed or candid pictures were not allowed at the White House without special permission. No photos were permitted beyond the public areas of the White House. The living quarters were off limits.[29]

Early set precise limits on how close the photographers could be to the president. Usually it was a minimum of 12 feet but the distance grew to 30 feet when the president was speaking to large groups. Early said he didn't want potential assassins to get too close, but PR was also on his mind. He wanted to limit the effect of blinding photo flashes, which bothered Roosevelt greatly, and provide open space around the president to lend more drama to the visuals.[30]

Early even set strict rules for covering the president at his Hyde Park estate during the 1940 reelection campaign, a move designed to make Roosevelt look happy and relaxed and cultivate positive feelings about him. Early issued these detailed instructions to the newspaper photographers and their handlers on the White House staff, and they amounted to forerunners of the news management techniques and stagecraft of today. "If the President will get in his car and go out to the stables," Early wrote, "have them lead a riding horse or two up to him so that he can be petting them while he is photographed." Also encouraged were "pictures of the President's little cubbyhole office; pictures of the President with any of the children that may be there; with his mother; with Mrs. Roosevelt; around the fireplace; on the porch; out in the yard."[31]

On one occasion when the news photographers went too far, Early was furious and clamped down on them aggressively. The photographers had taken pictures of FDR as he took off his spectacles and rubbed his eyes, after being bothered by flash bulbs during a session to mark his birthday. The captions used to explain the moment were distortions, Early said. One read, "Thinking over the Farm Problem," a reference to his embattled agricultural agenda. Early immediately imposed a rule that the photographers could snap their shots only when Early specifically said to proceed. This was aimed at forcing the photographers to focus only on what the president wanted.[32]

White House officials insisted on a conspiracy of silence or omission among news reporters and photographers to create the illusion that FDR was not as disabled as he really was.

Millions of Americans probably realized FDR suffered from polio—there were occasional newspaper or magazine stories about it—but they didn't realize his legs were paralyzed. For his part, Roosevelt didn't want to show vulnerability or weakness. Specifically, he didn't want to be seen in a wheelchair or using crutches or, worst of all in his mind, seen being lifted by his bodyguards from one place to another such as onto or off a stage, a car, or a speaker's platform. On rare occasions, some photographers rebelled, but overall the extent of media cooperation was remarkable as the photographers willingly became part of the White House public-relations operation.

Pictures of FDR's disabled legs or reminders of his affliction, including his crutches and wheelchair, were rarely published, although he was sometimes pictured with a cane. When FDR took a bad spill that left him lying full-length on the ramp of a speakers' platform at the 1936 Democratic National Convention in Philadelphia, "not a single picture or cartoon was published," Winfield reports. "In fact, there was no public mention of the incident, even though many people knew and many photographers were around the president."[33]

*   *   *

FROM THE PHOTOGRAPHERS' perspective, such collusion was justified as a way to get more access. "In 1933," White House photographer George Tames of the *New York Times* wrote in a memoir, "when Roosevelt first came into the White House, Steve Early, his press secretary, called in all the regular photographers for a conference, a number in the neighborhood of twenty-five. He told them that he had a request from the president of the United States. If the president's friends, the photographers, would refrain from photographing him while he was being carried or in any other situation that showed how incapacitated he was, Early said, then Roosevelt in turn would make himself available for picture taking more than any other president in the history of the United States."

"The deal was struck, and the conspiracy of silence began, but of course it turned out to be a one-sided deal. Roosevelt became less and less available, and every time in a very controlled situation. Still, the photographers kept their end of the bargain and, however tempted, made no pictures of him being carried or wheeled in his chair. The president's request was now the rule."[34]

Tames added: "I have heard that only two pictures were made of Roosevelt being carried, even though about 150 photographers shot him in and around the White House, and about twenty-five photographers from the agencies were regularly assigned there during Roosevelt's twelve and a half years as president. Neither of the two photographs ever ran—because of the extreme pressure exerted by the White House, which minimized the opportunities for such pictures, and because of an unwritten rule against making any such picture."[35]

Tames admitted he "became part of that great conspiracy to conceal from the general public the true physical condition of the president of the United States."[36]

Tames also wrote in his memoir: "In late 1944, while covering a small meeting at the White House, I looked through my long lens and observed that the president appeared very enfeebled. At a point when one of the other speakers was holding the stage, his mind seemed to drift off and his jaw slackened a bit. I came back to my office shocked by what I had observed." He also noticed that FDR was losing too much weight. Tames felt the president was dying.[37] He was correct. FDR suffered a fatal stroke in April 1945.

The media's conspiracy of silence under FDR underscored the close relationship and affection that the news photographers enjoyed with the president during the era of Franklin Roosevelt and Harry Truman, who succeeded to the presidency after FDR died.

Perhaps it was a patriotic feeling, a desire to support the commander in chief during very difficult times, or a wish to curry favor, or simply a matter of positive chemistry, but the photographers in those days felt close to the presidents, and did what they could to help them.

*   *   *

THE RELATIONSHIP was particularly close with Harry Truman, a former haberdasher who appreciated how hard the photographers worked. He got along very well with them. In addition to being president of the United States, Harry was also president of what he called the "One More Club," his name for the cadre of news photographers who covered him and were always requesting "one more" picture.

White House photographers at first found that Truman's heavy bifocal lenses made his eyes look distorted and unnatural, and they recommended that he give them a pair of his eyeglasses so plain glass could be inserted, to make his face look better in pictures. But there were still reflections in the lenses, so the photographers removed the lenses altogether and gave the president empty frames.

Truman didn't like his new look after he saw the prints. "This is not me," he said. "I will not go to Hollywood. I will be myself. I am what I am and these glasses are what I am and from now on, we'll just have to do with what I have."[38]

Presidents today have moved far beyond Truman and do whatever they can to look good. Partly it's their own vanity and partly it's an effort to look "presidential" for the general public. But for Harry Truman, before the era of television and the onset of today's emphasis on visuals, it was different. Image-making was not something he was interested in.

"There were times when the Trumans wanted pictures taken at the White House, but didn't want newsmen to do the job," writes Ollie Atkins, President Richard Nixon's photographer. "They couldn't call in a commercial man because of the political implications. So instead they used a military photographer who worked for the Navy and shot with a Speed Graphic. He took pictures of birthday parties—that kind of thing."[39]

*   *   *

DWIGHT EISENHOWER, who followed Truman in office, also had little understanding of or interest in his own visual record. And he didn't aim to be a glamorous, exciting figure, in keeping with what the country sought from him after a generation of economic depression and world war: normalcy.

"The Eisenhower years in Washington were orderly, peaceful, and dull," recalled Tames. "Wednesdays in particular were usually light days at the White House. The president's schedule was cut short so he'd have the whole afternoon free. Everyone knew it and planned accordingly. Ike would go out to Burning Tree [a golf course in Maryland] to play golf, and the whole city seemed to lie back with a sigh. In later years with other administrations, when crises seem to come tumbling over one another endlessly, I yearned for those long, lazy, sweet Eisenhower Wednesdays."[40]

Tames added: "The White House policy that photographers become deaf while in the president's office was strictly adhered to under Eisenhower. Every word was privileged, including the few exchanges he had with us."[41]

Eisenhower continued Truman's tradition of using a Navy photographer and then changed to one from the Army so he wouldn't show a preference between the major armed services. This photographer didn't have much extra access, however; he stayed with the news photographers outside the White House, and took other photos inside for the personal use of the president and his family.[42]

Under Eisenhower, the White House began handing out free copies of grip-and-grin photographs, paid for by the Interior Department and taken by Interior Department photographer Abbie Rowe. Before that, news photographers had charged the visitors a fee for a souvenir copy of their moment with the president.[43]

There were disagreements over coverage. Ike's press secretary James Hagerty angered print reporters by starting out in 1953 with a policy barring the reporters from some photo shoots with the news photographers, and this was the beginning of a long struggle between the photojournalists and the writing press about which contingent should have access to different events.[44]

The next year, Eisenhower took up a "speed camera" himself, with the aim of shooting candid pictures of his family. The news photographers offered informal lessons in the technology, as Eisenhower had considerable trouble with the lighting. Mamie, his first lady, preferred to appeal directly to the news photographers to obtain snapshots of grandson David and other family members for her green-leather family photo album. They were happy to oblige.[45]

An awkward situation arose when Eisenhower, trying to be sociable with the lensmen, attended the annual stag dinner sponsored by the White House News Photographers Association in 1956. But he had to be taken to Walter Reed hospital for intestinal surgery after the meal.[46]

News photographers filed a protest when they were banned from the president's swearing-in on January 20, 1957. They were kept out of that private family ceremony in the White House on Sunday, but allowed to cover a second, public oath on the steps of the Capitol the next day.[47]

Late in his administration, Eisenhower referred to the news photographers jokingly as "slave drivers" while posing with a visitor. He noted that they were forever asking him to move here or there, or to make a gesture or look in a certain direction, to improve their pictures, but he understood they were serious about their jobs. "They are the slave drivers around here, but they are my pals," the president said.[48]

*   *   *

OFFICIAL WHITE HOUSE photographers—members of the staff whose full-time job was specifically to chronicle the president and his family—didn't come on the scene until the PR-oriented Kennedy took office in 1961. He brought in Cecil Stoughton to be his visual historian and hired celebrity photographers from the outside, such as the esteemed Jacques Lowe. This changed presidential image-making forever.

Notes

1. Harold Holzer, *Lincoln at Cooper Union: The Speech that made Abraham Lincoln President*, New York: Simon & Schuster Paperbacks, 2004, pp. 1–2.
2. Ibid., pp. 2–3.
3. Ibid., p. 179.
4. Ibid., p. 5.
5. Ibid., pp. 92–93.
6. Ibid., pp. 93–94.
7. John Bredar, *The President's Photographer: Fifty Years Inside the Oval Office*, Washington, D.C.: National Geographic Society, 2010, pp. 45.
8. Carl Sferrazza Anthony, *America's First Families: An Inside View of 200 Years of Private Life in the White House*, New York: Touchstone, 2000, p. 340.
9. Bredar, *The President's Photographer*, p. 45.
10. Holzer, *Lincoln at Cooper Union*, p. 99.
11. Ibid., pp. 243–244
12. Richard Lowry, *The Photographer and the President: Abraham Lincoln, Alexander Gardner, and the Images that made a Presidency*, New York: Rizzoli Ex Libris, 2015, p. 2.
13. Ibid.
14. Ibid., pp. 8–9.
15. Ibid., p. 13.
16. "Abraham Lincoln's Love Story: Did a Waltham Man make the Last Portrait of Lincoln?" *Boston Daily Globe*, Feb. 12, 1904, p. 3.
17. "Gotthelf Pach, 73, Dies in His Sleep," *New York Times*, Apr. 18, 1925, p. 15.
18. "Amateur Photography in Washington," *Photographic Times and American Photographer*, vol. 18 (1888), p. 34.
19. "Photographer is Given Rebuke by Roosevelt," *Chicago Daily Tribune*, Sept. 23, 1901, p. 5.
20. Jos Ohl, "Snapped Miss Alice as She Played Ponies," *Atlanta Constitution*, Apr. 6, 1904, p. 1.
21. Augusta Prescott, "The Home Coming of the President: He Weighs Ten Pounds Less and is Three Shades Darker," *Atlanta Constitution*, June 14, 1903, p. D3.
22. "B.M.F. Clinedinst, Photographer, 90," *New York Times*, Mar. 18, 1953, p. 31; see also "Our Strenuous President," *Photo Era*, vol. 9, no. 1 (1902), p. 44. For a photo of TR jumping his horse, see 'Theodore Roosevelt Jumping, 1902', *Susan Barsy:*

The New Jeffersonian, July 21, 2015, https://susanbarsy.com/2015/07/21/theodore-roosevelt-jumping-1902.

23. Betty Houchin Winfield, *FDR and the News Media*, New York: Columbia University Press, 1994, pp. 11–12.
24. Ibid., p. 16.
25. Ibid.
26. Ibid., p. 111.
27. Ibid., p. 86.
28. "The President at Work," *Time*, Feb. 25, 1935.
29. Winfield, *FDR and the News Media*, pp. 111–112.
30. Ibid., p. 112.
31. Ibid.
32. Ibid., pp.112–113.
33. Ibid., p. 115.
34. George Tames, *Eye on Washington: The Presidents Who've Known Me*, New York: HarperCollins Publishers, 1990, p. 20.
35. Ibid., p. 19.
36. Ibid., p. 20.
37. Ibid.
38. Ibid., p. 39.
39. Ollie Atkins, *The White House Years: Triumph and Tragedy*, Chicago: Playboy Press, 1977, p. 11.
40. Tames, *Eye on Washington*, p. 52.
41. Ibid., p. 53.
42. Atkins, *The White House Years*, p. 11.
43. Dayton Moore, "Windsor uses Oddest Clubs in Playing," *Statesville Daily Record*, Aug. 11, 1953, p. 7.
44. Dayton Moore, "Press Secretary James Hagerty Snubs Newsmen," *Brownwood Bulletin*, July 21, 1953, p. 2.
45. "Eisenhower Tries Hand with Camera," *Kingsport Times-News*, Jan. 3, 1954, p. 8.
46. "Ike Undergoes Operation Early Today after 16 Doctors Confer," *Lubbock Morning Avalanche*, June 9, 1956, p. 1.
47. "Photographers Protest Ban on Swearing-In," *The Times* (Hammond, Ind.), Jan. 10, 1957, p. 2.
48. Associated Press, "Backstairs to White House," *Daily Times* (New Philadelphia, Ohio), Apr. 25, 1958, p. 10.

Chapter Two

Behind the Scenes with John F. Kennedy, Cecil Stoughton, and the Glamor Lensmen

Cecil Stoughton was the first official White House photographer.[1] President Kennedy wanted someone to visually record his activities for history and use pictures to expand on his popularity as a political celebrity. The man he selected was a lieutenant in the public information office of the U.S. Army Signal Corps who had been a military photographer during World War II. This was considered good preparation for the unpredictable and demanding atmosphere in the White House. Kennedy once told a staff member, "When you are around here, you have to eat fast, read fast, think fast and sleep fast or else you won't get anything done."[2] Stoughton filled the bill.

Stoughton arrived at the White House in early 1961, after he was recommended by Major General Chester Clifton, Kennedy's military aide. As Stoughton recalled, "Major General Clifton provided logistical support for the president and was present at all functions. He knew about my photographic abilities and told the president and Jackie that they would be in the public eye and needed someone in-house to capture various occasions and release the pictures to the press."[3] Beyond this, General Clifton and JFK wanted the photographer to provide a visual record of the Kennedy presidency, and Stoughton did so in a manner that was compelling and vivid. Stoughton also changed the nature of insider White House staff photography, moving from covering formal or official moments such as the president meeting with heads of state or members of Congress, to capturing private moments, informal scenes, and unusual events in the president's life to which Americans hadn't been privy up until then.

Journalist Richard Reeves, referring to Kennedy's cultivation of an image of glamor and grace under pressure, wrote: "Kennedy seemed to be bringing out the best in the American people. Perhaps he was just the end of an old America, but he wanted to be seen as the beginning of the new—and photographs were the record of that ambition. So it was not surprising that one of the new president's early actions was to appoint an official personal photographer—a first." This was Stoughton, 41 years old, roughly Kennedy's age.[4]

Jack and Jacqueline Kennedy were celebrities and wanted to feed the public's desire to know more about them. The goal was to enhance their appeal as young, dynamic people with fresh ideas and new approaches and to help popularize the president's agenda.

"Prior to JFK we had [President Dwight] Eisenhower, and there was no need for a photographer," Stoughton once told *National Geographic*. "He was about 63 years old and he didn't have the charisma and charm of President Kennedy, and he didn't have a young family that engaged the American public."[5]

"Americans living at the time were forever transformed by the contrasting stories of January 20, 1961 [when Kennedy took office], and November 22, 1963 [when Kennedy was murdered]," wrote journalist Harvey Lawler, who interviewed Stoughton extensively before the photographer's death in 2008. "Cecil Stoughton was among the select few who stood at the epicenter of those stories and the 1,036 days in between John F. Kennedy's inauguration and assassination."

"Stoughton played a role unlike any other individual attached to the Kennedy administration. He was the first official White House photographer. Just as remarkable, he also evolved to become the Kennedys' trusted chronicler of their personal lives. Stoughton was ever present, yet undetectable as he photographed and filmed virtually everything the first family did. This unprecedented privilege wasn't just Stoughton's job, it was his life. Daytime, nighttime, and on weekends, he continuously examined the Kennedys through his lens."[6]

Lawler also wrote, in a fashion typical of the glowing coverage of the Kennedy era, that Stoughton's hallmark "was the photography of joy:

the exuberance of the Kennedy children; the dazzle of Mrs. Kennedy, at home and abroad; the eagerness of crowds of Americans, reaching out simply to touch their president; the magnetism of a youthful leader who could send entire foreign cities into a welcoming frenzy. Stoughton framed it all for us; his legacy is our legacy."[7]

To make sure he didn't miss anything, Stoughton arranged for Evelyn Lincoln, the president's personal secretary, to have a buzzer attached to his desk in an office directly below the Oval Office where the president worked. That way, Lincoln or another staffer or the president could summon Stoughton immediately when something important or interesting was going on, and he would sprint up the stairs to the Oval Office in about 10 seconds. Stoughton also would hover outside the Oval Office, waiting for developments. He became so omnipresent that Kennedy, his senior staff, and the first family scarcely noticed when he was there, which helped Stoughton to get natural pictures. This "hidden in plain sight" approach has been adopted by White House photographers ever since. Sometimes, as with any news photographer, Stoughton got lucky and was in the right place at the right time. At other moments, his instinct for news and for interesting images drew him to where the action was.[8]

Stoughton discovered a PR gold mine when he realized that John Kennedy Jr., the president's young son, had found a door on the front of his father's desk in the Oval Office. From then on, the toddler considered this his special "cave." He would hide there, open the door and peek out, images that Stoughton and photojournalist Stanley Tretick were able to capture. On other occasions, the boy would keep the door closed. Visitors, from cabinet secretaries to White House staffers, would hear giggles and thumps from under the desk. If young John got too rowdy or if there was a meeting on a very serious topic, the president would ask his friend and aide Dave Powers to take John Jr. back to the White House residence.[9]

One of Stoughton's most famous photos was among 12 frames that he shot of Kennedy and his two children during three minutes inside the Oval Office in October 1962. Stoughton was outside the Oval waiting for something to happen, when he heard the president talking sweetly to his daughter Caroline and John Jr.[10] They had dropped by to see their dad, immersed in the Cuban Missile Crisis, and their presence gave their father a break from his confrontation with the Soviet Union. After stopping at a candy jar on Mrs. Lincoln's desk, the kids stepped into the Oval Office. "The next thing I knew," Stoughton said,

"I heard the president clapping and singing out, 'Hey, here's John-John.'" The photographer ducked into the inner sanctum and said it "looked like a fun thing I should be making a picture of," and Kennedy waved him in.

He took a dozen pictures of the president sitting in a wooden armchair and clapping his hands as the children danced and hopped around the room. JFK authorized the release of one photo to the press, and it was used around the world, "providing a rare glimpse of the young President and his kids at play and forever expanding our idea of a modern President," observed documentary filmmaker John Bredar.[11]

"I never made a bad picture of the children," Stoughton once recalled. "You couldn't. All you had to do was aim the camera and shoot. You always got something. I became such a part of the scene that many times I didn't even need a telephoto lens. I was close enough just to take pictures normally. And they expected it." Little John made a repeated request of the photographer, by then an Army captain: "Take my picture Taptain Toughton," and Cecil made hundreds of them, and also photos of Kennedy's daughter Caroline, to their parents' delight.[12]

Photography was in the Kennedy family: First Lady Jacqueline Kennedy had been a photographer herself, and she knew the PR value of pictures.

After attending Vassar College, the Sorbonne, and George Washington University in Washington, Jackie got her first job as an "inquiring photographer" for the *Washington Times-Herald* in 1951, about ten years before she became first lady. Her assignment was to approach people on the street and ask them questions about everyday life or current events, such as whether they approved of joint bank accounts between husband and wife, or "Do you think a wife should let her husband think he's smarter than she is?" Among the many people she interviewed was Senator Richard Nixon, the California Republican whom her husband would defeat in the 1960 presidential election. Later, as first lady, she showed an appreciation for good photos and also took a role in hiring renowned photographer Jacques Lowe to cover parts of the presidency and the first family as a personal photographer for the Kennedys.[13]

Mrs. Kennedy had strong ideas about how the first family should be depicted to the public. Just before her husband's inauguration in January 1961, Jackie sent a lengthy memo to her press secretary Pamela Turnure outlining the new rules for news coverage and photography. "I hate that tub-thumping-everything-is-great-about-my-boss kind of press relations," Mrs. Kennedy wrote. "Everyone is trying to get at us—but you will be there as a buffer—to shield our privacy—not get us in the papers. . . . I feel so strongly that publicity in this era has gotten so completely out of hand & you must really protect the privacy of me and my children." She added: "None of this is meant to sound reproachful—it is just that I had suddenly realized what it means to completely lose one's privacy—everyone is so interested in us—SO BE DISCREET."[14]

There were exceptions. After a snowfall in 1961, the Kennedys' first year in office, she drove her two children across the South Grounds in a pony-drawn sleigh and arranged for photos to be taken. The White House released a charming picture to the media, which was widely used across the country.[15] This was the start of the nation's love affair with John and Jackie Kennedy and their kids.

But, as indicated in her memo, Mrs. Kennedy was generally very careful about exposing her children to the media spotlight. Pierre Salinger, JFK's White House press secretary, recalled, "She was always in touch with me because she didn't want the press to do photography of the kids. And I said, 'If they're outside the White House I can't do anything about it.' . . . But . . . John Kennedy had another mentality. Every time that Jackie went on a trip somewhere, he'd say, 'Well, now's the time to get good pictures of the kids.' And that was something he wanted to have done."[16]

Mrs. Kennedy sent her husband and others numerous memos on the kind of photographs she wanted released in general and what she disliked. In January 1963, she sent her husband a note saying, "I was passing by Mrs. Lincoln's [the president's secretary's] office today and I saw a man being photographed in the Rose Garden with an enormous bunch of celery. I think it is most undignified for any picture of this nature to be taken on the steps leading up to the president's office or on the South Grounds. If they want their pictures taken they can pose by the West Lobby. This also includes pictures of bathing beauties, etc." The man with the celery turned out to be U.S. Representative Wayne Aspinall of Colorado, a powerful legislator with influence on issues important to the Rocky Mountain West. He was apparently trying to promote the region's agriculture.[17]

*   *   *

STOUGHTON WAS given other tasks beyond photographing the president for posterity. He was once asked to take motion-pictures of JFK as he played golf at the Hyannis Golf Club. Kennedy wanted to review the film to improve his game. After he hit the ball, he would signal whether it was a good shot or had gone badly, all so he could adjust his swing after viewing the home movie. It showed how serious Kennedy was about golf. His problem, however, was chronic lower-back pain that kept him from playing as often as he wanted or as well as he could.[18]

In September 1962, the first lady asked Stoughton to attend a fashion show at New York's Chez Ninon. Mrs. Kennedy explained that if she attended, she would disrupt the show with all the attention she would get, so she wanted Stoughton to take pictures of the new styles so she could review them at her leisure. She sent him a thank-you note that read, "Don't leave us for *Harper's Bazaar*."[19]

One of Stoughton's most popular activities was to take pictures of visitors with the Kennedys and send the guests photo albums to remind them of their time with the president and his family. The Kennedys and the visitors loved it because it strengthened the bond between them.[20] Since then, sending such pictures to visitors has become commonplace.

Kennedy liked to joke, often at other people's expense, and his photographer played a part in the merrymaking. "Back from his second European trip, Kennedy was eager to see the movies which Stoughton had made and, since his sisters had traveled with him, he eyed the rerun of their performances with special interest," reported journalist Hugh Sidey. "He roared with laughter when the film revealed that Jean Smith and sister-in-law Lee Radziwill had turned up in Great Britain wearing identical white coats. One picture showed their backs as they stood side by side, sister Jean's coat considerably longer than sister-in-law Lee's. Kennedy had the movie stopped to study the scene. Perfect, he decided, for a family gag. He had Stoughton make a life-sized blowup of that particular frame and swore him to secrecy. Then, the next time that the family gathered, Kennedy had Stoughton suddenly thrust the huge picture through a door. The gag brought the house down."[21]

Kennedy once observed his brother Teddy compete in a regatta and was stunned at all the mistakes Teddy was making as a sailor. The president told Stoughton to take pictures of the race, and later the president spent an evening using the film to show his brother his many errors.[22]

In all, Stoughton took nearly 12,000 photos during his time working for Kennedy. This was considered a huge number at the time but is meager compared with the millions of digital pictures taken by the White House chief photographer and his assistants today.

Many photographs were released to the press and seen widely around the world. Others were kept private until years after Kennedy's death. One such shot was the only surviving picture of JFK with movie star Marilyn Monroe. Stoughton took the photo at a private reception after the president's huge birthday celebration in New York's Madison Square Garden on May 19, 1962. (This was 10 days before his actual 45th birthday on May 29.) Monroe had caused a sensation in the garden when she appeared on stage and sang Kennedy a sultry rendition of "Happy Birthday, Mr. President." Stoughton took many pictures of the two at the reception but the FBI and Secret Service later confiscated all but one. This lone negative was in a film dryer when the authorities arrived, and they missed it.[23]

The surviving photo shows Monroe in a skin-tight, low-cut, glittery dress—the same show-stopping outfit she had worn at Madison Square Garden—standing between the president and his brother Robert. Monroe is listening intently to the president, who is seen from the side with his head lowered and apparently talking in a low voice. Robert Kennedy, the attorney general, is listening awkwardly. The photo shows that Monroe was a dazzling presence at the party and attracting lots of attention.

The picture isn't a good one, and it's not clear exactly what the three principals—JFK, Marilyn, and Bobby—were doing at that moment or what the president was saying. But it has become an iconic image thanks to rumors that the president and the movie star, two of the most famous and glamorous people of the era, were having an affair. Marilyn died of a barbiturate overdose less than three months later.

The Kennedys imposed restrictions to protect their image as an elegant, graceful couple. Pictures of the president or the first lady looking foolish were out of bounds. So were photos of Jack and Jackie kissing in public or engaging in other public displays of affection, which were extremely rare for them because they considered such displays in bad taste.[24]

Jackie and Jack also had a limited tolerance of photographs taken of them relaxing on Cape Cod aboard their yacht, the *Honey Fitz*. The first lady enjoyed water skiing or sunning herself, but wanted the staff and Secret Service to keep the press boat too far away to get good pictures. When the president slipped over the side for a swim, he wore a back brace to prevent further injury to his back and it was arranged that no photos could be taken of him until he was submerged to the neck.[25] This was part of the White House effort to hide JFK's many physical problems, which included Addison's disease and severe gastrointestinal maladies.

As for his back condition, foreign leaders noticed in private what was kept from the American public. British Prime Minister Harold Macmillan wrote in his diary in December 1961, after talks with Kennedy in Bermuda: "In health, I thought the president was not in good shape. His back was hurting. He cannot sit long without pain."[26]

There were other PR-oriented restrictions beyond the efforts to hide JFK's physical afflictions. Among them was Kennedy's insistence that he not be photographed with certain people if he believed the association would hurt his political standing in some way. For a while, one of those excluded from photos with the president was the Reverend Martin Luther King Jr., the rising civil-rights leader. Kennedy initially feared bad publicity because the FBI reported that King was a communist. But Kennedy relented. After watching King deliver his powerful "I Have a Dream" speech at the Lincoln Memorial in August 1963, he invited him to the White House with other civil rights leaders and they were photographed together. Kennedy recognized another media star when he saw one.[27]

Sammy Davis Jr., the brilliant African American entertainer, was placed on the "no pictures" list because his wife was white. Also banned from photos with the president was economist Leon Keyserling, who had observed that "Kennedy is as bad as Eisenhower" in setting economic policy.[28]

Kennedy spent hours perusing the White House pictures and deciding which ones should be released and which should remain private.

* * *

THE ROOTS of Kennedy's preoccupation with imagery ran deep. "It really goes back to Rose Kennedy, and the fact that her father, John F. ['Honey Fitz'] Fitzgerald, was mayor of Boston and a [Democratic] congressman," says Barbara Perry, chairwoman of the presidential history program at the University of Virginia's Miller Center. Rose, the mother of John F. Kennedy, learned the importance of image and photography from her dad. "He had a sense of the visual art of stills and moving pictures," Perry says.[29]

Rose's husband Joseph Kennedy, the future president's father, also had an understanding of visual imagery through photography and how vital it was for public figures who wanted to be popular. Joe Kennedy wasn't just an investor, he was also a movie producer. Between them, Rose and Joe inculcated in their children, especially the ambitious boys, an affinity for public image-making.

Joe arranged for his big, attractive, active family to be photographed often by the newspapers and popular magazines of the time such as *Life*, just as he had done as a film producer with entertainment-industry stars. The pictures were often of the family in informal scenes, not posed on a staircase or in groups, which was the standard in those days. Ted Kennedy, one of Joe and Rose's sons, once said *Life* magazine became "our family photo album."[30]

When Joe Kennedy was named by President Franklin Roosevelt as the first Irish-Catholic American ambassador to the Court of St. James's, it caused a sensation in the United Kingdom and the United States. Joe kept up his family PR campaign, and the Kennedys became international celebrities. Their images were frequently featured in the newspapers, magazines and newsreels.

Throughout the 1950s, long after he realized his own presidential ambitions would never be fulfilled, Joe Kennedy vigorously promoted his son Jack. He lined up many flattering photo sessions with the mass media in Washington and at the family estate in Hyannis Port, Massachusetts.

"Kennedy, exploiting his beautiful, young wife, Jacqueline, and a baby girl named Caroline, was never quite what he seemed: one of us," journalist Richard Reeves has observed. "He was, in fact, a child of privilege and a chronically ill one at that. But Kennedy and his family—his father had been president of RKO Pictures—understood the publicity and public relations that sold entertainment, specifically movies, and they used that savvy in the political world. Witness the film and stills of Kennedy, the young candidate with pants rolled up, walking barefoot on the beaches of Cape Cod. [Kennedy rival Richard] Nixon, who resented and envied the Kennedy grace his whole adult life, at one point tried to echo that apparent ease, walking along the Pacific surf for photographers. He was wearing black wingtip shoes."[31]

During a visit to the USS *Kitty Hawk* as president, Kennedy burst into laughter when Governor Pat Brown of California spilled some hot coffee in his lap and jumped to his feet as news photographers captured the embarrassing moment. But Kennedy offered his guest some friendly PR advice. "Pat," he said, "if I spilled boiling oil on my crotch in front of those guys, I would sit there and just keep smiling."[32]

Kennedy's obsession with public relations extended to his wife. Former Secret Service agent Clint Hill, who helped to protect the first family, said JFK was always trying to shape Jackie's public image and he even issued orders on how she should be photographed on her trip to Italy in 1962. "Before we went," Hill said, "he made sure I understood that he didn't want any nightclub scenes, no scenes with glasses or bottles of wine on the table and no bikini shots. The only photographs of Mrs. Kennedy in a bathing suit, other than long distance lens sometimes, were arranged by myself with the press [and she wore a modest, full-coverage swimsuit]. They said they'd back off if we could arrange for them to get a good photograph."[33] In the end, President Kennedy felt the trip occurred with no embarrassment.

*   *   *

KENNEDY WAS SO eager to enhance his image that he approved special access for several independent photographers, such as Bob Davidoff, who took many charming pictures of Kennedy and his family at their vacation home in Palm Beach, Florida, where Davidoff lived. Davidoff also was the house photographer at the Breakers, Palm Beach's grand hotel at the time, and he developed rare trust with many rich and famous people who vacationed there, including entertainers Frank Sinatra and Bob Hope. Later, Davidoff and his sons became the official photographers at Mar-a-Lago, the luxurious resort of billionaire Donald Trump, who was elected president of the United States in 2016.[34]

Davidoff was known as a "society photographer," and he always wanted to make his subjects look as appealing as possible. He was known never to release unflattering pictures of his subjects. This is what the Kennedys wanted too, so the match was perfect for both photographer and family. Davidoff was often invited to the Kennedy home on North Ocean Drive to take formal portraits and visually chronicle family birthdays and holiday parties. He took many photos of President Kennedy looking tanned and fit, playing with his children, laughing with his brothers, and attending church services.

Davidoff was particularly close to Jacqueline Kennedy and remained friends with her after her husband was killed and she was no longer first lady. "If I took a bad picture of her, I would kill it," he once said. "She trusted me and would not duck me."[35]

For a few years the family's favorite photographer was Jacques Lowe, a talented freelancer who was admired in particular by Jacqueline. Lowe became the unofficial personal photographer for the Kennedys during Jack's successful 1960 campaign and at the start of Kennedy's presidency.

Lowe got to know Robert F. Kennedy, the future president's brother, when Bobby was chief counsel for the Senate Committee on Government Operations. Three different magazines commissioned Lowe to photograph RFK because of his growing reputation as a crusading reformer taking on labor racketeers. Lowe spent a week in 1956 taking pictures of Bobby Kennedy, and they got along well.

Their friendship gradually blossomed and Lowe spent many weekends at Hickory Hill, Bobby Kennedy's estate in suburban McLean, Virginia. Lowe always brought his camera and took hundreds of pictures of Kennedy and his big, rambunctious family. RFK had five children at the time along with a pet menagerie of dogs, cats, ducks, and donkeys and there were regular football games and cavorting in the swimming pool. It added up to what Lowe called "a photographer's paradise."[36]

After a year, Lowe reviewed his pictures, chose 124 of the best images and made each into an 11-by-14-inch print. He sent the photos to Bobby to thank him for his hospitality.

Bobby loved them, and asked Lowe for another set of prints to give his father as a birthday gift.

Two months later, Lowe got an unusual phone call.

"I was working in my studio in New York one evening in early September 1958," Lowe recalled. "It must have been well [after] midnight when the phone rang. A strangely familiar but slurry voice asked, 'Is this Mr. Lowe?'"

"'Yes,' I said cautiously."

"'This is Joe Kennedy speaking.'"

"I was sure someone was playing a prank on me; Joseph Kennedy was an almost mythic figure at the time, far more famous than any of his sons. I said, 'Well, if you're Joe Kennedy, I'm Santa Claus.'"

"'No, no, no. This is Joe Kennedy. Today's my birthday and Bobby gave me those pictures you took of his family. They are the greatest photographs I have ever seen.'"

"Now I knew it was Joseph Kennedy and it was clear he had celebrated his birthday with a few drinks."

"'Those pictures are the most wonderful birthday present I've ever had. I want you to promise me you'll photograph my other son.'"

"'Which one is that?' I asked."

"'Jack. Will you call me at my office in two days?'"

"I agreed, mainly to be polite and to get him off the phone. When I called two days later, I expected that Joe would have forgotten all about me. To my surprise he invited me to come up to Hyannis Port [the family compound in Massachusetts]."

"And that is how my great adventure with the Kennedy family began."[37]

Lowe, who was 28 at the time, met John F. Kennedy during that trip. Kennedy was tired and out of sorts and was barely civil to this stranger. Lowe proceeded to take pictures of the then-senator, his wife, and their daughter Caroline. He returned home to New York City, developed the film and sent contact sheets to Kennedy along with his bill. He didn't hear anything immediately and figured he had "bungled the job."[38]

But he got another midnight call several weeks later. It was Jack Kennedy. "I'm in New York," the senator said. "Can you come see me tonight because I'm leaving in the morning?"

Lowe got dressed and took a cab to a Park Avenue building owned by Jack's father where Kennedy was staying. Kennedy opened the apartment door for Lowe wearing only a towel. He had just taken a shower and down the hall Lowe could hear water splashing—Jackie taking a bath. "Is that Jacques?" she called. "Oh, those wonderful pictures!"[39]

Kennedy retrieved the Hyannis contact sheets and spread them on the floor. Lowe got down on his hands and knees to sort through them as Jack stood, still clad in the towel, and made his selections, some for political purposes, and one that became the family Christmas card. Lowe's pictures were again a big hit, especially a shot of Jack, Jackie, and their daughter Caroline together in what was supposed to be a formal portrait, but with Caroline impishly putting her mother's pearls in her mouth with her tiny hand. This became an iconic image of the beautiful, charismatic family with an endearing, common touch.[40]

There was good chemistry between Lowe and John and Jackie. The Kennedys were drawn to Lowe's youth, his good looks, and his unusual, even exotic, background, including the fact that he was born in Germany to a German father and a Russian Jewish mother in 1930 and spent years hiding from the Nazis in Germany. The family emigrated to the United States in 1940 when Jacques was 9. He became a successful photojournalist whose work appeared in top publications and his career blossomed. His relationship with Jack Kennedy took off, too and eventually grew into a friendship.

Kennedy hired Lowe during his 1960 presidential campaign against Vice President Richard Nixon. Lowe's job was to "feed TV stations, small dailies and rural weeklies with pictures of the candidate and the campaign as frequently as possible," he later said.[41]

* * *

LOWE PROVIDED an insightful portrait of Kennedy as an individual, both in his pictures and in his personal recollections. One trait that stood out was Kennedy's vanity.

Take the matter of the missing hat. Kennedy never wore one, even on the coldest days. He felt hats made him look silly (and later, he wouldn't wear one at his frigid inauguration ceremony in January 1961). "People treated the 'hat controversy' as an amusing distraction during the campaign," Lowe said, "but as a photographer, I understood: Kennedy had an instinctive sense for projecting an image of a youthful, athletic man. The contrast could not have been greater; Eisenhower was a sort of grandpa and Nixon, too, was part of that old-fashioned, hat-wearing world."[42]

Several photographers who knew Kennedy have noted that he preferred not to be pictured head-on because he didn't think this was his best angle. After reviewing hundreds of photos of JFK, I have concluded that he had "lazy eye," a condition that causes one or both eyes to wander. This would certainly have embarrassed Kennedy, who was always very aware of his appearance and wanted to give the impression that he was the picture of health. This was untrue since he had Addison's disease, severe back problems, and other ailments.

Kennedy's youthful image and his personal charm resonated with women of all ages, Lowe wrote, explaining: "At some campaign stops there was a level of hysterical adulation that could get a little scary. In upstate New York, a blonde mother of three evaded the police detail and kissed Jack on the cheek. Mike DiSalle, the governor of Ohio, had his coat ripped as he tried to shield Jack from his fans and another campaign worker had his pants nearly pulled off. Jack loved to plunge into crowds and he often had buttons torn from his jacket. Sometimes the long fingernails of his fans bloodied his hands. There were also young women who would simply burst into tears as he approached."[43]

"One disadvantage of being so close to Jack was that he never carried any money," Lowe added. "He was constantly turning to me, or whoever was closest, and asking for fifty cents or a dollar. One particular time when we were checking into a big hotel, Jack leaned over on top of me and whispered: 'Jacques can you give me a dollar for the bellboy?' I only had a five-dollar bill so the bellboy got a nice tip and I was out of pocket five dollars." Kennedy never paid Lowe back.[44]

Others have noted that Kennedy had trouble in his marriage, which Lowe ignored in his memoir of the Kennedy years. Instead, Lowe accurately portrayed Kennedy as a loving father who doted on his kids and who was deeply committed to his extended family. Lowe portrayed Jackie as a loving mother in addition to being a stylish and glamorous first lady.

Kennedy's time at the family estate in Hyannis was filled with family activities, including jaunts on the private yacht anchored in the nearby harbor. Jack enjoyed the huge family picnics, which sometimes included 15 adults and 30 children, plus nurses and nannies.[45]

Often the large, boisterous group would visit a picnic site by yacht. "They would haul along several hampers of hot dogs and hamburgers and French fries and Coke," Lowe recalled. "Jackie maintained a kind of elegant reserve. She didn't try to keep up with the constant activity— the football and softball games, pulling each other into the swimming pool—but she did go on the picnics. She would pack her own hamper with champagne, foie gras, and *oeufs a la Russe*. Jack wouldn't have touched her stuff if his life depended on it; he stuck to the hamburgers and hot dogs."[46]

* * *

ON ELECTION DAY 1960, Jack and Jackie filled out their ballots in Boston and then flew to Hyannis Port to await the results. "Once more I felt incredibly privileged to have complete access to the family compound while most the press corps, some two thousand strong, hung around the Hyannis National Guard Armory," Lowe said. "After the hectic clamor of the campaign, Election Day was almost eerily calm. I went to the local polling station with Bobby and Ethel Kennedy and later in the day I got Jack and Jackie to pose with Caroline."[47]

"By the time I woke up at 7:50 a.m., Kennedy's lead was just a hundred thousand," Lowe related. "I went over to Bobby's house and found Ethel alone downstairs. The rest of the family had gone for a walk. The maids were all out, so the two of us made coffee and cooked enough eggs and bacon to feed a dozen exhausted people who were hanging around the house. Later, we joined the family on their walk. Bobby carried a football and tossed it around with Ted to relieve the tension."[48]

After it was clear that Kennedy had won a very narrow victory, Lowe thought it would be a good time to take a picture of the whole family in the flush of their triumph. "Now they were all here and it was a momentous occasion," he recalled. "I knew this would be my only opportunity but as I tried to get them all together they kept wandering away. Finally, I realized how to pull it off: I enlisted Joe Kennedy to set the thing up and he ordered everybody to assemble in the library. When they were all there, Jack asked, 'Where's Jackie?'"

"She's down by the water," Lowe responded. He had seen her leave the house in a raincoat and start walking alone in the drizzle along the beach.

"I'll go get her," he said. He came back with her, and she went upstairs to get dressed while the family waited. When she came back down and entered the room everyone got up and applauded the new first lady. "It was a wonderful moment," Lowe said.[49]

In Lowe's telling, JFK was admittedly a patrician whose father was one of the richest men in the country, but he liked informality and didn't talk down to people. He enjoyed entertaining and preferred the company of journalists to politicians, people such as Ben Bradlee, Walter Lippmann, James Reston, and Joe Kraft. Kennedy was brilliant with a nimble mind, "a speed-reader who seemed to retain almost everything that he read," Lowe said.[50]

Kennedy had a keen and hard-nosed political sense. Lowe wrote: "At one point *Vogue* wanted Jack to pose for some pictures, which Jackie much favored. But Jack said to me, 'To hell with them. What am I going to do with three hundred thousand Republican ladies?' Instead, *Modern Screen*, with a circulation of five and a half million, got the pictures. When the issue came out, Jackie was furious. Though Jack okayed it, I was the one who got the blame."[51]

Lowe was under no illusions about his role. He wasn't there as a journalist, to fully inform the country about the candidate, flaws and all. He was a PR man for Jack Kennedy. "The point of my job was to place my photographs in the media where it would do the most good to get him elected President," he said.[52]

It was an enormous undertaking, little understood at the time. "I developed each day's photographs in a portable dark room, selected the useful images myself, and sent them to the Democratic headquarters in each of the fifty states plus about one hundred key television stations," Lowe said. "I was also providing images for small rural newspapers that didn't employ photojournalists. I was turning out hundreds of pictures every night as we rolled from Wisconsin to West Virginia, California, Illinois on our way to the convention."[53] And it got more intense after Kennedy was nominated.

Lowe's access was amazing.

The biggest question after Kennedy won the presidential nomination at the Democratic National Convention in July 1960 in Los Angeles was who Kennedy would choose as a vice-presidential running mate. And Lowe was an insider during that drama.

"I arrived in Jack's suite in the Biltmore Hotel at eight in the morning just as Jack phoned Lyndon Johnson to request the meeting where he would feel Johnson out about the Vice Presidential nomination," Lowe recalled. "For the rest of that extraordinary day I stayed on the scene as the process played out in a series of meetings. Bobby, who detested Johnson, went back and forth a number of times between Jack's suite and Johnson's, which was two floors below. I was there when Bobby and Jack had it out about choosing Johnson. When it was all finally worked out and time to seal the deal, there were just the three of us in the room—LBJ, JFK, and me. Johnson poured himself a healthy drink. Then Bobby came into the room and stood silently by, regarding Johnson with a look of deep suspicion." This photo was one of Lowe's most revealing. The distrustful look on RFK's face was priceless as he stood between LBJ, drink in hand and talking, and JFK, his hands on his hips, listening, with his eyes fastened on Johnson's. Bobby clearly had little use for LBJ.

Lowe added: "Only with hindsight, and because of the assassination, can we see just how much history flowed from that moment, from the great progressive legislation that Johnson passed to his tragic and disastrous conduct of the war in Vietnam."[54]

Look magazine published several of Lowe's pictures and Jack Kennedy wrote the captions, in another example of their special relationship. Lowe recalled that getting these photos was "a coup" for him in his career.[55]

After the convention, the Kennedy family gathered at the family estate in Hyannis Port for a break before the fall campaign. Lowe took lots of pictures, including a series of Jackie in a swimsuit and bathing cap. They weren't the most flattering images of her, but *Vogue* magazine heard about them and wanted to run a photo spread. Lowe felt that the Kennedys wouldn't like the images of Jackie in the bathing cap, which was gaudy and hid her glamorous hairdo. (Lowe felt that "its charm was its unstylishness.") Rather than run afoul of Jack and Jackie, he never gave the pictures to *Vogue*.[56]

* * *

AFTER KENNEDY won, Lowe's job was to continue to make President Kennedy look as good as possible, and he did it well. He said he was offered the job of official White House photographer but didn't want to put up with the endless ceremonial obligations such as ribbon cuttings and receiving lines.[57] The official job went to Stoughton.

But as the unofficial personal photographer, Lowe was given such close access that the news photographers got jealous and nicknamed him, derisively, "Jacques-Strap Lowe."[58]

"During those early months I had an extraordinary entrée to the entire administration," authorized by President Kennedy, Lowe recalled. "If someone asked for a photograph, he'd say, 'Call Jacques Lowe.' He would tell them he'd let me into the White House to take the photograph but no one else. When NBC wanted to follow Jack around with a 16mm camera and document the early days, Jack said no. 'I'll let you do the story in stills and I'll allow Jacques to follow me around.' They had no choice; they had to hire me. Jack was the best agent I ever had."[59]

Lowe was privy to many private moments that were revealing of the internal workings of the White House. He heard Kennedy aides refer to Vice President Johnson as "Uncle Cornpone," indicating the low status that LBJ had. Johnson was shut out of many decisions, and he wasn't happy about it.

Lowe saw that members of the Joint Chiefs of Staff had little respect for the young commander in chief. Kennedy found ways to "show his contempt for their self-importance," such as allowing Lowe into their national-security discussions. The chiefs didn't like this even though Lowe had a high-level security clearance, but there was nothing they could do about it and they followed the president's wishes.[60]

Kennedy was a voracious reader of newspapers, mostly to read about himself and see what images were being used. And he and Jackie valued photography in different ways.[61]

"Jackie was very aware of the power of photographs," Lowe wrote. "To Jackie an image was a piece of art; composition, light, and shadow interested her and she had photographer friends such as Peter Beard and Mark Shaw. Jack looked at content. For him a photograph was a document. . . . Jack would have extended conversations with me debating the relative merits of a *Time* magazine cover of him versus a *Newsweek* one."[62]

But Lowe eventually got into hot water with the Kennedys when he sold a picture of the president to the *New York Times Magazine* without clearing it with the president or the first lady. It was an image of Kennedy in his office with a pair of eyeglasses pushed on the top of his head. JFK thought the glasses made him look like an old man, and when it ran in the magazine, Kennedy complained to magazine photographer George Tames. Summoning Tames to his office, Kennedy jumped to his feet holding a copy of the magazine, turned to the offending photo and angrily said, "Why did you publish a picture of me like this?" Tames replied, "Mr. President, I did not make that picture. It was made by Jacques Lowe and sold to the *Times*."[63]

Kennedy phoned White House Press Secretary Pierre Salinger and called him to his office, according to Tames. He told him to inform Lowe that he no longer had free access to the president, and Kennedy explained, "Jacques Lowe shit in the nest, and he's got to go."[64] Lowe remembered this differently. He said Kennedy called him personally and complained but after that "it was forgotten."[65]

Whether this incident was truly forgotten or deeply harmful to Lowe's standing with Kennedy, there was a fundamental change in Lowe's desire to stay on at the White House. He left JFK's orbit in mid-1961. He felt "it was time to leave and reestablish my studio in New York," he recalled. "Documenting the new administration had been very exciting but after a while I realized that the same routine happens each day. I missed the crazy energy of the campaign, where something new occurs every minute and people are shouting and screaming at each other. New York had so many more possibilities for a photographer."[66]

Stoughton remained on the job and his access was so extensive that, in nearly 12,000 photos over about three years, he was able to capture some of the most iconic images of Kennedy and vivid scenes from the administration.[67]

*   *   *

AS HIS ADMINISRATION proceeded, Kennedy showed more of his private side to the staff photographers, including his sometimes strange sense of humor. He asked White House cameraman Robert Knudsen, one of Stoughton's deputies, to make a home movie depicting his death, two months before he was killed in Dallas. Knudsen said Kennedy wrote the script and it was supposed to be a joke, albeit a macabre one. "He just called me over one day and said they wanted to have someone and shoot a movie" during a weekend in Newport, Rhode Island, in September 1963, according to Knudsen.[68]

Ralph G. Martin, in his book *A Hero for Our Time*, reported that the film showed Kennedy stepping off the *Honey Fitz*, a family yacht, and walking down a long pier. Kennedy suddenly clutched his chest and fell. Family members stepped over him nonchalantly and continued walking toward shore. Even his wife Jackie stepped over the body and walked on. Red Fay, a Kennedy friend, stumbled and fell on the president's body, and at this point a blood-like liquid gushed from Kennedy's mouth and onto his shirt.

Knudsen, who was traveling with the family as a member of the photo staff, shot the scene several times to get it right. The film remains something of a mystery, as it is not stored in the archives of the John F. Kennedy Presidential Library and Museum in Boston, according to the Associated Press.[69]

Knudsen refused to give more details of the incident, saying he felt it was done in confidence, but, referring to the account in Martin's book, he told the AP, "I wondered if it was a premonition he had, or a quirk of fate."[70]

*   *   *

WHAT PEOPLE remember best about Stoughton's work came at one of the saddest moments for the presidency and the country—the now-famous photo he took on November 22, 1963 that showed Lyndon B. Johnson's swearing-in as president after Kennedy was assassinated in Dallas. It was Johnson's first big decision to have his picture taken under these crisis conditions. LBJ, the vice president who had accompanied Kennedy to his home state of Texas, wanted the world to know there had been a smooth transition of power and that he was firmly in charge as the nation's 36th president.

Stoughton was in the seventh car behind Kennedy's limousine in the Dallas motorcade, much too far back for him to effectively observe the president. It was a warm, sunny morning and the sidewalks were thick with crowds eight to ten people deep, the air full of cheers as the motorcade made its way into downtown Dallas. Stoughton checked his camera and saw that he had used up half a roll of film after taking pictures of the president and first lady disembarking from *Air Force One* and greeting well-wishers at Dallas' Love Field. Stoughton had also taken pictures of the crowds along the motorcade route.[71]

The motorcade left the downtown office district with its canyon of buildings and began to pass Dealey Plaza, an open area, when Stoughton heard three loud noises. Stoughton recognized them as gunshots but at first wasn't worried because he guessed that they were just part of the welcoming atmosphere. "Hey, Art," he said to another photographer in his car, "these Texans really know how to welcome a guy, don't they?" Stoughton later recalled: "In my mind I saw a guy on the roof in a ten-gallon hat with a six-shooter—bang! bang! bang! bang! That's what I thought."[72]

At 12:30 p.m., Stoughton's car turned a bend and entered Elm Street, near the Texas School Book Depository building, and he saw that all the cars ahead of him were gone. As his vehicle came to a stop, he jumped from the car when he spotted four people lying on the ground in fear, and he took a picture of them and also took pictures of a couple of other photographers on the scene snapping their own photos. Then he jumped back into the car and called, "Let's get the hell out of here!" Bystanders began shouting that the president was being taken to Parkland Memorial Hospital, and some local police agreed, so that's where they sped. Upon arrival, Stoughton noticed Secret Service agents surrounding the president's bloodied limousine, and he snapped two frames.[73]

By this time, the injured had been moved inside the hospital.

Malcolm Kilduff, the assistant White House press secretary, ran out to the emergency entrance, weeping, and said: "The President has been shot. We think he's dead."[74]

Stoughton went inside and stationed himself with General Chester V. Clifton, Kennedy's military aide, outside the swinging doors of the emergency room, to help in any way they could.

Stoughton was too distraught to take pictures of the weeping aides in the corridors of Parkland Hospital, but when Lyndon Johnson rushed by, surrounded by a knot of bodyguards, Stoughton asked where they were going. "The President is going to Washington," he was told. It was at this point that Stoughton realized that JFK had died and LBJ had succeeded him. He decided he should be with the nation's new leader.[75]

"I knew I had to be there for the oath of office whenever it was to take place," Stoughton recalled. "Two Johnson men and myself got a police officer to drive us to the airport. The policeman went to the only entrance he knew. It was close to the active runway."[76]

Stoughton continued: "We drove out on the runway and headed for *Air Force One*. I read later we were almost machine-gunned. No one knew who we were or what we were up to. I went to the cabin. Kilduff ran up the aisle and said, 'Cecil, thank God you're here. You're going to take the picture of the swearing-in and give it to the press.'"

The plane's engines began to roar in preparation for takeoff. Stoughton looked out a window and saw a large bronze casket containing Kennedy's body, and the photographer snapped several pictures of Secret Service agents carrying the heavy casket up the stairs of *Air Force One* and onto the plane—images that many Americans still remember today.[77]

Johnson asked Stoughton, "Where do you want us, Cecil?" And the photographer told the new president and others where to stand. "Kilduff made a dictaphone recording of the ceremony," Stoughton said. "I made the picture."[78]

LBJ's swearing-in aboard the presidential jet at 2:38 p.m.—about two hours after Kennedy was shot—was really just a formality. There was no question that Johnson had already succeeded to power according to the Constitution. But Johnson wanted to send a message that there would be no crisis. "He wanted to have a picture taken of the ceremony so it could be flashed around the world when he landed, as a symbol that the Constitution works and that the light in the White House may flicker but it never goes out," recalled Jack Valenti, an LBJ confidant who was on board. "And Johnson wanted Mrs. Kennedy in the photograph with him, to show that the Kennedy legacy was still intact."[79]

Johnson saw Stoughton as he was about to take the oath, and motioned for him to snap the historic picture. The strapping photographer climbed on top of a sofa that rested against a wall in order to get the best angle in the cabin crowded with two dozen people. One of his images became one of the most iconic photographs of any presidency, capturing a moment of national trauma. LBJ towered over everyone else and looked determined and solemn, his right hand raised as he took the oath of office. Sarah Hughes, a Dallas federal judge, presented an incongruous figure in a polka dot dress. A friend of Johnson's, she was called in at the last minute to administer the oath. Lady Bird Johnson, the new first lady, was holding back tears as she stood at LBJ's right side.

And, most compelling and poignant of all, the photo captured Jacqueline Kennedy, the slain president's widow, grief-stricken and looking dazed as she stood to Johnson's left. She insisted on wearing the pink suit she had on when JFK was shot a few hours earlier, and the jacket and skirt were stained with the dead president's blood.[80] It was traditional for the person taking the oath to place one hand on a Bible, but none could be found aboard the plane. Someone located a Catholic missal (Kennedy had been Catholic) and this was substituted.[81]

Unknown to the rest of the witnesses or to the new president, there was a potentially serious mishap. Stoughton snapped six pictures of the crowd milling about, before Jacqueline Kennedy arrived, and then began using his favorite camera, a Hasselblad, known in photographers' circles as one of the best. But the first time he tried to take a shot, the camera failed. "I almost died," Stoughton recalled. "I had a little connector that was loose because of all the bustling around, so I just pushed it in with my finger, and number two went off on schedule." To play it safe, he used another camera as backup, in addition to the Hasselblad, to make sure he had properly documented the event, taking a total of 20 frames including eight that showed the actual swearing-in ceremony.[82]

Stoughton had other challenges that day. "When I left the plane," Stoughton recalled, "Kilduff gave me the dictaphone belt [part of a recording system]. For a few seconds I felt I was the only person in the world who knew what had happened. I had the visual and sound proof. I then gave the belt to a signal corps man. I flipped a coin to see which local office—AP or UPI—would process the film."

"AP got the toss. I went into the darkroom with the man who processed the film. I found a negative where everyone had their eyes open and you could see he had a hand on the [missal]. UPI sent a motorcycle man over to get a copy."

"I got both AP and UPI offices in New York on the phone. Holding both phones to my ears, I waited until I thought the motorcycle man had made it back to his office."

"Holding the two phones open, I said, 'On my signal, start your photo drums transmitting.' It took *Air Force One* an hour and 40 minutes to fly to Washington. As the plane was landing at Andrews, the television station was projecting the picture I had taken. President Johnson saw it."[83]

The day wasn't over for Stoughton. At the airport in Dallas, he boarded an Air Force jet sent from San Antonio to pick him up and, with one photographer from AP and one from UPI also aboard, flew to Washington in one hour and 35 minutes. Stoughton went straight to a darkroom and printed a couple of sets of the negatives of the swearing-in and gave them to Ken O'Donnell, Kennedy's aide and longtime friend. He also learned that the president's body would lie in state in the East

Room. He arrived there, placed a ladder in the East Room and stationed himself nearby to take pictures starting at 3:30 a.m.[84]

Stoughton's final photo of Kennedy had been at a fence in the Dallas airport, with Jackie at his side. "I have that picture on my wall at home," Stoughton said. "I consider that to be the last picture of him." Actually, bystanders took photos and home movies of Kennedy and his wife in their limousine during the motorcade when he was shot.[85]

*   *   *

ABOARD *AIR FORCE ONE*, Johnson took immediate command of the presidency. "Now let's get airborne," he declared over the roar of the idling jet engines after he took the oath. And even though his aggressive exercise of his new powers alienated the Kennedy family, in retrospect his actions were the right ones. While Mrs. Kennedy and the slain president's aides kept vigil with his casket in the rear cabin, Johnson was extremely busy up front. He conferred with Larry O'Brien, Kennedy's chief congressional lobbyist, asking him to stay on the Johnson team and jumped immediately into legislative strategy. They talked about a pending amendment in the Senate to a foreign-aid bill that Johnson feared would damage the program: Johnson ordered O'Brien to fight the amendment.

Johnson coordinated by phone with Cabinet officers and ordered meetings with the nation's governors, congressional leaders, and former Presidents Eisenhower and Truman. He also talked with Rose Kennedy, the slain president's mother, and Robert Kennedy, his brother and the attorney general. This phone call to Robert Kennedy caused lasting hard feelings. Johnson expressed his grief, but he also asked Robert Kennedy pointed questions about the legal issues involved in taking power, such as who should have administered the oath. LBJ wanted to make sure everything had been done lawfully. (It was.) This was appropriate in a technical sense, since Kennedy was attorney general, but other officials could easily have handled such matters.

LBJ's insistence that Jackie Kennedy stand next to him during the swearing-in also angered Kennedy associates because they thought it was too much to ask of the obviously distraught widow, according to historian Robert Dallek. Mrs. Kennedy participated willingly but the episode started Johnson on the wrong track with the Kennedy family.

"Robert Kennedy was less cooperative," Dallek writes. "In a state of profound shock and grief, he was in no mood to indulge anyone's needs beyond those of his immediate family. When *Air Force One* landed at

Andrews Field in Maryland, Bobby, 'his face . . . streaked with tears,' hurried by the Johnson party to Jackie's side." Johnson later admitted he felt snubbed: "He ran [past LBJ] so that he would not have to pause and recognize the new President," Dallek observed.[86]

The first hours of Johnson's presidency were typical of his entire administration—moments of brilliance, strong leadership, and civic-mindedness, mixed with bouts of insensitivity, egotism, pettiness, and insecurity.

The first dramatic photo had a big impact on Johnson. It persuaded LBJ to have "comprehensive, documentary-style coverage [by White House photographers], a trend that has continued, to a widely varying degree, through to today," says documentary filmmaker John Bredar.[87]

* * *

ON THE MOST SOMBER of notes, Jackie Kennedy was determined to surround her husband's funeral in Washington with photographic images of the family's dignity, pride, and courage. Standing on the steps of St. Matthew's Cathedral as her husband's flag-draped casket passed, she nudged her son John Jr. forward to salute his father's body, a dramatic moment that many Americans wept over and still remember today.[88]

It was Jacqueline Kennedy who invented the image of Camelot to summarize her husband's time in office and his legacy. She came up with the metaphor—capturing romantic visions of a noble and courageous King Arthur and the Knights of the Round Table—shortly after JFK's death, and the image has remained indelible. It has been reinforced over the years by innumerable photos of the young president in action, making decisions, meeting with other world leaders, yet finding time to have fun and play with his children. All this imagery deepened Kennedy's image as a leader struck down in the prime of life, before he could reach his full potential.[89]

* * *

IT TURNED OUT that Stoughton had a problem with President Johnson—LBJ didn't like his pictures. Shortly after he became president, Johnson sat in the Oval Office making his way through a pile of official 11-by-14-inch prints from the previous day's activities, provided by Stoughton, and he found only a few that he liked. He kept these in a small pile on his desk and threw the others, one by one, onto the floor. "Goddam it!" Johnson raged. "Why can't they make good pictures of me like they did with Kennedy?" The new president then yelled at a press aide, "Get me that Jap photographer!"[90]

He meant Yoichi R. Okamoto, then the director of photography at the United States Information Agency. LBJ quickly installed him as his official photographer, sending Stoughton to work for the National Park Service. Okamoto turned out to be one of the best and most influential photographers to ever hold the job.

Notes

1. "Biographical Profiles: Cecil Stoughton," John F. Kennedy Presidential Library and Museum, www.jfklibrary.org/research/research-aids/ready-reference/biography-art-profiles.
2. John Bredar, *The President's Photographer: Fifty Years Inside the Oval Office*, Washington, D.C.: National Geographic Society, 2010, p. 51.
3. Ibid.
4. Richard Reeves, *Portrait of Camelot: A Thousand Days in the Kennedy White House*, New York: Abrams, 2010, p. 8.
5. Quoted in Jackson Krule, "All the Presidents' Photographers," *New Yorker*, Feb 17, 2021, www.newyorker.com/culture/photo-booth/all-the-presidents-photographers.
6. Reeves, *Portrait of Camelot*, p. 342.
7. Ibid., p. 343.
8. Cecil Stoughton and Chester V. Clifton, *The Memories: JFK, 1961–1963*, New York: W.W. Norton & Company, 1973, p. 137.
9. Ibid.
10. Bredar, *The President's Photographer*, p. 51.
11. Ibid., p. 52.
12. Stoughton and Clifton, *The Memories*, p. 137.
13. Evan Andrews, "10 Things You may not Know about Jacqueline Kennedy Onassis," *History*, July 28, 2014, www.history.com/news/10-things-you-may-not-know-about-jacqueline-kennedy-onassis.
14. Barbara A. Perry, *Jacqueline Kennedy: First Lady of the New Frontier*. Lawrence: University Press of Kansas, 2004, pp. 78–79.
15. George Tames, *Eye on Washington: The Presidents Who've Known Me*, New York: HarperCollins Publishers, 1990, p. 71.
16. Perry, *Jacqueline Kennedy*, p. 71.
17. Reeves, *Portrait of Camelot*, pp. 8–9.
18. Stoughton and Clifton, *The Memories*, p. 115.
19. Bredar, *The President's Photographer*, pp. 52, 55.
20. Stoughton and Clifton, *The Memories*, p. 60.

21. Ibid., pp. 103–104.
22. Ibid., p. 104.
23. Lesley Ciarula Taylor, "Only Known Photo of Two Icons for Sale," *Toronto Star*, June 3, 2010, p. A13; see also Associated Press, "Rare Monroe Shot Among Trove of Kennedy Photos Sold in NYC," *Hamilton Spectator*, Dec. 10, 2010, p. A17.
24. Stoughton and Clifford, *The Memories*, p. 84.
25. Ibid., p. 115.
26. Quoted in Reeves, *Portrait of Camelot*, p. 58.
27. Ibid., p. 9.
28. Ibid.
29. Barbara Perry, telephone interview with author, Sept. 21, 2016.
30. Ibid.
31. Reeves, *Portrait of Camelot*, p. 7.
32. Ibid, p. 9.
33. Liz McNeil, "Former Secret Service Agent Clint Hill Reveals why JFK didn't want Jackie Kennedy Photographed in a Bikini," *People*, May 3, 2016, http://people.com/celebrity/clint-hill-jfk-didnt-want-jackie-kennedy-photographed-in-bikini.
34. Matt Schudel, "Bob Davidoff, 78; Florida Photographer of the Kennedys," *Washington Post*, Oct. 17, 2004, p. C10.
35. Ibid.
36. Jacques Lowe, *The Kennedy Years: A Memoir*, New York: Rizzoli, 2013, p. 14.
37. Ibid., p. 9.
38. Ibid., p. 15.
39. Ibid.
40. Ibid.
41. Robert McNeely, *The Clinton Years: The Photographs of Robert McNeely*, New York: Callaway, 2000, pp. 23–24.
42. Lowe, *The Kennedy Years*, p. 123; see also 'John F. Kennedy Demonstrates His Exotropia', *Tywkiwdbi*, June 28, 2012, http://tywkiwdbi.blogspot.com/2012/06/john-f-kennedy-demonstrates-his.html.
43. Lowe, *The Kennedy Years*, p. 130.
44. Ibid., pp. 154, 203.
45. Ibid., p. 26.
46. Ibid., p. 119.
47. Ibid., p. 155.
48. Ibid., p. 165.
49. Ibid.
50. Ibid., p. 26.
51. Ibid., pp. 26–27.
52. Ibid., p. 26.

53. Ibid., p. 83.
54. Ibid., pp. 85, 111.
55. Ibid., p. 85.
56. Ibid., pp. 120–121.
57. Ibid., p. 185.
58. Tames, *Eye on Washington*, p. 71.
59. Lowe, *The Kennedy Years*, p. 185.
60. Ibid., pp. 187, 203, 191, 194–195.
61. Ibid., p. 197.
62. Ibid., p. 202.
63. Tames, *Eye on Washington*, p. 71.
64. Ibid., p. 72.
65. Lowe, *The Kennedy Years*, p. 195.
66. Ibid., p. 247.
67. Don Nardo, *Assassination and Its Aftermath: How a Photograph Reassured a Shocked Nation*, North Mankato, Minn.: Compass Point Books, 2014, p. 32.
68. Associated Press, "Kennedy Played His 'Death' for Home Movie," *New York Times*, Aug. 14, 1983, www.nytimes.com/1983/08/14/us/kennedy-played-his-death-for-home-movie.html?
69. Ibid.
70. Ibid. ·
71. Nardo, *Assassination and Its Aftermath*, pp. 4–5.
72. Ibid., p. 7.
73. Ibid., pp. 7–8.
74. Stephanie Fuller, "JFK's Photographer: Memories Flash Back thru his Camera's Eye," *Chicago Tribune*, Nov. 22, 1973, p. E4.
75. "Historical Notes: The Full Record," *Time*, Feb. 24. 1967, http://content.time.com/time/subscriber/printout/0,8816,899410,00.html.
76. Fuller, "JFK's Photographer," p. E4.
77. Nardo, *Assassination and Its Aftermath*, pp. 9–10.
78. Fuller, "JFK's Photographer," p. E4; see also Cecil Stoughton, interview, *Antiques Roadshow*, Jan. 11, 2016, www.pbs.org/wgbh/roadshow/stories/articles/2016/01/11/john-f-kennedy-documents-interview; Bredar, *The President's Photographer*, p. 55.
79. Jack Valenti, interview with author, Jan. 15, 2002.
80. Nardo, *Assassination and Its Aftermath*, pp. 11, 37.
81. Ibid., p. 39.
82. Ibid., pp. 39, 42, 44.
83. Fuller, "JFK's Photographer," p. E4.
84. Ibid.
85. Ibid.

86. Robert Dallek, *Flawed Giant: Lyndon Johnson and his Times 1961–1973*, New York: Oxford University Press, 1998, p. 50.
87. Bredar, *The President's Photographer*, p. 15.
88. Tames, *Eye on Washington*, p. 74.
89. Reeves, *Portrait of Camelot*, p. 10.
90. Tames, *Eye on Washington*, p. 87.

CHAPTER THREE
BEHIND THE SCENES WITH
LYNDON B. JOHNSON AND YOICHI OKAMOTO

Yoichi R. Okamoto was born of Japanese parents in Yonkers, New York, in 1915 and graduated from Colgate University. After that, he was a photographer for the *Post-Standard* (Syracuse, NY) from 1938 to 1942 and then served as a photographer with the U.S. Army Signal Corps during World War II. He worked in Italy and other battle zones in Europe—one of the rare Japanese Americans to do so—and then was assigned to the U.S. Information Service, later the U.S. Information Agency, in Vienna, Austria, and in Washington, D.C.[1]

Okamoto was a reserved man who rarely talked about himself. But he had a fascinating personal story, perhaps the most interesting of any White House photographer. As a small boy visiting Japan, he was evacuated on an American warship after an earthquake in 1923. And as a child of 8 he toured with a Red Cross unit telling of his experiences in the disaster, which struck while he was walking in a park.[2]

Prior to his assignment at the White House starting in 1964, he was already known to the photographic cognoscenti as a brilliant practitioner of visual arts. His work as a government photographer eventually came to the attention of celebrated photographer Edward Steichen, and this gave Okamoto a burst of fame. When Steichen opened a photo exhibit called "The Family of Man" at the Corcoran Gallery of Art in

Washington, D.C., he included an Okamoto photo of dancer Harald Kreuzberger, made in 1950 while Okamoto was covering a cultural festival in Salzburg.[3]

Okamoto was also praised in a *Washington Post* review of a one-man show he held in 1958. "Okamoto is chief of the visual materials branch of the Press Service of the United States Information Agency and has had a distinguished career, first as Gen. Mark Clark's photographic officer with the United States forces in Austria and later, with the State Department's information program in Vienna," the reviewer wrote. "In 1954 he was given the Silver Award of the Austrian Photographic Society for 'contributions to the advancement of photography' in that country."

The reviewer added: "Okamoto is a photographer whose work is interesting on every level. He specializes in strong contrasts of black and white, with asymmetric compositions designed to give great emotional impact to the work. His photos reflect his Oriental background in their use of a single isolated object held in tension against great space. Studies of ballet dancers, of artists, of rooftops and tenements, of strange corners of European countries, all give him his opportunity to compose and design. He is more of an artist with a camera than are most painters with a brush."[4]

*   *   *

OKAMOTO GOT TO KNOW then-Vice President Lyndon B. Johnson when he took the official pictures of LBJ on a visit to West Germany, including the Berlin Wall, in August 1961. Johnson loved the photos and arranged for Okamoto to repeat as the official photographer on other Johnson trips while LBJ was vice president.

"JFK was this really good-looking young guy with a beautiful wife and his gorgeous kids," observed David Kennerly, who served as President Gerald Ford's White House photographer. "The marriage of JFK and still photography was made in heaven, for both, because JFK came across so beautifully in pictures, and he knew it. . . . LBJ wanted pictures like JFK was getting, and so he remembered Okamoto photographing for the United States Information Agency on his trips overseas. LBJ just let him in to do whatever he wanted to do. And LBJ did that out of a sense of vanity and out of a sense of history."[5]

Okamoto, at that time the chief photographer of the U.S. Information Agency, was reassigned on a temporary basis to the White House.

Okamoto, known by the nickname "Oke," had his own problems with Johnson's impatience and temper. "I sent some of my pictures up to him," Okamoto recalled, "And he sent one of them back [saying], 'It's the worst picture of me I've ever seen, except one.' [This apparently was a reference to his official portrait painted by Peter Hurd, which LBJ detested.] And I sent a note back: 'I'm still the best damn Japanese photographer you have on your staff.'"[6]

Okamoto told Johnson when he took the job that he wanted to "try to document history in the making," not just settle for grip-and-grin shots, such as the endless handshakes at official receptions and meetings, or staged official images.[7]

The new photographer was promised and given enormous access to the president, more than JFK had allowed. He reported directly to Johnson, not the press secretary or White House chief of staff, and he could walk into the Oval Office whenever he wanted, in order to "document history in the making."

"He let me walk in on him at any time," Okamoto once said. "There were only two people at the White House, Marvin Watson, the appointments secretary, and myself, who had permission to walk in on the President of the United States at any time. Well, once he let me do that, I figured out that the responsibility would be to the historian 500 years from now."[8] His goal was to "get an honest picture of a crucial moment."[9]

And the countless pictures of those moments included LBJ meeting with the Reverend Martin Luther King, Robert Kennedy, and Richard Nixon, getting a haircut, in the hospital during and after surgery, lecturing his aides, lobbying members of Congress, and meeting with staff while still in bed in the morning.

"Yoichi Okamoto has done the best job of anyone who was in that position," says Kennerly.[10]

Kennerly met with Okamoto over lunch to get advice when he became Ford's photographer. Okamoto told him: "Remember one thing: that when you're here, everybody will be your friend, the cabinet officers and all that. But what they really want are the pictures." Okamoto also told Kennerly: "You got to just be there all the time; 16 hours a day. That's how you're going to get the good pictures. . . . There's only so much time you'll be in that job. You'll never have another opportunity like that."[11]

Oke considered himself a visual storyteller. "He captured the tension and the fatigue on the face of LBJ," Kennerly said. "When you look at the pictures, you just feel like you're there. Oke became the godfather of White House photography. Nobody had done it that way before, and pretty much nobody's done it since. Oke had the combination of a great subject, a really difficult time in American history with the Vietnam War going on, with civil-rights problems. He was photographing the heart of all these things that were happening during that presidency, and how LBJ just dealt [with them] on a day-to-day basis."[12]

"I'd always known Oke was a good photographer," Kennerly added, "but when I went through the contact sheets at the LBJ library, what I saw was greatness. I saw a photographer who not only took really good individual photos, but he thought and he photographed as a storyteller. . . . When I look at Oke's pictures, I see magic. And I think it underscores the value of the White House photographer in the hands of someone like him."[13]

*   *   *

OKE'S STRATEGY within the White House, replicated by the most effective White House photographers since then, was to be unobtrusive. "He wasn't an in-your-face kind of person," said Mike Geissinger, a young assistant to Okamoto. "He was very laid back; he was very quiet and I think that translated directly into his photography so that he was able to work in that unobtrusive manner. And quietly. I don't want to say behind the scenes, because he wasn't behind the scenes. He was right up front."[14]

Okamoto said his objective was "training the president" not to realize he was there. "I made it a point to be in his office when he walked in the first thing in the morning," Okamoto said, "and I intentionally did not say good morning to him unless he said good morning to me. The main purpose of that was that he'd consider me as part of the furniture. After a while he never saw me."[15]

"Several times, I would go into the Cabinet Room and the people were there before he arrived and I'd take pictures because people behave differently before the President and after he is in the room and I found that interesting. And then he'd come in the room and I'd cover the whole bit, take pictures from both sides and even take a 21mm or 20mm [a very wide-angle lens] six or seven inches from the back of his head and then I'd figure I'd shot my wad and go down to the office. And I'd get there and the buzzer would buzz [the same buzzer installed during Stoughton's time] and I'd dash back upstairs. As I walked in with my camera he'd say, 'All right now, everybody comb their hair and look good 'cause this fellow's going to take your picture.' And everybody in the room of course had already seen me." But LBJ didn't realize this.[16]

Okamoto had a sudden falling-out with the notoriously mercurial Johnson. Four months after he arrived at the White House as a staff photographer, the media reported that LBJ had authorized the expenditure of $5,000 for pictures of himself on a single weekend. Oke had revealed this to a reporter without thinking that the information would embarrass his boss, and LBJ suspected Oke of the leak. When *Newsweek* reported that Johnson was about to name Okamoto his permanent personal photographer, the president went ballistic, called Oke into the Oval Office and fired him for talking to the media without authorization.[17] Okamoto was so devoted to his job that he kept taking pictures of LBJ in the Oval Office for several minutes even after his dismissal.[18]

But famous photographer Edward Steichen intervened. Several months later, Steichen found himself as an invited guest at a White House reception and he used the occasion to urge the president to rehire Oke, whom Steichen knew and respected. Steichen advised the president to have Oke make a photographic record of the Johnson presidency to save for history. Okamoto was brought back immediately but with a major warning. Johnson ordered Oke to "mind his own business and not talk to the media." Johnson also told Oke he had his "pecker in his pocket and could rip it out at any time and throw it to the dogs."[19] Okamoto once said LBJ always treated him as a "flunky" or "subordinate" and they had no personal rapport.[20]

Johnson made life difficult for his photographer day in and day out. He felt that the left side of his face was more attractive than the right side, and he wanted as many photos as possible to be taken with that in mind.[21] Johnson took a great interest in projecting as good an image as he could.

He insisted on having photos taken with virtually all his visitors, and he would have his staff send out the autographed prints as White House mementos, to cement his relationships, and to provide personalized LBJ keepsakes. "President Johnson realized the political value of a photo," said Okamoto. "He had a unique sense of history. He understood man's vanity. He was almost always available for photos, and he authorized me to walk into his office without knocking . . . to record some very precious moments of history."[22]

"So obsessed was LBJ with photographs of himself that almost daily, until the end of his term of office, he edited all White House pictures that were to be released, and woe to anyone who acted without his authorization," wrote photographer George Tames of the *New York Times*, who knew Okamoto and the LBJ White House well.[23]

Tames also observed: "I don't believe LBJ ever came to grips with the power of television. 'They are learning to smile and act on TV,' he remarked to me one day, talking about political friends and enemies, 'when they really should be learning ass kissing and ego rubbing, the only way to really get things done.'"

"The great compromiser would not compromise with his new electronic opponent. LBJ needed to wear glasses but refused to do so and appear 'old.' To see, he had to squint, which gave him a perpetual scowl and grumpy countenance. His teleprompters had one-inch-high letters, but still he had to strain to see."

"On one occasion in the East Room, during a diplomatic reception and television broadcast, LBJ tried using contact lenses," Tames added. "It was a disaster. His eyes watered and his vision blurred. At the end of the broadcast, he stalked in a menacing manner into the Green Room, where he tore the contact lenses from his eyes and stomped them underfoot. The air turned blue with curses."[24]

LBJ insisted on controlling the settings and staging the pictures as much as possible. "The only picture I can recall which does not fit this classification is the picture Charles Gorry of Associated Press made of LBJ as he picked his pet beagle up by the ears," said Ollie Atkins, a news photographer who became Richard Nixon's chief shooter. "It was far from being artistic or truly great as a photograph but it certainly will be remembered."[25]

What particularly rankled the press shooters was Johnson's decision to forbid still photography while he was speaking at press conferences. "Still photographers must make all their pictures in the first few seconds before the President speaks and then there follows a lot of mad arm flailing by the press aides cutting the still photographers off," Atkins said at the time. "Live television and news reels continue to photograph him through the entire press conference. The explanation for this restriction on still pictures is that LBJ feels the cameramen will shoot pictures of him with his mouth open while he is scratching an ear or wiping the perspiration from his brow and these single shots will be used on the front pages to illustrate his pronouncements."[26]

Atkins added: "Probably the best known photograph made of President Johnson is the one called 'old scarbelly' by the press corps and this picture of LBJ exhibiting the incision scar of his gall bladder operation is certainly not great photographically nor can I imagine that it is cherished by the President himself."[27] This was probably true, but Atkins didn't recognize the value of this picture. It showed Johnson as the earthy, larger-than-life figure that he was.[28]

This brings up a broader point—that Okamoto was limited by his role of hired hand, as all staff photographers are. *New York Times* critic Andy Grundberg wrote in 1990 that Okamoto did not really aim to show Johnson's dark or unappealing sides, but was essentially a PR man with a camera even if his images could be brilliant. Referring to an exhibit of 120 LBJ photos at the International Center of Photography in New York, Grundberg noted that "the notorious photograph of Johnson pulling up his shirt to reveal his scar from [a gallbladder] operation—the scar was later transformed by a political cartoonist into a map of Vietnam—was taken by a United Press International photographer, not by Okamoto or any other photographer on his staff. This suggests that there were limits to the candid approach the White House photographers employed."

"Indeed, the image of Johnson portrayed throughout the exhibit—of an avuncular, high-spirited but sincere and caring man who tried to make the Presidency more human and humane, in the tradition of Andrew Jackson—is at radical odds with the portrait of venality and chicanery meticulously traced by Robert A. Caro in his best-selling biography of Johnson's political rise, *Means of Ascent*. One might even say that the pictures of 'L.B.J.: The White House Years' [by Okamoto] resemble a public relations campaign as much now as they did when they were first taken."[28]

Grundberg added: "Johnson's Presidency could be said to have ended as it began, in tragedy. The war in Vietnam led to domestic protest and discontent, and the projected Great Society never materialized. A picture in the exhibition of Johnson with his head down while listening to a tape-recorded account of action in Vietnam speaks eloquently (albeit metaphorically) of the war's impact on his state of mind. But overall the show masks the extent to which the war had become a major public and political preoccupation by 1968."[29]

* * *

DESPITE THE CHALLENGES, Okamoto's body of work was remarkable and remains much admired by his successors. In photo after photo, President Johnson comes alive at a historic moment or when a seemingly trivial but revealing incident is captured on film. Okamoto estimated that Johnson made 200 to 300 decisions a day and took papers to the residence with him each night, with many having approval or disapproval boxes for him to check at the bottom: "yes," "no," and "see me."[30]

"LBJ had seen all these pictures of JFK from outside photographers like Jacques Lowe and Stanley Tretick," says David Kennerly, the White House photographer for President Gerald Ford. "They had John Jr. under the desk. George Tames [of the *New York Times*] had the famous picture from behind the desk, 'The Loneliest Job' [showing Kennedy with his head bowed, alone at a window]."[31] LBJ wanted similar photos of himself.

Kennerly, a Pulitzer Prize winner for feature photography for his coverage of the Vietnam War for United Press International in 1972, recalled some of Oke's best pictures—and there were many—such as his insider's shot, taken while Oke crouched under a table, when LBJ met with then-Soviet leader Aleksei Kosygin during a superpower summit at Glassboro, New Jersey. There was also Oke's picture of LBJ looking weak and vulnerable in the hospital after gallbladder surgery.

"He had astonishing moments," Kennerly said. "He had the photographs that really showed the relationship between RFK and LBJ, neither of whom liked each other, and the pictures showed that." In one particularly revealing shot, LBJ is seated in what appears to be John Kennedy's trademark rocking chair—a move sure to get under RFK's skin because he could never fully accept Johnson as his brother's successor. The two antagonists apparently are alone (except for Oke) in the Oval Office, sitting stiffly an awkward distance from each other, each of them like a coiled spring.[32]

One sees the contemplative Lyndon Johnson in Okamoto's famous picture of LBJ with civil-rights leader Martin Luther King Jr. during a discussion of the civil-rights movement in the Cabinet Room in March 1966. King is shown in the forefront of the frame, sitting at a big table, clearly defined, while Johnson is in the background, intentionally blurred as if he were just an observer. King has a hand resting gently on the side of his face as he talks to LBJ, while Johnson has a big fist planted in his left cheek as he listens, seeming depressed. It looks like a very serious moment. There is no hint of levity or distraction in either man. It reveals how sober, even solemn, these discussions were. People's lives were at stake as the protests grew. The nation's soul was also at stake as America painfully moved toward equal justice amid enormous obstacles.

Okamoto also captured Johnson's massive personality and effort to dominate everything around him. Typical was the "Treatment"—LBJ's way of invading the personal space of people he was talking to, one on one, leaning into his target so their noses were almost touching and often resulting in the other person leaning backward in reaction to the president's looming presence. A perfect illustration was Oke's picture of Johnson lobbying Senator Richard Russell, (D-Ga.), to get his support for the Civil Rights Act. Johnson has locked eyes with Russell, and the senator is trying to stand his ground, remaining almost at attention while Johnson seems an irresistible force.

In another series of photos, LBJ is giving the "Treatment" to Senator Theodore Green (D-RI), and the diminutive senator seems almost fearful as the six-foot-four Johnson leans more and more, invading Green's personal space. There is nowhere for the senator to go, no way to escape. LBJ has him pinned against a table, intentionally no doubt. Senator Barry Goldwater (R-Ariz.), once said Johnson was the only man he ever knew who "when he'd talk to you would breathe into your mouth."[33]

In another, lesser-known photo, Johnson crouches down and inspects something left behind by his dog Yuki on the fancy rug in the Oval Office. The president, Oke later explained, was inspecting the stool for worms. Yuki, seeming understandably nervous, is standing at a safe distance from the president.[34] Johnson's crudeness was part of his nature. He sometimes chatted with visitors while he was doing his business on the toilet. He caused a stir among animal lovers when he picked up one of his beagles by the ears, a scene which unfolded in front of news photographers, who sent the image around the world.

LBJ never seemed to stop working, and that was evident in a photo snapped by Okamoto of the president getting a haircut in the White House barber shop and giving an interview at the same time. LBJ's shoulders are draped in a piece of fabric as barber Steve Martini snips at the back of his head. A stern-looking, rubber-faced Johnson is making a point as he looks intently at his interviewer, Arthur Sulzberger, publisher of the *New York Times*, who is sitting at LBJ's knee taking notes on a spiral pad.[35]

In one of the most poignant images of all, LBJ is shown during the turbulent summer of 1968, a season of massive demonstrations against the Vietnam War. He is sitting alone in the Cabinet Room as he listens to a tape recording from his son-in-law Chuck Robb, a Marine captain in Vietnam. Robb was reporting to his father-in-law about conditions in that embattled country, and the commander in chief is apparently deeply troubled by what he is hearing. His head is hung low and his forehead rests on his clenched right fist planted on a table, his left hand leaning on the arm of a chair. The viewer can't see his face but his demeanor speaks of anguish and exhaustion. The photo was taken by Jack Kightlinger, one of Okamoto's deputies, on July 31, 1968. It revealed the amazing access that Johnson granted to his visual historians and the doubts that he hid from the public regarding how badly the war was going despite his public expressions of optimism.

Okamoto's final major project as White House photographer was a photo spread in *Life* magazine published on November 15, 1968, after the unpopular LBJ decided not to run again. Republican Richard Nixon had gained the White House, defeating Democratic Vice President Hubert Humphrey. Okamoto's pictures illustrated LBJ's decision-making process during a 23-day period leading up to his suspension of U.S. bombing of North Vietnam. Amid all the photos of Johnson listening, gesticulating, and scowling at his advisers (all men—an insight into the times when women had not yet reached the top echelons of power) or sitting alone as he talked on the phone, two images stand out. Both involved his 1-year-old grandson, Lyn Nugent. In one, taken on Halloween, October 31, the boy is standing next to the president's desk in the Oval Office, wearing a "super president" mask and costume and carrying a plastic pumpkin to hold his trick-or-treat candies. Johnson is barely paying attention to the boy as he talks on the intercom. In the other standout image, taken on the same occasion, Lyn is shown gently kissing his grandfather's image on a television screen in the Oval Office, apparently as a way to get LBJ's attention.[36]

After his stint in government, Okamoto worked as a freelance photographer at operated Image, Inc., a custom photo lab in Washington, D.C., until he retired in the early 1980s.

* * *

A FINAL WORD about Okamoto: He died at age 69 on April 24, 1985 at his home in Bethesda, Maryland. Police ruled it a suicide by hanging.[37] His successor Kennerly observed: "He was a very quiet, professorial kind of guy. . . . Oke was very reserved and incredibly tight-lipped. . . . And you know, Oke ultimately killed himself in 1985. I don't know why. From what I've heard, he had a history of depression."[38]

He must have been troubled for years by the difficulties and pressures of his job and also by the stereotypes Oke faced all his life as a Japanese American, going back to World War II and LBJ's later reference to him as "that Jap photographer." The flare-ups of prejudice could erupt at the oddest times, such as at a visit with LBJ to the home of former President Harry Truman in 1966. Johnson and his entourage were walking into the house when Bess Truman stopped a group of news photographers, including Oke on LBJ's staff, from entering. "I don't allow photographers in my house," Mrs. Truman announced. Okamoto asked her why. "Well, I've got furniture that dates from World War I, old furniture. It suits me. It suits Harry. But I don't want anybody taking pictures of it. I don't want anybody making fun of it. We're not going to have it. You, you little old Japanese boy, you get off my porch." Okamoto protested: "Look, I'm the White House photographer. I'm working for President Johnson." But Bess Truman held firm: "I don't care who you work for, you get off my porch," she ordered. Okamoto was fuming but took a few frames on the porch and then stepped off into the yard. He never mentioned the incident to Johnson.[39]

Occasionally, Oke pushed back. When German Defense Minister Gerhard Schroeder visited the White House in July 1968, he spotted Okamoto and, noting he had been Germany's ambassador to Tokyo, began speaking to the cameraman in Japanese. Okamoto, who had spent 11 years in Vienna, said to Schroeder in German, "Mr. Minister, can we try a language I understand?"[40]

Notes

1. "USIA Official Revisits P-S, Former Employee," *Post-Standard* (Syracuse, N.Y.), Nov. 20, 1961, p. 26.
2. "Japanese Native of U.S. Enlists," *New York Times*, Jan. 7, 1942, p. 14.
3. "Steichen Exhibit has Portrait by D.C. Man," *Washington Post*, June 29, 1955, p. 18.
4. "A One-Man Photo Show," *Washington Post*, Jan. 5, 1958, p. E7.
5. James Estrin, "Photographing the White House from the Inside," *New York Times*, Dec. 10, 2013, https://lens.blogs.nytimes.com/2013/12/10/photographing-the-white-house-from-the-inside/?_r=2.
6. John Bredar, *The President's Photographer: Fifty Years Inside the Oval Office*. Washington, D.C.: National Geographic Society, 2010, p. 85.
7. Ibid.

8. Ibid., p. 201.
9. Ibid., p. 202.
10. David Kennerly, interview with author, Apr. 27, 2016.
11. Estrin, "Photographing the White House from the Inside."
12. Ibid.
13. Ibid.
14. Bredar, *The President's Photographer*, p. 86.
15. Ibid., p. 119.
16. Ibid., pp. 119–120.
17. George Tames, *Eye on Washington: The Presidents Who've Known Me*, New York: HarperCollins Publishers, 1990, p. 88.
18. Bredar, *The President's Photographer*, p. 89.
19. Ibid., pp. 89–90.
20. Robert McNeely, *The Clinton Years: The Photographs of Robert McNeely*, New York: Callaway, 2000, pp. 24–25.
21. Tames, *Eye on Washington*, p. 88.
22. Lloyd Shearer, "Photographing the President," *Salt Lake Tribune*, Sept. 5, 1971, p. 46.
23. Tames, *Eye on Washington*, p. 88.
24. Ibid., p. 91.
25. Ollie Atkins, "Photographing the President," *U.S. Camera World Annual 1968*, New York: U.S. Camera Publishing Corp., 1967, p. 8.
26. Ibid., p. 200.
27. Ibid., p. 202.
28. Andy Grundberg, "Review/Photography: The Personal Side of Johnson as President," *New York Times*, June 1, 1990, pp. C1–C26.
29. Ibid., p. C26.
30. Atkins, "Photographing the President," p. 202.
31. Estrin, "Photographing the White House from the Inside."
32. Ibid.
33. Tames, *Eye on Washington*, p. 91.
34. Bredar, *The President's Photographer*, pp. 92–93.
35. Ibid., p. 202.
36. "The Bomb Halt Decision," *Life*, Nov. 15, 1968, pp. 84A–97A.
37. "Photographer Yoichi Okamoto Dies at 69," *Washington Post*, Apr. 25, 1985, www.washingtonpost.com/archive/local/1985/04/25/photographer-yoichi-okamoto.
38. Estrin, "Photographing the White House from the Inside."
39. Jack Albright, oral history interview II, June 10, 1981, pp. 3–4, Lyndon Baines Johnson Library Oral History Collection, www.lbjlibrary.net/assets/documents/archives/oral_histories/albright_j/Albright2.pdf.
40. "Photographer Yoichi Okamoto Dies at 69."

Chapter Four
Behind the Scenes with Richard Nixon and Ollie Atkins

President Richard Nixon was indifferent to pictures and considered the work of Ollie Atkins, his chief White House photographer, an intrusion. He gave Atkins a rule: "Six and out." This meant Atkins could take six pictures and then would have to leave the room. Nixon would listen for the frames to click off on Atkins' camera and then nod for his shooter to exit. Sometimes, Nixon would dismiss Atkins in a gruff and even angry way, as if the photographer himself was a nuisance.

Atkins, originally from Wellesley, Massachusetts, and a 1938 graduate of the University of Alabama with a journalism major, was a former *Saturday Evening Post* photographer and a talented shooter. He had earlier worked for the *Birmingham Post* and the *Washington Daily News*. Atkins, a tall, genial man who wore large black-framed eyeglasses, had taken pictures as a news photographer of Presidents Franklin Roosevelt, Harry Truman, Dwight Eisenhower, and John F. Kennedy. He also had been president of the White House Press Photographers Association so he knew his way around the East and West Wings.[1]

Atkins, who had been Nixon's campaign photographer during his successful 1968 campaign, said in a 1971 interview: "He's accustomed to posing for news photographers. But he doesn't like to ham it up. He won't wear Indian hats or pose in shorts or violate what he consider his domain of privacy. I would say he is cheerfully reconciled to the necessity of having photographers around. But he is not particularly interested in the outcome of a photo session. He just takes them in stride. I don't believe I've ever submitted contact sheets to him so that he can pick out the best shots. Unlike other presidents who've exercised their right of approval, he assumes no photographer is trying to do him in."[2]

Atkins described his hiring this way: "I had worked for Nixon's election committee during the campaign of 1968. Actually, I was with the candidate for a little over two months, during which time he had a chance to look at me, and, of course, I had a chance to work on the campaign and to get to know everybody. Herb Klein, chief of the Office of Communications, later told me that the President wasn't even sure he wanted an official photographer. . . . He figured making so many photos in the White House was needless work."[3]

"However, it was pointed out to him that he would need a photographer to do two things: make pictures of guests from time to time; and create a photographic history of his administration. On that basis, the President changed his mind and decided to select a photographer, approving me for the job."[4]

Atkins was hoping for the kind of access that Lyndon Johnson had given to Okamoto. "But Ollie's dreams died aborning when he was placed under the direct thumb of the president's press secretary, Ronald L. Ziegler," recalled longtime *New York Times* photographer George Tames: "No top-secret clearance, no personal and direct access to the president, all picture opportunities cleared with the press secretary."[5]

Atkins' relationship with Ziegler quickly deteriorated because of Ziegler's arrogant manner and the many restrictions he imposed. At one point, the press secretary called Atkins' office and demanded to see him immediately. Atkins was in the restroom. A young staffer ran in and yelled, "Ollie! Ollie! Come quickly! Ziegler wants to see you and he's really mad!" Atkins' voice was then heard from a stall, saying, "Tell him I can only handle one shit at a time!"[6]

Ziegler's dismissive, even abusive, attitude came from the top. "It's weird, but you don't think of Nixon being a navel-gazer, you know, that he was that self-aware," says Don Carleton, director of the Briscoe Center for American History at the University of Texas. "But actually I think Richard Nixon was very self-aware. I think there's a lot of evidence that he had a full understanding, particularly of his dark side. And I think he struggled with his dark side his entire life, frankly. And I think he was scared to death to reveal that to people and I think that's why he was afraid of a camera. I think that's the reason he was such a control freak with his White House photographer."[7]

Atkins has written: "On some occasions, the President paid very little attention to me. In fact, he seemed to ignore me completely. However if he hadn't really broken the ice with his visitor yet, he used me as a kind of conversation starter."

" 'By the way,' he'd say 'this is Ollie Atkins, my official photographer. He's going to make a couple of official photographs of us. You'll get one in the mail.' "[8]

Time observed in 1970, mid-way through Nixon's first term: "John Kennedy and Lyndon Johnson spoiled news photographers assigned to the White House. Nowadays the cameramen are thinking wistfully of the good old days: of shots of John John playing under his father's desk, of a husky Kennedy in bathing trunks on a Southern California beach, of L.B.J. raising his shirt to show his surgical scar or hoisting his beagles by the ears."

"Richard Nixon is not about to be caught by anyone's candid camera. Laments one White House photographer: 'We pretty much do the ceremonial stuff in the office—bill signings, Cabinet meetings. The photographic image of Richard Nixon is of a man taking a shower with his suit and vest on.' "

"That is precisely the way Nixon wants it. He may be the most exceptionally private President since Calvin Coolidge—and of course he may be scarred by a 1960 memory of what a camera can do with his image [when he was pictured as haggard and shifty-eyed during his presidential debate with John Kennedy]. These days, even Ollie Atkins, the official White House photographer, pleads vainly for some 'humanizing' shots of Nixon boating off Key Biscayne. The President may be inhibited here, too, by the memory of a 1955 fishing expedition in the Florida Everglades when he fell overboard and was pictured for posterity hauling himself out of the drink. Last week when Nixon clambered ashore at Key Biscayne from a boating trip, he sported a small bandage over his left eyebrow, having apparently banged his head when the boat pitched. The forlorn photographers were left to dream about yet another shot that they had missed."[9]

*   *   *

IN 1972, when President Nixon was running for reelection, Julie Nixon Eisenhower, his daughter, published *Eye on Nixon*, a coffee-table book of photos about her dad. But his indifference to photography showed. The volume, for which Nixon speech writer William Safire provided the text, mostly contains shots of formal events, such as the commander in chief greeting foreign leaders and posing in other official or stilted situations. Sometimes he is shown reading in private or meeting with aides, all apparently designed to demonstrate his work ethic for the electorate.

There are some shots of a warmer, more engaging Nixon, such as the president at his daughter Tricia's White House wedding and walking with his wife Pat on a beach. But when compared with the kind of fascinating, emotionally charged images disseminated of JFK and LBJ, the Nixonography falls flat. There is very little of the behind-the-scenes feel that Kennedy and Johnson allowed and that enhanced their images as approachable, interesting people.

Julie provides a valuable insight when she writes in the book that her father never was interested in photography, even of his family, and neither was his wife Pat.

She writes: "Photographs are sometimes the best way to show what a person is really like because they catch fleeting moments."[10] But she adds: "It is ironic that I am doing a book of photographs, because the truth is that we have never exactly been a family of photophiles. . . . David once asked where my baby pictures were and I had to admit I had none to show him. My father just never took them. . . . My mother has always been indifferent about photographs. During the war, when my father wrote asking her to send a picture of herself, she had none available and had to go to a neighborhood photographer—she has never been one to have her picture taken. . . . So we have few family pictures. . . . My father never looks at books of Presidential photographs, just as he does not watch himself on television."[11]

The book, which covers Nixon's first term, is heavy with staged photos, especially those showing Nixon meeting with other heads of government such as British Prime Minister Edward Heath, Canadian Premier Pierre Trudeau, French President Charles De Gaulle, South Vietnamese President Nguyen Van Thieu, and General Francisco Franco of Spain. But there are no compelling images and nothing that reveals the private Nixon. Nixon's historic visit to China is given six pages of photos but none are memorable. They include Nixon shaking hands upon arrival in Beijing with Premier Chou En-lai, shaking hands later with Chairman Mao, and standing stiffly on the Great Wall for the obligatory tourist shot. The only interesting photo shows Nixon skeptically inspecting a morsel of food he holds at the end of his chopsticks during a dinner with the Chinese leaders.[12]

Even the photos of the president at the White House wedding of his daughter Tricia are nothing special. They show a happy father and family, but no private moments. One caption, however, gives a slight hint of the impatient and brusque Nixon that others have described: "Though the day was overcast, both father and daughter were determined to hold the ceremony outdoors in the Rose Garden. As Julie describes it, the tension built toward the time of the ceremony; the President paced around in the upstairs living room, looking out the window down at the Rose Garden and glowering back at the sky. Then he said, 'Where are the chairs? Why aren't those chairs out there?' and barked orders into the phone."[13] Nixon's attitude about photographs severely damaged the ability of his official staff to do their jobs. He felt that pictures were frivolous and just took him away from his work. He didn't feel that a visual record of his presidency was a pressing concern and it certainly wasn't a priority.

While Lyndon Johnson would personally review the official photographs and select those to be released to the public each day, Nixon thought this would be a waste of his time. He had a few formal portraits taken of him by New York photographer Philippe Halsman, and they were reproduced 200 or 300 at a time to be sent to government agencies, post offices and individuals who requested photos of the president.[14]

*   *   *

RICHARD NIXON was the polar opposite of his predecessor, far more reserved and private than LBJ. He never would have shown off a surgical scar or lifted his dog by its ears as Johnson did. He didn't like "candid" shots, feeling he wouldn't look natural no matter what the photographer did and suspecting that such sessions would open him up to ridicule. He understood the need for photographs to promote himself and create a positive image but he didn't make it easy for Atkins, his chief photographer, and Atkins' two assistant photographers, Bob Knudsen and Jack Kightlinger.

Akins, in his 50s during Nixon's presidency, described Nixon as "a business-oriented gentleman, conservative in dress and camera demeanor."

Atkins observed in his memoirs: "One of the most interesting things I observed about the President was the extent of his careful preparation for every event on his calendar. If possible, he never did anything that he wasn't completely prepared for.

"Even for a minor meeting with a noncelebrity he demanded extensive briefing by means of well-researched background papers. Nixon didn't want anybody to walk in his office about whom he wasn't thoroughly briefed.

"He had his staff people arrange a backgrounder ahead of time for all his meetings. After studying it carefully, he reread the material just a few seconds before the meeting actually took place."[15]

Atkins also found that Nixon had a "double personality."

"I mean that he had two sides to his personality," Atkins wrote. "One was his professional, business personality; the other, his family personality. He never mixed these two. In fact, a lot of businessmen I know are the same way. It doesn't make it easy to summarize such a man for the public.

"There's the story, for example, about the time he was meeting one of his political aides at an airport during the campaign. The aide, quite excited, ran up to Nixon and embraced him happily, slapping him on the back exuberantly. When Mrs. Nixon, who was on the plane with the aide, came up, Nixon shook hands with her.

"But that's the way he was. He just wasn't a glad-hander."

"Richard Nixon was a very distant man, and even though I'd known him for some time, I really didn't feel close to him as a personal friend," Atkins said. "I was and always would be an employee. As a matter of fact, I don't think that any of the people on the White House staff were personal friends of his, or became personal friends.

"The only exception was Rose Mary Woods. She was a special, very special, staff person, the only one of the staff who was a personal friend of the Nixons—and "I mean the whole family. As the President's secretary, she handled all his correspondence. She did other chores for him too, things that he trusted her with because he knew that anything he asked her to do would be done properly and with dispatch."[16]

Recalled George Tames: "Certainly Nixon resented Kennedy's love affair with the press and never understood the clublike atmosphere of the Kennedy Press Room.

"Suspecting rightly that he was never considered one of the boys with whom reporters would feel free to talk about anything, from politics to women, Nixon kept them at arm's length, deepening the isolation and suspicion on both sides.

"I am not aware, for example, of any member of the media's receiving a midnight call to come join Nixon and friends in an informal political roundtable discussion of current events, as happened with Presidents Kennedy and Johnson. When he got into trouble, he had no one in the media who knew the real Nixon, the human being. His isolation and brusque manner led to additional misinterpretation and misunderstanding.

"Only with the [news] photographers did Nixon feel any remnant of affinity. We—particularly the wire service photographers—had captured his triumphs in Russia and China, and thus shared them."[17]

But even the photographers felt shut out eventually, especially in comparison with their access under JFK and LBJ.

* * *

IT EVENTUALLY BECAME CLEAR that Nixon's affinity for any photographers went only so far. Take the case of Cecil Stoughton, who had enjoyed such close access in the Kennedy administration and was reassigned by Lyndon Johnson. During the Nixon years, Stoughton was an Army major and chief still cameraman for the National Park Service.

He attended Nixon's second inauguration in January 1973 and planned to shoot pictures from the stands behind the presidential party. But a Secret Service agent ordered him to move, and Stoughton found his way to a spot behind the president and first lady as they faced the crowd. Wearing a vivid blue and brown plaid coat, he dropped to his knees and shot a few frames. Unfortunately for him, he was visible very clearly in the photos taken by his colleagues of the actual swearing in. Nixon and his men were furious, arguing the Stoughton had spoiled the historic shot. Even though Stoughton wrote an apology to Nixon, his job was abolished and he retired in April 1973.[18]

* * *

ATKINS BECAME an expert on the president's daily routine. This was important because he needed to know what the president was doing, minute to minute, in order to plan what he would record visually and what might turn into an important or interesting photo opportunity.

Nixon got up each morning between 7:30 and 8:00 a.m. He quickly dressed and ate his breakfast in the East Wing residence unless he had a guest for the meal, such as national security adviser Henry Kissinger or a member of Congress. In that case they would eat in one of several small dining rooms downstairs. When the president ate alone, which he did on most days, he would gulp his food—most likely a half grapefruit or other fresh fruit, cold cereal, skim milk, orange juice, and coffee—in two or three minutes and then head for the Oval Office or sometimes his hideaway office across the street from the White House at the Executive Office Building. He would generally arrive at the Oval Office at 8:00 a.m. or a few minutes later, preceded by his valet, Manolo Sanchez who carried the president's attaché case and anything else Nixon needed for work.[19]

Nixon would begin by reviewing the paperwork left for him overnight by Bob Haldeman, his chief of staff. He also read a daily news summary prepared by his staff, often 50 typewritten pages, single-spaced. Nixon's meetings started with a senior-staff session at 8:30 a.m.

For lunch, he had a regular dish—cottage cheese with a pineapple ring or other fresh fruit. For dinner, he liked meatloaf. But Nixon had little interest in food, Atkins said. He was driven almost totally by his work.

White House speechwriter William Safire wrote: "The President builds thinking time into his calendar. Wednesdays, for example, are kept relatively clear of appointments to allow time to ponder, to read and to ask a few searching questions."

"He can be interrupted. Oddly, you are not expected to knock on the door when entering the President's office, presumably on the theory that you would not be there if you should not be. But when he's chewing things over, it's not a good idea to go in with something trivial."[20]

* * *

TAKEN AS A WHOLE, the photos of Nixon during his presidency have an antiseptic and staged quality. With a small handful of exceptions, there is no visual record of a likeable, approachable, appealing Richard Nixon behind the scenes, and this hurt him with the public.

Atkins wrote: "One of my main photographic problems with President Nixon was to get him to appear casual and to show him at ease with people around him. We had been after Ron Ziegler to get the Chief Executive to take a walk on the beach near the Western White House at San Clemente for months. Finally, on June 7 [1971], the President said he'd take a stroll for us and show us just how casual he really was. A group of us went down to set up our cameras and photograph him walking along the sand."

"He came down from his residence on a switchback wooden stairway built into the steep bank. He was wearing what he considered casual clothes: shoes and socks and long trousers; a light-blue windbreaker jacket with a big Presidential seal on the front. He looked like the chairman of the board out for a walk in between acquisitions. For the record, that's about as casual as Richard M. Nixon ever got.

"He went walking along the beach at the point where the waves stop, where the sand is the firmest. It's a hazardous place for walking because from time to time a wave unexpectedly comes up farther than the others. And sure enough, just about the time he got within camera range, one of those bigger waves came along and he was suddenly up to his ankles in water. He did a little dance trying to get out of the surf as we snapped our pictures."[21]

But the gambit didn't work. There was so little interest by that time in the supposed private side of Nixon that the news media ignored the photos, Atkins said.

*   *   *

ATKINS' MOST FAMOUS photo was a bizarre occurrence: Nixon meeting Elvis Presley at the White House in October 1970, which has become one of the most requested pictures in the Richard Nixon Presidential Library and Museum archive.

Elvis, the king of rock and roll, was an admirer of law enforcement and he wanted to become a "federal agent-at-large" in the Bureau of Narcotics and Dangerous Drugs, so he could help catch drug dealers. The irony is that Elvis had a secret problem with overusing prescription drugs at the time.

By prearrangement with White House aides, Elvis showed up at a front gate on December 21, 1970, dressed in a resplendent purple velvet cape and a white shirt open halfway down his chest, a gold chain, and big sunglasses. Nixon at first had been hesitant to meet with this pop-culture icon because he didn't like rock and roll music and wasn't sure what he would talk to Elvis about.[22]

But the meeting went well, even though it was more than a bit awkward. Nixon referred to his guest as "Mr. Presley" and Elvis called Nixon "Mr. President." Elvis showed the president photos of his wife Priscilla and daughter Lisa Marie and produced several police badges he had collected. "I really support what our police have to do," Elvis said. Nixon replied, "They certainly deserve all the support we can give them. They've got tough jobs."[23]

As part of the chitchat, Nixon said, "You dress kind of strange, don't you?" And Presley replied, "You have your show and I have mine."[24]

Presley got his law enforcement badge and Nixon got a picture with "the king."

*   *   *

THE DOMINANT IMAGES of Nixon were of the workaholic, and innumerable photos were released of Nixon at his desk, on the job, reading or conferring with other white men in business suits. "He comes in in the morning and sits down in that chair, and that's where he stays all during his working day," said an aide.[25] There wasn't much opportunity for vivid photography in that pattern.

Wrote Fred J. Maroon, an outside photographer who was hired by the White House to document some of the Nixon presidency: "It was very quiet in the president's office; the only interruption was the sound of rustling paper as he finished reading each page. I knew that anything that had made it this far for his consideration had to be important, as indicated by his solemn concentration. I used a range-finder Leica M camera so the sound of the shutter clicking would not be so distracting as to get me thrown out of the office."[26] But the results of Maroon's work were a series of dull shots that added no luster to the Nixon presidency.

He rarely loosened up; at least that's the only way he allowed photographers to see him. His personal relationship with his wife, Pat, and his daughters, Tricia and Julie, was close and affectionate, his aides said, but he refused to reveal very much about this side of his life. He seemed to think that such moments should remain private because the news media were against him and would find a way to make such pictures an embarrassment to him or his family.

Atkins observed: "I'll tell you frankly, I always felt on the outside of everything that happened in the East Wing of the White House, where the family lived."[27] This was unfortunate for Nixon and for history, because it kept the public from seeing the way the family truly lived and kept their warm relationships with one another from becoming well-known. This distance between the presidential family and the official photographer added to the impression that Nixon was at heart a recluse who didn't really like people, which was probably more accurate than White House public-relations managers liked to admit.

Privately, Nixon was preoccupied with getting even with what he considered his enemies and the White House seemed a humorless, even grim place. As columnist Tom Wicker wrote: "Nixon had always seethed with anger at slights real and imagined, and had expected, as president at last, to avenge himself against his enemies: liberals, reporters, anti-war activists, Kennedyites—Nixon-haters all. . . . It was perhaps for all these and no doubt other frustrations, as if they had been combined into one, that he had so frequently flailed at his perceived enemies and turned to action outside the law—electronic surveillance; infiltrating radical groups; briefly approving then abandoning the 'Huston Plan' for 'combatting terrorism' by numerous illegal methods; and creating the 'Plumbers,' an unauthorized covert unit within the White House, designed supposedly to stop 'leaks,' but actually to carry out all sorts of intelligence gathering."[28]

This atmosphere led to the May 1972 Watergate burglary in which covert operators broke into the offices of the Democratic National Committee in Washington's Watergate Hotel, to plant listening devices. The burglars were caught, and the operation was linked to supporters of Nixon and eventually to the White House. Nixon approved a cover-up. This was uncovered by congressional investigators moving to impeach Nixon for obstruction of justice, and in August 1974 Nixon was forced to resign.[29]

Atkins observed in his 1977 memoir, three years after Nixon's resignation: "I still have no idea whether the President knew or did not know about any of the shenanigans connected with the Watergate break-in. However, I do know that after the hearings on the Hill started, a great gloom descended on the White House and all of us working in it. Day after day the Committee questioned people who had been dragged down into this thing to become its victims."[30]

But as a close observer of Nixon, Atkins saw the mistakes that were being made in handling the crisis and the toll it was taking on the president, whom he said looked "haggard and tired."[31] On August 14, 1973, Atkins recalled: "He left for Camp David in the afternoon to put the finishing touches on his speech [to update the country on the ongoing controversy]. As the official White House photographer, I did not make a single shot of Mr. Nixon at work on what might prove to be the most important speech of his career. That disturbed me. The President had sealed himself up with a handful of close advisors. I'd put in requests both at Camp David and at the White House to make some sort of a photograph showing him working on this major address, but my requests hadn't even been answered."[32]

The speech didn't go over well, and Nixon's mood worsened. On August 20, 1973, he lost his composure during a trip to New Orleans.

En route to speak at a convention of the Veterans of Foreign Wars, the Secret Service at the last minute rerouted the president's motorcade ride to back streets instead of through central areas where thousands of bystanders were expected. There had been an assassination threat and the Secret Service was doing its job. But Nixon was angry at being deprived of what he expected to be a few minutes of positive crowd reactions.[33]

When he arrived at the convention center, Nixon was in a foul mood. White House Press Secretary Ron Ziegler was four or five feet behind the president but suddenly Nixon swung around and angrily pushed Ziegler toward the press corps, ordering him to prevent the media horde from entering the doorway that the official party was about to use. "I don't know what his actual words were," Atkins recalled. "I was watching him closely and he seemed to be shouting at Ziegler, holding him by both shoulders. Then he suddenly swung him around and gave him a one-handed but powerful shove in the back."[34]

"I did not shoot the scene," Atkins added. "My instincts were to raise the camera and bang off a few frames. But at the same moment I knew that the President would see me clearly, and the sight of his own photographer taking a picture of him in a bad mood might double his anger.

"It was the first time that I had ever seen the President lose his cool. To me, it was a disturbing thing. There were some television people right behind Ziegler; they caught the action on film."[35] The incident showed how the Watergate scandal was clouding Nixon's judgment and adding to the tension in the White House.

Atkins recalled that the incident with Ziegler prompted a wave of speculation in the press corps that the president might be drinking heavily or on drugs. Atkins was asked about it and he told his reporter colleagues that he really didn't know whether Nixon was on drugs or drinking too much alcohol, but it was very much out of character for him to do such things.

The rumors got so intense that White House spokesman Jerry Warren felt he had to address them. He assured reporters at a briefing the next day that the president was not abusing drugs or alcohol but Nixon was understandably on edge.[36]

Atkins also had some choice words about the press corps, which he observed closely throughout his stint at the White House. "Ironically enough, in the press corps the supporters of the President are the technicians, the sound men, the lighting men, and the cameramen—*not* the reporters," Atkins wrote. "The photographers in many cases despise the reporters and commentators they work with, especially the television cameramen."[37]

*   *   *

DURING THE NIXON YEARS, the staff photographers and favored outside photographers were occasionally given access to moments when they could make good pictures, even though they were few and far between.

Maroon was allowed to photograph the president and first lady in black-and-white—the lensman's preference because he considered black-and-white images more compelling—as they prepared to enter a White House reception in February 1971, two years after his inauguration. Nixon looked dapper in a tuxedo, and Pat was lovely in a flowing light-colored gown with white gloves, but they were standing awkwardly looking in opposite directions. Commenting on the photo, Maroon wrote: "Presidents of the United States do a lot of formal entertaining, and these receptions and dinners are always grand occasions. The Nixons carried on the tradition, changing one small detail. They had served soup at the first state dinner, but because Nixon spilled some of it on his tuxedo, soup was never again to be on the menu! The press tended to dwell on the stiffness of the First Couple, but those who knew them better attributed it to their fundamental shyness."[38]

Maroon did better with his pictures of the couple at their seaside home in San Clemente, California, in January 1971. In one shot the president and first lady sat stiffly on a bench overlooking the water on a blustery day. Nixon had his right arm around his wife's back, a rare display of affection from him. They were surrounded by trees and lush bushes and seemed serene, and they appeared lost in their own thoughts.

Maroon recalled: "The president told me there was a bench at San Clemente overlooking the Pacific Ocean that was a favorite spot of his. He asked if I would photograph him there with his wife. After he resigned and returned to San Clemente, I often saw the two of them on this bench in my mind's eye, and I wondered what they must have thought as they reflected on the highs and lows that life had dealt them."[39]

In another picture, taken during the same 1971 photo session, Nixon is holding an umbrella over Pat's scarf-draped head as they cope with the drizzle on a deserted beach. It doesn't look like much fun, but it was reflective of a larger reality— that the president found it difficult to relax. Commenting on this photo, Maroon wrote: "Even though it was drizzling, the president and Mrs. Nixon went for a walk along the beach-front of their San Clemente retreat and agreed to be photographed. It was a challenge to capture the president in a moment of relaxation, but here on the beach the interplay between his wife and him was both natural and affectionate."[40]

The problem for Nixon was that he still looked ill at ease in the wind and rain. It was a remarkable contrast to the glowing photos of President Kennedy and his wife and family on the beach at Hyannis Port, Massachusetts, where they had a family compound. Kennedy of course was very camera-savvy and photogenic. Nixon wasn't.

Even when he allowed a photographer to have "special access" during his work days in Washington, the results were underwhelming. On October 7, 1970, Maroon was given the opportunity to take pictures of Nixon working on a television speech in his hideaway office in the Executive Office Building across the street from the White House, where he frequently went for seclusion. The main photo showed Nixon sitting in a plush easy chair with a sheaf of papers on his lap. He was wearing his suit jacket, his tie was not loosened but was perfectly knotted at his collar, and two family photos sat on a table behind the chair. A phone sat on a side table to his left. Maroon remembered it this way: "Nixon had a hideaway office in the Executive Office Building, next door to the White House, and I was taken there to photograph him as he prepared for a television address. He scarcely moved from his seat the entire time I was there. I kept hoping he might answer the telephone or walk around the room, so I could get some variety, but it didn't happen. Later, in the Press Room, I overheard some White House correspondents commenting on how formal the president always was. One said, 'I bet he takes a shower in that suit!' Another added: 'If a photographer ever photographed him with his feet up, it would be worth a million dollars.'"[41] In the main picture, which Maroon later published in a book, Nixon has his feet up on an ottoman, but it wasn't a compelling shot and wasn't worth a million dollars.

The culture of the Nixon White House was that of a fortress, built to protect the president rather than to promote him, to guard him from his "enemies" in the liberal world, in the media, in the popular culture. Maroon wrote that "I was not the only one who had difficulty gaining access to the Oval Office. [White House Chief of Staff] H.R. Haldeman himself admitted to having constructed a protective wall around the president; some outsiders characterized it as a 'Berlin Wall.'"[42] The crew-cut, buttoned-down Haldeman saw his role as being Nixon's "SOB," the supreme gatekeeper, and he was very effective at it.[43]

With such an emphasis on secrecy, many photos taken by the official photographers or the contract shooters seemed bland and lifeless. Small moments were dissected to find larger meanings, especially when something happened that was out of the ordinary. In a Maroon photo from February 10, 1971, Nixon is shown in an unusual circumstance, not at his desk but walking in the White House with his hands in his pockets. He rarely did this. In the photo, his head was slightly down and he was scowling. Maroon wrote, "I loved being a fly on the wall in the Oval Office, waiting for that perfect fleeting moment. Steve Bull, the president's appointments secretary, was gesturing to someone as the president, with hands in pockets, and with his own seemingly dark thoughts, walked toward him."[44] No one could be sure what the hands-in-pockets walkabout meant, if anything.

In a snippet of video from Nixon's final hours in office, one gets an even more vivid idea of what Atkins and all the other photographers were up against. The video was shot moments before Nixon gave his address to the nation announcing his resignation in 1974. Nixon is seen sitting at his desk and he curtly orders Atkins out of the room. "That's enough!" Nixon says. Then he looks into the TV camera set up to record his departing remarks and adds: "My friend Ollie, always taking my picture. I'm afraid he's going to catch me picking my nose." Nixon pauses, and adds: "You wouldn't print that, though, would you, Ollie?"[45]

Atkins, off camera, asks if he can remain, and the president impatiently says, "No, no, Ollie. Only the CBS crew will be in the room. No, there will be no picture. No. After the broadcast. You've taken your picture. Didn't you just take one? That's it. You got it?" He orders Atkins out of the room, with words of irritation and urgency, "Come on."[46]

* * *

NIXON'S LAST DAYS in office were painful for the country and for the president and his family. As the House of Representatives moved to impeach the president for a variety of crimes related to Watergate, Nixon's options dwindled and the pressure depleted him. "Nixon tried to maintain a bold front as the summer of '74 wore on," wrote journalist Tom Wicker. "He held meetings and made a major speech on inflation (another national concern that summer), even spent weekends at Camp David that were apparently routine (in fact, they were anything but routine). He was visited by the West German foreign minister, and during part of the summer Pat Nixon and her friend Helene Drown redecorated the Garden Room and Queen's Room in the White House.

"Richard Nixon was not sleeping well, however," Wicker wrote. "Often, in the middle of the night or early in the morning, he was awake and on the phone, or scribbling on one of his ubiquitous yellow legal pads. Those who saw him almost always commented on his pallor and wan appearance. Henry Kissinger, visiting San Clemente on July 26, was 'shocked' at his condition and convinced 'the end of Nixon's presidency was now inevitable.'"[47]

Atkins documented this as best he could, but he was not allowed much access to the wounded president or his family for most of this period.

Neither was the press corps. On August 8, the day Nixon announced that he would leave office, the media, reporters and photographers, were confined to the press room in the West Wing in an enormous crowd of restless, resentful journalists. Maroon was among them.

"The week beginning August 4, 1974, was unlike any I had ever experienced," Maroon wrote. "It defined what was one of the most politically momentous events of the century. To this day I cannot remember when I sensed such dark foreboding in the White House. By the evening of August 8 we all knew we were in the final countdown and that something climactic was imminent. We, like the rest of America, had to watch television to find out what was happening just a few steps from us. Regardless of one's political persuasion, it was an emotional and sad moment that evening when President Nixon appeared on television to announce his resignation."[48]

Yet the access suddenly opened up for Atkins and he managed get a series of very personal photos of Nixon at his most vulnerable. The moment came at the very end of his presidency and it happened almost by accident.

It was the evening of August 7, 1974, and Atkins was told by White House Press Secretary Ron Ziegler to go to the solarium in the Residence and take some pictures of the president and his family having dinner. Atkins came upon a historical and poignant scene—the president's final hours in the White House. It turned out that Nixon had decided to announce his resignation the next day, August 8, because of the Watergate scandal and leave office August 9.[49]

The family wasn't in the mood to have dinner, and so Atkins photographed Nixon, his wife, Pat, his daughters, Julie and Tricia, their husbands, David Eisenhower and Edward Cox, standing together in a show of solidarity. All the family members knew of Nixon's decision, but no one told Atkins.

He went about his business and shot photos of the family standing tightly and uncomfortably in a row, their arms around each other. Everyone was wearing forced smiles, although the daughters were clearly near tears. They were dressed for a casual evening, with the women in floral dresses and David and Edward in shirtsleeves. Nixon always wore a suit and tie. After the group photo, Atkins snapped a frame of Julie hugging her father in an emotional moment that was rarely seen in the Nixon White House. He also got photos of Nixon with his longtime assistant Rose Mary Woods, who was with them that evening. Nixon told him to release whatever family picture he liked best.

Despite Atkins' objections, none of these images of sadness and defeat was immediately released to the media. Noting that Ziegler had initially thrown all the prints in the garbage, Atkins wrote: "The pictures I had made on one of the most crucial days of the Presidency, pictures that were absolutely exclusive, had been chucked in with the trash; it was a difficult situation." He called it "a crying shame," but he saved the negatives and they were stored in the National Archives.[50]

Atkins published the photos and described the incident in his book, *The White House Years: Triumph and Tragedy*. It was one of his lasting memories of Nixon and his family.[51]

One of his staff photographers took a picture of Nixon's final meal as president—his standard fare of a pineapple ring with a scoop of cottage cheese in the middle, presented upon White House china. It captured the sad and forlorn end of a presidency that Nixon had believed would be an exalted part of history.

Notes

1. Ollie Atkins, "Photographing the President," *U.S. Camera World Annual 1968*, New York: U.S. Camera Publishing Corp., 1967, p. 7.
2. Lloyd Shearer, "Photographing the President," *Salt Lake Tribune*, Sept. 5, 1971, p. 46.
3. Ollie Atkins, *The White House Years: Triumph and Tragedy*, Chicago: Playboy Press, 1977, pp. 11, 16.

4. Ibid., p. 16.
5. George Tames, *Eye on Washington: The Presidents Who've Known Me*, New York: HarperCollins Publishers, 1990, p. 110.
6. Ibid.
7. John Bredar, *The President's Photographer: Fifty Years Inside the Oval Office*, Washington, D.C.: National Geographic Society, 2010, p. 124.
8. Atkins, *The White House Years*, p. 22.
9. "The White House: Camera Shy," *Time*, Apr. 13, 1970, http://content.time.com/time/subscriber/printout/0,8816,904274,00.html.
10. Julie Nixon Eisenhower (ed.), *Eye on Nixon: A Photographic Study of the President and the Man*, New York: Hawthorn Books, Inc., 1972, p. 6.
11. Ibid., pp. 6–7.
12. Ibid., pp. 72–77.
13. Ibid., p. 52.
14. Atkins, *The White House Years*, p. 23.
15. Ibid.
16. Ibid. p. 27.
17. Tames, *Eye on Washington*, p. 111.
18. Patricia Sullivan, "Cecil Stoughton, 88: Kennedy White House Photographer," *Washington Post*, Nov. 6, 2008, http://washingtonpost.com/wp-dyn/content/article/2008/11/05/AR2008110504258.
19. Atkins, *The White House Years*, p. 30.
20. Eisenhower (ed.), *Eye on Nixon*, p. 39.
21. Atkins, *The White House Years*, p. 56.
22. Tevi Troy, *What Jefferson Read, Ike Watched, and Obama Tweeted: 200 Years of Popular Culture in the White House*, Washington, D.C.: Regnery Publishing, 2013, pp. 69–73.
23. Ibid., p. 103.
24. Ibid.
25. Fred J. Maroon, *The Nixon Years: 1969–1974: White House to Watergate*, New York: Abbeville Press, 1999, p. 21.
26. Ibid.
27. Atkins, *The White House Years*, pp. 48–49.
28. Quoted in Maroon, *The Nixon Years*, p. 78.
29. Ibid., p. 80.
30. Atkins, *The White House Years*, p. 151.
31. Ibid., p. 154.
32. Ibid., p. 151.
33. Ibid., p. 155.
34. Ibid., p. 156.
35. Ibid.
36. Ibid.

37. Ibid., p. 153.

38. Maroon, *The Nixon Years*, p. 61.

39. Ibid., pp. 54–55.

40. Ibid.

41. Ibid., p. 25.

42. Ibid., p. 66.

43. Ibid., p. 136.

44. Ibid., p. 68.

45. See "White House Photographers," panel discussion at the Lyndon B. Johnson Library, Austin, Texas, Jan. 20, 2010, www.c-span.org/video/?291502-1/white-house-photographers.

46. Bredar, *The President's Photographer*, p. 124.

47. Maroon, *The Nixon Years*, p. 171.

48. Ibid., pp. 176–177.

49. Atkins, *The White House Years*, pp. 215–219; see also Bredar, *The President's Photographer*, p. 124.

50. Atkins, *The White House Years*, p. 220.

51. Ibid., pp. 215–219.

CHAPTER FIVE
BEHIND THE SCENES WITH GERALD FORD AND DAVID KENNERLY

David Kennerly, the personal photographer for Gerald R. Ford, always felt like a member of the presidential family, trusted and welcomed to inner sanctums like few other staff members of any president.

He had won a Pulitzer Prize for his photography during the Vietnam War, and later was assigned by *Time* magazine to cover Ford when he was a Republican member of the House of Representatives from Michigan. Ford was rumored to be a possible choice for vice president to replace Spiro Agnew, who was under investigation for alleged tax evasion and corruption.

Agnew resigned in October 1973, and Ford was then named by embattled President Richard Nixon to replace him.

As a photojournalist, Kennerly covered Vice President Ford very closely and quickly earned the trust of the former congressman and his family. Kennerly recalls that "Vice President and Mrs. Ford and their kids welcomed me into their world, and after a while it felt like we were all running away together to join the circus."[1]

During a Ford ski vacation in Vail, Colorado, Kennerly had dinner with the then-vice president and his family at a Chinese restaurant. After the meal, Ford opened his fortune cookie, read the prediction, fell silent, and placed the tiny piece of paper on the table and covered it with his hand. But Kennerly, in a playful act of familiarity, pried the fortune from Ford's grasp and read it out loud: "You will undergo a change of residence in the near future." Ford, embarrassed that someone might think this meant he would move to the White House to replace Nixon, blurted out, "I hope not," and added: "You can't believe these things."[2]

Eight months later, in August 1974, Nixon resigned and Ford moved into the White House.

Kennerly, then 27, was hired to be the chief White House photographer on August 9, Ford's first day as president.[3] After an evening celebration with his family and very close friends—Kennerly included—Ford met privately with Kennerly in the living room of his modest suburban home at 514 Crown View Drive in Alexandria, Virginia. (The White House wasn't quite ready for him to move in at that point.) Puffing on his pipe as they sat on a sofa, Ford mentioned the possibility of naming Kennerly as his photographer and asked, "What would you think about the job?"

Kennerly said he would love to do it—on two conditions. First, he would report directly to the president with "no staff in between," and, second, he would have "total access to everything that happens in the White House."

Ford replied with a quip: "What, no use of *Air Force One* on the weekends?"

Ford said he would think about it and check back with Kennerly the next day.

The following day, Kennerly was at the *Time* Washington bureau, lounging in the mailroom with his feet up on a desk, when a switchboard operator paged him and announced urgently, "The president wants to talk to you!" Kennerly joked that he'd have to call him back, but the operator said, "He's on the line!"

Ford greeted him, "Hi, Dave, how would you like to come work for me?"

The young photographer replied, "I'd love to, Mr. President."

And Ford said, "Well, you better get over here right away because you've already wasted half a day of the taxpayers' money."

Kennerly walked the few blocks from the *Time* bureau to the White House, and started his historic journey with Ford."[4]

* * *

"YOU CAN'T take great pictures every day in the White House," Kennerly says. "They are meeting, people talking, blah, blah, blah, all day long. That's what they do over there. The only time there are really good meetings is when there is some shit hitting the fan that makes it dramatic. The best pictures come then—there's an important event and you're inside it."[5]

Kennerly adds: "It was quite a switch: from outside to inside in the bat of an eye. Inside was a place news photographers rarely reach, but it's where they always want to be. All the frustration I had experienced trying to get an exclusive during the Nixon days was washed away with that one phone call [offering him the job]. Every day was going to be an exclusive from now on, and the way I worked that meant sixteen hours a day, seven days a week."[6]

Kennerly resents any implication that he was a PR man. "What I did was deliver a straightforward, honest record of what they were doing [in the Ford White House]. I did not compromise my journalistic ethics and instincts to make Gerald Ford look good. To imply that is unfair and wrong. . . . What I tried to do is be a documenter of history. That's what I was in it for, not to make him look good."

And he had a glowing assessment of his number one subject: "He was an intelligent guy, a shrewd person, a strong leader who made decisions not based on politics, certainly not on the basis of party. . . . He never would call anybody names; he didn't use slurs like Nixon. He was the kind of person we should all aspire to be."[7]

Kennerly has written: "Photographs define a president. In the case of Gerald Ford, the real Ford—the solid, steady-as-she-goes leader—came across honestly in pictures. He let me into his life with my camera to document his time in office, unafraid of what would be revealed. I have never met anyone with less guile or vanity. I truly believe he gave me that historic opportunity because he liked having me around not because he felt that his every move should be preserved for posterity—that just wasn't the kind of thing he thought about."[8]

*　*　*

PRESIDENTIAL PHOTOGRAPHERS often learn what their bosses are like better than anyone outside a president's family, and this was true for Kennerly.

The Mayaguez incident was a benchmark. "Being so close to the president on a daily basis gave me the unique opportunity to watch him grow into the office," Kennerly said. "Here was a man whose first public statement after Nixon announced that he was quitting was, in effect, 'Don't worry, Henry Kissinger is right here running the world.' That changed and I saw it happen. Although it didn't evolve overnight, there was a tectonic shift in the presidential plates, and Gerald R. Ford firmly seized the reins of power once and for all. That shift had a name: the SS *Mayaguez*.

"The cargo ship *Mayaguez*, its captain, and thirty-nine other American sailors were captured by Khmer Rouge rebels off the coast of Cambodia on May 12, 1975. It was up to the president directing the forces at his command to get them safely released. After diplomacy failed, President Ford, who had only been in office for nine months, eschewed the advised military option, which involved massive B-52 bombing raids around Cambodia's ancient capital of Phnom Penh. Instead, he ordered strong and precise air strikes near where he thought the crew was being held. The action ultimately secured the crew's freedom.

"There was no bloodlust in him. He knew Vietnam had been a debacle and had the unfortunate duty to oversee the end of that horrible chapter in American history. But he refused to kill innocent Cambodians to make them pay for America's mistakes in Vietnam. . . . The incident was the fulcrum of his presidency and the moment where he came of age as commander in chief. And I was a privileged observer of that remarkable metamorphosis."9

*　*　*

KENNERLY got along well with Ford's wife and children, and they gave him remarkable access. "I hit it off with them from the start," Kennerly told me. "It was like I was a favorite cousin. It was a professional relationship but it was also a personal relationship. You can't describe it in a conventional way. . . . They certainly appreciated my photographic ability but the personal side made it all happen. . . . President Ford liked the fact that I was not a bullshit artist."10

Kennerly knew where to draw the line in protecting the family's privacy, and this in turn generated more trust for him with the Fords. For his part, when it came to official events, Ford imposed limits on Kennerly only in rare cases. One was when he reprimanded a high-ranking military officer and two other occasions when he fired members of his cabinet. Kennerly agreed, saying later that "having a third party there would have been excruciating" and mortifying for the principals.11

But he did have to push back a bit when Ford let his innate courtesy interfere with Kennerly's work. "Early on the president needed some training in the ways of photographers," Kennerly recalled. "Because he was one of the most polite people who ever walked the Earth, he was constantly introducing me to everyone who entered the Oval Office. 'Senator Goldwater, this is my White House photographer, David Kennerly,' and so on. Finally, after a couple of days of this, I told him that as much as I appreciated being introduced to everyone, it was kind of getting in the way of my pictures and that ignoring me was okay—imperative, in fact. So, reluctantly, and with a few relapses, he learned to pay me no mind, and I truly became the ever-present but invisible man. It was perfect."[12]

*   *   *

IN 1974, not long after her husband was sworn in as president, First Lady Betty Ford learned that she had a marble-sized lump in her right breast. Two days later, surgeons removed her breast in a radical mastectomy. Breaking a taboo at the time, she talked openly about her condition and the surgery and encouraged other women to have the operation to save their lives.[13]

But the president took the news hard. When aides told him that his wife Betty needed the breast-cancer surgery, he broke down and began to weep. Kennerly was in the room with him but says: "I did not photograph that."[14]

Still, there were many Kennerly photos that showed a very personal and unassuming side of the first couple. One, taken before work during his first days in office, shows the new president standing in shirtsleeves at his kitchen table before the family moved to the White House, the room cluttered with plates, saucers, two coffee cups, a "Lazy Susan" laden with flowers, half a stick of butter on a dish, salt, pepper, and bottled salad dressing. Betty Ford, the new first lady, is shown in a bathrobe seated at the kitchen table, smiling at her husband and wearing a transparent shower cap over her hairdo.

In the spring of 1975, Ford ordered General Fred Weyand, the Army chief of staff, to assess the deteriorating situation in Vietnam. Kennerly asked if he could go and Ford approved. A UPI article in the *Los Angeles Times* reported the insider story: "Kennerly photographed the Oval Office meeting at which the generals and diplomats got their orders from Ford and watched them depart. He turned to Ford."[15]

" 'Mr. President, I would like to go with them,' said Kennerly, winner of a Pulitzer Prize for his news photography for UPI in the Vietnam War.

" 'Why?' asked Ford. Kennerly said it was his job to record for history the doings of the Administration.

"The President said OK adding: 'Besides, I'd be interested to hear your view of what's going on when you get back.' "[16]

" 'Uh, ah,' said Kennerly. 'One thing, sir. The mission is leaving right now, and I've got no money.'

"Ford reached for his wallet and pulled out $47. 'It's all I've got on me. Take it,' said the President. Kennerly took it.

"As the photographer was going through the door, Ford jammed a hand into a pocket and summoned him back.

" 'Here's a quarter. You might as well clean me out.' "[17]

When Kennerly returned, he showed Ford his photographs of civilian victims of the war, including graphic pictures of dying children and buses and ships full of refugees. Kennerly said Ford was "devastated." These apparently helped to convince Ford to begin an airlift of Vietnamese orphans out of the country.[18]

* * *

KENNERLY, with his beard, blue jeans, and irreverence, became a celebrity in his own right, attracting considerable attention in the news media because he stood out so much from the buttoned-down White House staff and from the low-key President Ford.

Kennerly's luster brightened even more when he escorted actress and part-time photographer Candice Bergen aboard the chartered press plane during Ford's trip to Atlanta in February 1975. In one of many stories about Kennerly as a celebrity, the *New York Times* wrote: "Escorted by David Kennerly, the bearded bachelor who serves as the White House photographer, Miss Bergen took some pictures in the President's hotel suite, flew back to Washington on *Air Force One* and then attended a White House dinner [with Kennerly]. Her presence caused a bit of a stir among the regular press corps but veteran newsmen attributed it more to envy of Mr. Kennerly than to objection to Miss Bergen's special privileges."[19]

The *Los Angeles Times* noted: "Kennerly's ready wit led some to call him the court jester. His bachelor life-style, complete with a healthy fondness for fast cars, fine scotch and attractive women, earned him a reputation with Washington gossip columnists as the *enfant terrible* of the White House staff." And his closeness to the first family caused some envious aides to nickname him David Ford, as if he were really related to the president.[20]

Kennerly's brashness and sense of humor were highly unusual in any staff member, let alone in a photographer who said he preferred to be unobtrusive doing his work of snapping pictures. After President Ford escaped injury on September 22, 1975, when a woman tried to shoot him in San Francisco, Kennerly greeted his boss aboard *Air Force One* immediately after the incident with the quip: "Other than that, Mr. President, how did you like San Francisco?"[21]

UPI observed: "The care and feeding of the President's sense of humor formed part of the service the White House photographer rendered the Ford Administration. Kennerly could be depended on to say, when the President sat engulfed in problems in the Oval Office, 'You accepted the job, didn't you?'"

"Gossip columnists delighted in his bachelor doings," UPI added. "Even some veteran White House reporters judged his closeness to Ford as little more than the nearness of a pet. But students of power regarded Kennerly as no mere court jester."[22]

*   *   *

KENNERLY OPERATED the photo office with four deputy photographers: Ricardo Thomas, Bill Fitz-Patrick, Karl Schumaker, and Jack Kightlinger. But he felt he had another mission as chief White House photographer—to expand access for news photographers from the newspapers, magazines, and other outlets. Unlike Obama or Donald Trump in recent years and unlike Nixon earlier, Kennerly and Ford opened many doors to the news media's shooters. "Private access for photographers during Nixon's time outside of the staged 'photo ops' had been very limited," Kennerly explained. "I was able to change that, with President Ford as a willing and understanding participant. Dozens of photographers had the opportunity to document him up close and behind the scenes during his two-and-a-half years in office."[23]

Those shooters got their own special insights into Ford and found him refreshingly down to earth, as reflected in their imagery. Photographer Fred Ward spent three months behind the scenes for a book about Ford, and at one point was searching for an electrical outlet in the Oval Office for his strobe lights when he noticed President Ford on his hands and knees behind a couch. Ward at first thought the commander in chief had suffered a stroke or heart attack. But then Ford looked up and remarked that he thought there was a plug "somewhere around here." He was just trying to help out, a classic response from this very considerate man.[24]

*   *   *

THERE WAS a limit to what Kennerly or anyone else could do to showcase the president's best qualities and improve Ford's image. The voters didn't think he was doing enough to improve the economy and strengthen America's position in the world, and Vietnam was still a mess. In addition, many voters hadn't forgiven Ford for pardoning Richard Nixon for the abuses that he ordered or tolerated while in office. Ford argued that the nation was being ripped apart by divisions over Nixon, and he hoped the pardon would encourage Americans to move beyond the issue of Nixon's behavior, including the Watergate scandal. But the pardon caused more voters to turn against Ford.

He lost his bid to be elected on his own in November 1976. This ended not only a presidency but a period of remarkable access for the White House photographers.

Jimmy Carter, the Democratic victor, would handle his own visual history in a much more restrictive way.

Notes

1. David Hume Kennerly, *Extraordinary Circumstances: The Presidency of Gerald R. Ford*, Austin: Briscoe Center for American History, 2007, p. 14.
2. David Kennerly, interview with author, Apr. 27, 2016.
3. Ibid.
4. Ibid.
5. John Bredar, *The President's Photographer: Fifty Years Inside the Oval Office*. Washington, D.C.: National Geographic Society, 2010, p. 170; see also Corinna Wu, "A Leading Lady", *Cancer Today*, Sept. 27, 2012, www.cancertodaymag.org/Fall2012/Pages/betty-ford-yesterday-and-today.aspx.
6. Robert McNeely, *The Clinton Years: The Photographs of Robert McNeely*, New York: Callaway, 2000, p. 24.
7. David Kennerly, interview with author, Apr. 27, 2016.
8. Kennerly, *Extraordinary Circumstances*, p. 15.
9. Ibid., p. 17.
10. Kennerly, interview with author, Apr. 27, 2016.
11. Kennerly, *Extraordinary Circumstances*, p. 15.
12. Ibid.
13. Wu, "A Leading Lady," p. 1.
14. David Kennerly, comments at "White House Photographers," panel discussion at the Lyndon Baines Johnson Presidential Library, Austin, Texas, Jan. 20, 2010, www.c-span.org/video/?291502-1/white-house-photographers.

15. Richard H. Growald, "Ford Lensman had Access to History: Ford Photographer: Access to History," *Los Angeles Times*, Dec. 19, 1976, p. A28.
16. Bredar, *The President's Photographer*, pp. 135–136.
17. Growald, "Ford Lensman had Access to History," p. A28.
18. Bredar, *The President's Photographer*, p. 136.
19. "Headliners: The Press Corps," *New York Times*, Feb. 9, 1977.
20. Alex Riley, "Postscript: Former Ford Photographer now a Hustling Freelance," *Los Angeles Times*, July 15, 1978, p. D1.
21. Growald, "Ford Lensman had Access to History," p. A28.
22. Ibid.
23. Kennerly, *Extraordinary Circumstances*, p. 16.
24. Dennis Brack, *Presidential Picture Stories: Behind the Cameras at the White House*, Washington, D.C.: Dennis Brack, Inc., 2013, p. 106.

CHAPTER SIX
BEHIND THE SCENES WITH JIMMY CARTER AND A MISSING CHIEF PHOTOGRAPHER

Jimmy Carter didn't appoint a personal White House photographer. His aides said he didn't like the title or the concept because it seemed to indicate an imperial presidency such as the one created by the disgraced Richard Nixon.[1]

Actually, Carter did privately offer the job of "chief" photographer to *Look* magazine photographer Stanley Tretick, but Tretick turned him down because the president defined the role in a very limited way. "I didn't feel he wanted an intimate, personal photographer around him," Tretick explained later.[2]

Carter then lost interest in filling the post. He kept a handful of staff photographers on board, but gave none of them his trust. This meant that many opportunities to show a more appealing side were lost. "No one became personal photographer during the Carter administration and, to my mind, the result is obvious," writes George Tames, longtime White House photographer for the *New York Times*. "Almost no candid photographs came out of the White House in the four years of the Carter administration, and very few pictures that showed the innermost feelings of the man, his deep faith, his caring nature. Nothing to show a grieving Carter at the news of the abortive tragic action to free the American hostages in Iran. He mourned in private when he really needed public sympathy."[3]

The cost was substantial. "If you look at the photographs that came out of the Carter White House, there's nobody trying to tell Jimmy Carter's story," says Don Carleton, who has researched presidential photography as director of the Briscoe Center for American History at the University of Texas. "There's no candid kind of revealing sort of stuff like the Ford administration with David Kennerly. It's just sort of a kind of a chaotic accumulation of images that don't necessarily interconnect with one another."[4]

Carleton added: "I think that any President that does not have their administration photographically documented is really losing out in history. They're really shutting off a doorway, a pathway that people can take to understand their Presidency. And I think that was the mistake that Carter made."[5]

Because so few interesting or revealing photographs were released by the White House staff shooters, it fell to the news photographers to capture Carter's true persona as best they could. But they were confined almost entirely to staged events, such as public speeches and meet-and-greet sessions and didn't enjoy much access beyond this.

"He seemed to love humanity," wrote Dennis Brack, a photographer for Black Star and a contract photographer for *Time* and other publications who covered Carter's White House. "People who evoked his compassion were certain to receive a caring embrace and perhaps one of his forehead-to-forehead moments. President Jimmy Carter's love for other individuals who were close to him, even those who might be called on to give their lives to protect him—not so much. It was as if those people were not worth his time and attention. He simply did not want to be bothered with them; Secret Service agents and the executive mansion staff were some of the little people in the Carter White House, instructed to never say hello and never to speak unless spoken to. He ignored them as he passed. The lowest on his list of little people were the photographers."[6]

During his first day as president, walking from the Oval Office to address government employees, Carter slipped on a patch of ice. His briefcase went flying and he caught his balance awkwardly. The new president's misstep was captured by waiting news photographers and published on the front pages of many newspapers the next day. Carter and his aides were infuriated, and the incident started a White House feud with the news photographers that got progressively worse.[7]

Among the few telling images was Carter and Vice President Walter Mondale at one of their weekly lunches, both heads bowed in prayer as they said grace, reflecting the president's strong Christian faith.

There was also the shot of a jubilant Carter, a beaming Egyptian President Anwar El Sadat and a somber-looking Israeli Prime Minister Menachem Begin at the signing of the Camp David Accords at the White House in September 1978. The signing occurred after 12 days of tense and grueling negotiations over which Carter presided at Camp David, the presidential retreat in the Maryland mountains. The talks almost collapsed but Carter managed to guide Sadat and Begin to a compromise. A compelling visual record of those 12 days has been lost to history largely because of Carter's disinterest in it.

On the negative side was the indelible image of Carter collapsing while competing in a footrace in September 1979. The photo, captured by news photographers and transmitted around the world, showed the president looking dazed, his mouth gaping as he gasped for air, starting to crumple to the ground in obvious exhaustion.

It happened during the third mile of a grueling 6-mile race through Maryland's Catoctin Mountains. After his mishap, the president was given smelling salts and taken to the presidential retreat at nearby Camp David, where his doctor took an electrocardiogram, gave him an intravenous saline solution, and wrapped him in wet towels to cool him down. It turned out to be heat exhaustion.[8]

Carter had become an inveterate jogger as president and he agreed to participate in the run to encourage Americans to exercise and to demonstrate his own fitness. He started running up a hill about midway through the race when he staggered, his face turning white and his mouth hanging open. Doctor William Lukash, the White House physician, and a Secret Service agent, both of whom were jogging with Carter, supported him under his arms and helped him get to the crest of the hill, about 100 yards from the entrances to Camp David. Carter was then put into a car and whisked away into the presidential retreat. He emerged a short while later to present awards to the top runners, and seemed fine. He explained, "They had to drag me off. I didn't want to stop." But the incident made him seem like a man who didn't know his own limitations and reminded people of his stubbornness as president, which limited his effectiveness.[9]

Another embarrassing moment for Carter came in what the media referred to derisively as the "killer rabbit" incident. Carter was vacationing at his home in Plains, Georgia on April 20, 1979. A White House staff photographer noticed what Carter later called "a robust-looking rabbit" swimming toward his fishing boat on a pond and took pictures of it. The White House released a picture, adding fuel to the bizarre story, which was heavily covered in the media. Carter later explained that he thought the animal was trying to board his boat and he splashed water on it with a paddle, driving it away. Carter told newspaper editors at a Florida conference, "The rabbit I don't think was trying to attack me." The president was apparently trying to make light of the incident, but some news reports made it seem as if he was afraid, at least briefly, of the furry creature, and, as his domestic and international problems mounted, it was seen as more evidence that he was in over his head as president.[10]

Plagued by severe economic problems, a hostage crisis in Iran, and a rebellion against him within the Democratic Party, Carter refused to modify his views in the face of public and congressional opposition. He lost his bid for reelection to Ronald Reagan in 1980.

Notes

1. George Tames, *Eye on Washington: The Presidents Who've Known Me*, New York: HarperCollins Publishers, 1990, p. 132.
2. Nick Ravo, "Stanley Tretick, 77: Photographer of Kennedys at the White House," *New York Times*, July 20, 1999, www.nytimes.com/1999/07/20/us/stanley-tretick-77-photographer-of-kennedys-at-the-white-house.html.
3. Tames, *Eye on Washington*, p. 132.
4. John Bredar, *The President's Photographer: Fifty Years Inside the Oval Office*, Washington, D.C.: National Geographic Society, 2010, p. 158.
5. Ibid., p. 160.
6. Dennis Brack, *Presidential Picture Stories: Behind the Cameras at the White House*, Washington, D.C.: Dennis Brack, Inc., 2013, p. 107.
7. Ibid., p. 108.
8. "Jimmy Carter's Collapse in a Maryland Road Race Sparks a Moment of Fear in the Situation Room," *People*, Oct. 1, 1979, www.people.com/people/archive/article/0,,20074710,00.html.
9. Sarah Pileggi, "Jimmy Carter Runs into the Wall," *Sports Illustrated Vault*, Sept. 24, 1979, www.si.com/vault/1979/09/24/823995/jimmy-carter-runs-into-the-wall.
10. Don Irwin, "President Splits a Few Hares in Telling of Pond Encounter," *Los Angeles Times*, Sept. 1, 1979, p. A25.

Chapter Seven
Behind the Scenes with Ronald Reagan, Michael Evans, and Pete Souza

Ronald Reagan was a movie and television actor prior to his election to the presidency in 1980, and consequently he was already familiar with ways to look his best.

Marlin Fitzwater, his White House press secretary, once asked Reagan what was the key to always looking good before the cameras, and Reagan had a simple but savvy answer. "Always look directly into the lens," he said, "and never look down even if someone is tugging on your pants."[1]

There are more levels to this advice than might be immediately apparent. What Reagan meant was that a public figure needs to be disciplined and pay full attention to the photographers around him while they are snapping pictures and not get caught in silly, embarrassing, or off-message moments, such as squinting, eye-rolling, grimacing, or spilling food during meals. Even Reagan, the master communicator, couldn't always live up to his own advice—more than once, he was caught dozing in public, even during an audience with the pope. He was in his mid-70s by then, and perhaps had lost more than a bit of energy, but his original advice was sound: always pay attention to the cameras.

Reagan said he learned some other valuable tricks of the trade as a film star. One was to look as tall as he could. Stature usually conveyed a sense of power and dignity, he believed, and he always wanted to be the tallest man in the photograph, if he could. Years earlier, he starred in a movie with actor Randolph Scott, known for his height and long, lean physique. A publicity photo was scheduled for the press on the movie set. As the photographer rushed over, Reagan discreetly used his feet to push some dirt on the ground into a pile, and he stood on top of it during the shoot, adding an inch or two in height. Scott was left wondering how Reagan had gained so much stature over the course of five minutes.

During his presidency, Reagan liked to delegate, and he empowered Fitzwater to decide which photos to release to the media and which to keep stored in the White House archives. President George H.W. Bush, Reagan's successor, who kept Fitzwater on the job, maintained the same pattern of letting the press secretary make almost all of the decisions on the images that were released. Fitzwater said he sometimes reviewed the White House photographers' images but only rarely said no to releasing them.

*   *   *

MICHAEL EVANS, who became Reagan's chief photographer in the White House, was born in St. Louis, the son of a Canadian career diplomat and a nurse, and was raised mostly overseas.

He worked for years as a news photographer for the *Cleveland Plain Dealer*, the *New York Times*, and *Time*. Evans covered Reagan for *Time* during his unsuccessful bid for the Republican presidential nomination in 1976, and one of his photos was a shot that the Reagans loved from the moment they saw it. The image was taken at Reagan's California ranch by Evans while he was on assignment for an equestrian magazine. The picture showed Reagan in a cowboy hat, his face glowing with delight and a big smile on his face. It captured his affability, his good looks, and his charisma.

Evans couldn't recall exactly what he and Reagan were talking about while he was taking the shot, but the photographer said something that caused Reagan to break out into that famous lopsided grin. Reagan and his wife Nancy liked it so much that Evans gave them several prints as gifts.[2] The photograph captured the essence of the genial, upbeat Reagan and was used for campaign buttons and on the covers of *Time*, *People*, and *Newsweek* and in various newspapers to commemorate Reagan's death in June 2004 at age 93.

Evans also covered Reagan's successful presidential campaign in 1980 for *Time* and got to know Reagan even better. After he won, Reagan asked Evans to be his chief White House photographer, but it turned out that *Time* offered Evans the job of chief White House photographer for the magazine, a job which paid a much higher salary than the White House was offering. Nevertheless, Evans decided that the White House position would give him a unique opportunity to see a presidency "from the inside." He took the job with Reagan "and never regretted a day of it."[3] Evans said he had admired Reagan ever since he saw him give a televised speech for Republican presidential nominee Barry Goldwater in 1964, when Evans was a college photojournalism student at Queen's University in Kingston, Ontario.[4]

It developed that Evans became too close emotionally to his boss, and this hindered him at a very inopportune time. It happened on March 30, 1981, when Reagan was shot and almost killed as he left a speech to the AFL-CIO at the Washington Hilton Hotel.

Evans was walking a few paces behind the president just outside the entrance when John Hinckley Jr. fired six shots with a .22-caliber pistol, wounding Reagan, White House Press Secretary James Brady, Secret Service agent Timothy McCarthy, and Washington, D.C., police officer Thomas Delahanty. Evans didn't make the best pictures of the shooting—he was slightly out of position. This distinction went to Associated Press photographer Ron Edmonds, who was well placed to take three frames at the moment a shot ricocheted off the president's armored limousine. The bullet ripped into Reagan's chest as Secret Service agents began pushing him into the car to rush him out of the area. The first frame shows Reagan waving with his left hand; the second shows him startled by the shots as an agent puts his own left hand on Reagan's upper arm to guide him into the vehicle; and the third, and most dramatic, shows a stricken president being pushed aggressively into the limo. Edmonds won the 1982 Pulitzer Prize for spot news photography for these pictures.

But Evans got several important images, one showing the chaotic scene that included still photographers and TV cameramen trying to capture the moment. Brady, face down on the ground, was being helped by White House officials, and Delahanty, also lying face down, was unattended. A Secret Service agent scanned the crowd while holding an automatic weapon, poised to shoot. Police estimated later that Evans narrowly missed being hit in the stomach by a bullet.[5]

Evans hopped into a chase car that followed the president's ambulance to nearby George Washington University Hospital, where Reagan struggled for life. He saw the president wheeled to the operating room on a gurney but, he recalled, "I froze. I knew I had come to respect Ronald Reagan, but I didn't realize how deeply my affection ran until that moment in the hospital. It came as a complete shock. I felt as if my own father had been shot. I just sat there for an hour, devastated. It never occurred to me to take any pictures."[6]

Eventually, Evans developed an even stronger rapport with this man he so admired. He argued that a personal bond is vital for a White House photographer to succeed. "The job of photographing the president—sure, you have to be a good photographer," he said. "But in many ways the job is more like being a valet than like the secretary of state. You're often with him and his family in very intimate settings so you have to get along. They liked my photography, sure, but I think they liked my persona more."[7]

Evans was a master at what an admiring reporter called being "both ubiquitous and invisible."[8]

He fit in perfectly with the well-groomed, corporate atmosphere of the Reagan White House. "At 40, he has the conservative presence of a K Street lawyer, with his gray flannels, white button-down shirt and neatly graying hair," wrote *Washington Post* reporter Lois Romano in a January 1985 profile. "His is a demeanor and look not unlike that of the people he must photograph daily in the White House, but strikingly different from that of his most famous predecessor, David Hume Kennerly, who would show up in Jerry Ford's Oval Office wearing blue jeans."[9]

Evans said: "Someone wrote once that if Kennerly was like a son to Ford, I'm like the president's nephew. That's an accurate assessment of our relationship."[10]

Supervising a staff of four photographers, Evans captured many now-familiar images of Reagan, such as the president clearing brush and chopping wood at his California ranch and riding horses with his wife Nancy.

He estimated that he and his staff shot 37,000 rolls of film over four years and 70 percent of his job was taking "grip-and-grin" photos of the president with visitors.[11]

Evans wasn't given access to his "uncle's" private life, a level of access that David Kennerly had in photographing President Ford and that Pete Souza had in photographing President Obama years later. And Reagan was extremely self-controlled, always trying to look the part of a president. "Even in front of me, his personal photographer, he was the consummate pro," Evans recalled. "He knew history would remember every photo if I didn't."[12]

Evans found out how sensitive his photographs could be very early on. When Reagan turned 70 the month after he was sworn in during 1981, he attended a birthday party at the White House and Evans always enjoyed taking pictures of the Reagans and their Hollywood pals. "I released a terrific picture of Nancy dancing with Frank Sinatra and the president trying to cut in," Evans recalled. "It was a warm and funny picture and larger than life."[13]

But the next morning, seeing the picture, White House Chief of Staff James Baker and Reagan media adviser Michael Deaver were fuming, "It was like a bomb went off in my car," Evans said. The two aides were upset because the picture called attention to Reagan's friendship with Sinatra, who had been criticized for alleged ties to the underworld. The Reagans calmed Baker and Deaver down, however, when they said they liked the picture very much.

The Reagans didn't want Evans around after work, when they preferred to be alone. Evans didn't mind. "Quite frankly, catching them at home was sort of boring," he said candidly while George H.W. Bush was president. "Two elderly people with TV trays on the couch just doesn't generate the same excitement as having kids around the way the Bushes do."[14] Or the way the Kennedys did.

Vice President George H.W. Bush had a different problem, and Evans was blunt in describing it. "When George came in the room he would almost invariably say hello to me," Evans said. "Reagan, on the other hand, would not. It wasn't rudeness. It's just that he knew how to be aware of the camera and [seem to] ignore it. But George would feel this need to relate to me as a human being. Now when I see pictures of him, I see the difference even clearer in the two men. George isn't Hollywood. He understands as a practicing politician he has to demonstrate a sense of style yet he has to work at it. And when he gets unstuck is when he tries too hard." Evans sometimes longed for a crisis so he could capture another important moment in history similar to the assassination attempt. "Working down in the basement, I used to wish the Russians would invade Poland so that there would be an honest-to-God crisis."[15]

But he did manage to reveal what appeared to be the essence of Reagan, both in his photographs and in his personal recollections. Reagan was his own best PR man. At one point, Evans took a picture of the president in a finger-pointing exchange in the Oval Office with House Speaker Tip

O'Neill. White House media adviser Michael Deaver thought the image was too raw and ordered that it not be released. But it turned up on the front pages of several newspapers, and Deaver demanded to know what happened. Evans explained that Reagan had requested a copy and the president liked it so much that he had it forwarded to O'Neill. Evans told Deaver, "It was the 40th president of the United States. You're going to have to talk to him about it." This ended the matter.[16]

One of Evans' achievements while in Washington was what he called the "Portrait Project," a sort of capital yearbook containing nearly 600 pictures of people prominent in Reagan-era Washington and taken over two and a half years starting in 1982. The images included those of the president, cabinet members and Reagan advisers such as James Baker and Deaver, along with members of Congress, Supreme Court justices, journalists, and a Capitol Hill janitor. The collection was featured in a 1985 exhibit at the Corcoran Gallery of Art in Washington and in a book.

Evans worked for Reagan at the White House for four years, departing after Reagan's first term. During this time, he switched from black-and-white to color portraits. He also hired Pete Souza as staff photographer in 1983, and Souza would share photo duties with four other shooters during Reagan's second term, and then return to be President Barack Obama's chief photographer for all eight years of the Obama administration. Souza felt this multi-photographer approach of Reagan's second term limited overall access because none of the photographers could develop the close relationship with the president or the trust that a single chief photographer would have had.

Evans maintained he never had a political discussion with Reagan. He explained that they had "a personal relationship" but, more important, they both had "a reason to be there and . . . a job to do." And Evans felt that his job wasn't to chat with the boss.[17] Reagan liked it that way.

* * *

REAGAN UNDERSTOOD the importance of imagery and good public relations. But he was a television president and, strangely enough for a man who was so photogenic, wasn't fully comfortable with still pictures.

He told a visitor in 1985, four years into his presidency, why this was so. "On movie film or TV tape I can drop the ball and still recover with a little joke or gesture," Reagan said. "But with still pictures I am frozen in time, and it is much harder to project my true self or the part, the image, I am trying to create."[18]

Yet there is a strong still-photo record of Reagan's eight years, and much of it reflects Reagan's sense of humor. *Air Force One* was a good venue. When the president saw an aide asleep after a long day, he would approach the snoozing official and stand over him pretending to be angry, gesturing with his hands and scowling in mock fury amid the fake and silent harangue. The White House photographer on duty would take some snaps, all without awakening the victim. Later, a White House manila envelope would appear on the aide's desk, and inside would be the pictures, signed by the president. Nearly every aide would recoil in embarrassment at the practical joke, but they kept the photos, which are probably framed and displayed prominently in each subject's home.

* * *

REAGAN'S INTERACTIONS with the photographers provided many insights into his character and personality.

Whenever Reagan was hosting an event, his old-school sense of etiquette compelled him to invite the women to leave the room first. He felt it was the polite thing to do. But this graciousness also included Susan Biddle, one of the White House staff photographers. And she wasn't happy about the practice because it meant Biddle often had to leave the room while Reagan was chatting with some of his guests, and she couldn't record those moments with her cameras. At one point, she took the president aside and asked him to stop ushering her out because, she said pointedly, "I can't do my job." Reagan expressed surprise that he hadn't realized this and murmured with some embarrassment, "Oh well, OK." This changed the pattern and Biddle got better pictures as a result.[19]

The many weeks that Reagan spent at Rancho del Cielo, his 688-acre retreat near Santa Barbara, California, showed the more calculated side of his image-making.

Reagan went to the mountaintop retreat as often as he could, and it enabled him to escape from his duties as much as possible. His staff, knowing that the septuagenarian president needed time to relax, didn't bother him with official business unless they felt it was absolutely necessary. The main agenda day after sunny day was a horseback ride with his wife Nancy, but it was not what it seemed. As I wrote in my book *From Mount Vernon to Crawford: A History of the Presidents and their Retreats*: "He would go up the hill to the tack barn and prepare for his daily horseback ride. When everything was ready, he rang a bell outside the barn to summon his wife, and she would walk quickly to meet him.

"Then they would go for a leisurely horseback ride, the president on his white Arabian named El Alamein, a gift from the president of Mexico, and Mrs. Reagan on her less flashy brown quarterhorse, No Strings. Several Secret Service agents always followed, also on horseback. His code name was Rawhide; hers, Rainbow.

"But the rides were not as spontaneous as White House image makers made them appear in the photos released to the media. To protect him, the Secret Service insisted that he go over his riding route on a map in advance so his bodyguards would always know his whereabouts. And while official photos of the rides focused on the mounted president, the First Lady, a bodyguard, and a friend or two, there was actually quite an entourage tagging along. Several agents would ride at discreet distance, and behind the small column of horses, out of camera range, was a special four-wheel-drive vehicle containing even more armed agents, sophisticated communications gear, medical kits, and the 'football," a briefcase containing nuclear-missile launch codes—just in case.

"When they returned from their ride, Nancy would allow only her husband to help her dismount. Once a new Secret Service agent tried to lend a hand, but she wouldn't budge. Moments later, the agent was startled by a familiar voice behind him. 'That's *my* wife, and *I'll* be the one to help her,' the president said as he brushed past the bodyguard and gently eased the diminutive First Lady from the saddle to the ground, his hands firmly grasping her slender waist. They would end each ride with a hug and a kiss."[20]

Pete Souza, a deputy White House photographer under Evans, was also given unusual access to the Reagans at the ranch. Reagan felt liberated there and was more relaxed than anywhere else, free from the tedium and suffocating schedules of the White House. "The president called the shots on what he would do for the day," Souza has written. "Mornings usually meant horseback riding on his favorite horse, El Alamein. Afternoons usually were spent chopping wood, trimming trees, or working on a project like building a fence. When he dressed in blue jeans, a workman's shirt, and some sort of hat, one could easily mistake Reagan for one of his workers. The only giveaway would have been members of the Secret Service in the woods, not needing to conceal their Uzi machine guns."[21]

Souza captured Reagan's playfulness and sense of drama in a photo of him riding El Alamein at the ranch. "He was riding along with some close friends," Souza recalled, "and when he spotted me taking pictures out on the trail, he yelled out, 'Charge!' I think he was showing off for his friends." It was a great shot as Reagan, his black hair glowing in the sun, was shown smiling broadly and pointing his right index finger forward with a sweep of his arm as if leading a cavalry attack.[22]

Reagan would even get mischievous. "Reagan knew that some of the networks set up television cameras miles away on a ridge overlooking the ranch, which he viewed as an invasion of privacy," Souza wrote. "He once tricked the reporters by going to an area where he knew the cameras could see him and clutching his chest with both hands as if he were having a heart attack. White House Chief of Staff Donald Regan looked as if he might have heart attack when I later told him what his boss had done."[23]

* * *

EVANS left the White House in March 1985 when the imperious Donald Regan replaced easygoing James Baker as chief of staff. Regan made life quite difficult for Evans because the new chief of staff wanted to control everything, including the photography department. Evans returned to *Time* for several years and moved to Atlanta in 1989 to become photo editor of the *Atlanta Journal-Constitution*. He later formed his own photo and computer company.

Evans died of cancer at his Atlanta home on Dec. 1, 2005. He was 61.[24]

* * *

PETE SOUZA managed to establish a connection with Reagan although it didn't approach Evans' relationship with the president. Souza wasn't named chief photographer after Evans left the White House. No one got that title because Evans was considered irreplaceable. But the ambitious and creative Souza became what he called "one of Ronald Reagan's shadows"—the self-styled first among equals as one of the president's official photographers. "From June 1983 to January 1989. I followed him in public and in private, often in intimate moments known only to a few," Souza said. "Sometimes it was just Reagan, my camera, and me."

"I was an official White House photographer, and thus, I saw him when he was far less guarded and less scripted than he was in public. In private, I also came to admire how he treated people in all walks of life."[25]

"The president was comfortable with my presence and understood the historic value of documenting behind-the-scenes moments of his life on film. As a result of his trust, I had virtually unfettered access to the Oval Office. The only time he asked me not to photograph him was when I once saw him putting in his hearing aid."[26]

Souza observed and captured with his camera scenes that he described as "extraordinary for their sheer normalcy, except that they happened to include the president of the United States. They included feeding the squirrels on the White House colonnade [and] putting a golf ball [into a practice cup] aboard Air Force One."[27]

Souza's access to Reagan enabled him to see the president in ways virtually no one else did, as a man of simple tastes, with a youthful spirit, a strong marriage, and a desire for normalcy. Souza didn't share Reagan's conservative ideology, but the photographer said, "For whatever flaws he had, Ronald Reagan was as good-hearted a man in private as he appeared to be in public. There was not a prejudicial bone in his body. I admired him because he was genuine in showing respect to all people—whether they were a head of state or a White House butler."[28]

Souza was in Reagan's presence during many unguarded moments even though Reagan was a formal man and rarely let down his guard. Once, Reagan was watching the nightly news on TV and he complained to his photographer, "They always show a correspondent telling people what I said instead of showing me saying what I said." On another occasion, Reagan watched a news story and snapped that sometimes he'd like to "bash Congress over the head." [29]

In 1985, Souza overheard a rare argument between the president and the first lady. The issue was Nancy's belief that her husband should cancel a planned visit to a World War II cemetery in Bitburg, West Germany. Reagan had agreed to make the visit at the invitation of German Chancellor Helmut Kohl, but it was later revealed that Nazi soldiers were buried there. Nancy agreed with critics, including many American Jewish leaders, who said Reagan shouldn't go to the cemetery. But Souza overheard Reagan rebuff his wife's request. He said he had to follow through on his agreement with Kohl to make the visit or "my word means nothing." Souza interpreted the incident this way: "While those around him framed the visit as a political liability, Reagan was determined to keep a promise, political damage be damned. Even the first lady couldn't change his mind."[30]

The Bitburg disagreement was unusual because President Reagan and his wife were so devoted to each other and had such a close relationship. This became clear to Souza in many ways, such as in the way they held hands, exchanged gifts, traded love notes, and almost never argued.

On a flight to Europe aboard *Air Force One*, the president was traveling without Nancy, and he summoned Souza to his cabin to issue a request. "I have a picture I want you to make," he said. He explained that his wife knew he had trouble sleeping when he traveled without her and she had insisted that the president's aides make sure that he got some sleep on the plane. "Please get a picture of this," President Reagan said and then he stretched out on a bed in his compartment and pretended to snooze.

Souza took a few frames and faxed a picture to the first lady at the White House with a handwritten note: "The president got some sleep on the plane." When he returned to Washington a few days later, Souza asked Mrs. Reagan if she had received the picture. "She just smiled," he recalled.[31]

Reagan told Souza a few times that his wife was consulting an astrologer, but the president said it in a "lighthearted way" and Souza didn't take it very seriously. The photographer kept this tidbit to himself. But it became big news when Regan revealed it in a memoir after he was fired as White House chief of staff at Nancy's instigation. She felt he was too overbearing and alienated too many people in Washington.[32]

Souza captured Reagan in a playful mood as he threw a paper airplane from the 34th-floor balcony of the Los Angeles hotel where he was staying during a trip to California in 1986. The picture was shot from behind, with Reagan in a blue and white casual shirt, poised to launch the paper airplane, which he held delicately in his right hand as he looked out over the panorama of LA in a cloudless but smoggy sky. The plane, which was a blank sheet of White House stationary, landed on another balcony 25 floors below.

Reagan didn't like the picture at first; nor did his White House media handlers, considering it "unpresidential." But Souza released it two years later as Reagan was preparing to leave office, and it was published in *U.S. News & World Report*, where I was White House correspondent. Reagan had his doubts but Souza said: "Mr. President, it just shows there's a little bit of a kid in every one of us, even the president of the United States." Reagan warmed to the image over time. After Souza gave him a print and signed it with, "Mr. President, bombs away!" Reagan put the framed photo on his office shelf in California near a signed picture from Queen Elizabeth II.[33]

Souza's steadily increasing access paid off in a big way during October 1986 when Reagan and Soviet leader Mikhail Gorbachev tried to negotiate an arms-control agreement during their meetings in Reykjavik, Iceland. The talks broke down when Reagan refused to give up his Strategic Defense Initiative, known as "Star Wars," a system designed to shoot down enemy missiles, and Gorbachev refused to accept SDI.

Souza captured Reagan, wearing a tan raincoat, and Gorbachev, in a blue raincoat and dark grey fedora, both grim-faced, as they walked stiffly side by side to Reagan's waiting limousine for his departure from Reykjavik. One can see the deep disappointment on their faces. Souza's observations remain invaluable to historians' understanding of what happened. As Gorbachev walked with Reagan to the limousine, Souza, snapping photos, heard their final, poignant exchange as translated by an interpreter.

"I don't know what else I could have done," Gorbachev said.

"You could have said yes," Reagan replied dejectedly, and then he stepped into his vehicle.[34]

Souza reported this exchange between the two leaders to Pat Buchanan, the White House communications director, who passed the parting comments to White House Press Secretary Larry Speakes, who in turn released them to the media. They became part of the historical record.[35]

Souza summarized his own reaction later: "To me, that seemed like the height of the cold war."[36]

The presidential motorcade next sped to the U.S. ambassador's residence in Reykjavik for a reception with U.S. Embassy staffers there. Souza found himself alone with Reagan and a Secret Service agent for a few minutes, and the distraught president let his feelings of disappointment show. "I hope I didn't let people down," he said somberly.[37]

Reagan's personal aide escorted him into the reception but the president couldn't shake off his disappointment at the failure of the talks with Gorbachev. Souza recalled, "Reagan was always so good at this—posing for keepsake photos—a firm handshake, a twinkle in his eye as he looked at each person, a few words of thanks, and finally a nice smile. He always made people feel special in what was likely their only chance to meet a president of the United States.

"But Reagan was obviously distracted this day, which he explained to the embassy staff, apologizing for this rare difficulty in 'smiling for the camera.' "[38]

The Reagan–Gorbachev relationship and the relationship between the two superpowers would improve, however; and Souza was there to chronicle it as the two leaders eventually agreed on a pact limiting intermediate range nuclear forces.

*   *   *

IN POPULAR MYTHOLOGY, everyone defers to the president of the United States, who always gets the last word. Not with Ronald Reagan and then-British Prime Minister Margaret Thatcher. Souza saw it first-hand. "Thatcher and Reagan were usually aligned politically, and they became good friends," he observed. "Reagan also admired the fact that a woman had risen to become a prime minister in Great Britain. The two conversed frequently, both in person and on the phone. One time, I was in the Oval Office when the president happened to be talking to Thatcher on the telephone. He had the phone to his ear for a long time, and he was trying unsuccessfully to interrupt the caller. I could tell he was frustrated as he leaned back in his chair. When he finally hung up, he turned to me and said, 'That Maggie!' and lamented that he sometimes couldn't get in a word when something was on her mind."[39]

*   *   *

SOUZA'S PHOTOS captured the celebrity factor that the Reagans made a hallmark of their years in the White House. There was the picture of the president and the first lady having what seemed to be a serious talk while pop icon Michael Jackson stood awkwardly between them in the Diplomatic Reception Room. Jackson is shown standing stiffly with his hands clasped across his waist, wearing a faux military jacket with gold buttons and a dramatic gold sash across his chest. The back story, described by Souza, is that White House staffers were told in advance not to bring their children to the event, designed to discourage drunk driving, so Jackson wouldn't be mobbed. But the staffers ignored the directive and brought their kids anyway. Jackson was surrounded and took refuge in a men's restroom in the White House library until the Reagans appeared and Jackson joined them for the ceremony.[40]

Another moment highlighting the celebrity factor happened at a state dinner to honor British royalty. Souza took a memorable photo of actor

John Travolta swirling Princess Diana around the dance floor in the Grand Foyer of the White House, as a military band played a medley from Travolta's hit movie, *Saturday Night Fever*. Everyone, including the president and first lady, were in the background. They all stood aside to give the actor and the princess plenty of room to show their moves.[41]

There were also the private moments that Souza visually chronicled of the health crises endured by the Reagans, showing the access they granted him. Souza photographed Reagan in bed at what was then Bethesda Naval Hospital, looking chipper and strong, a few days after his 1985 colon cancer surgery. Souza also photographed Reagan being briefed by White House Chief of Staff Donald Regan and meeting with key aides at the hospital, all designed to reassure the country that Reagan was up to the job and in control. Many newspapers used these pictures on their front pages.[42]

And there was Souza's picture of the president visiting his wife at Bethesda Naval Hospital after her 1987 mastectomy for breast cancer. She was wearing a pink robe and had a giant get-well card on her lap as she sat up in bed to greet her husband. The president was dressed in a dark suit and tie as he leaned in to gently kiss her.[43]

These private moments showed the Reagans facing adversity with grace and optimism.

*   *   *

SUSAN BIDDLE joined the small group of White House staff photographers in late 1987, hired from the *Denver Post*, and stayed through Reagan's final year in 1988, then spent four years working for George H.W. Bush. She got a close-in view of both presidents.

Veterans of the Reagan administration considered her too journalistic and news-oriented at first. When she was introduced to White House Press Secretary Marlin Fitzwater during her first few days on the job, Fitzwater told her, "I wondered who that woman was running across the Rose Garden."[44] Relying on her news instincts, she didn't want to miss anything so she ran from one spot to another to get the best images. This wasn't necessary at the White House, since she would have a great spot reserved for her at each venue, and in any case such headlong rushes were frowned on by the no-drama, dignified Bush staff. She slowed her pace after that.

Her philosophy for doing the job was similar to other White House camera people: She wanted to be a storyteller. "Because I came from a newspaper background, I wanted to tell what the president was like, for history," Biddle told me.[45]

Biddle learned that Reagan in private had the same affable manner and sense of humor that he displayed in public. Just before one of Reagan's weekly lunches with then-Vice President Bush, Reagan and Bush were seated at a table in the small dining room adjacent to the Oval Office and Biddle got on her knees to get the best angle for a photo. Suddenly, Bush popped up and announced that he was going to the restroom, leaving Reagan at the table and Biddle kneeling awkwardly before him. The president looked over at her and quipped, "You really don't have to kneel. A curtsy would be fine."

Notes

1. Marlin Fitzwater, interview with author, Apr. 9, 2016.
2. Jay DeFoore and David Walker, "Reagan's Death Returns Photographer to Limelight," *Photo District News*, vol. 24, no. 8 (Aug. 2004), p. 14.
3. Ibid., p. 24.
4. "Tribute to Michael A.W. Evans," *ZUMA Press*, Dec. 1, 2005, www.zumapress.com/aboutzuma/newsletter_archives/2005newsletters/2005newsletter48.html.
5. Matt Schudel, "Reagan Photographer Michael Evans, 61," *Washington Post*, Dec. 3, 2005, www.washingtonpost.com/wp-dyn/content/article/2005/12/02/AR2005120201967.html.
6. John Bredar, *The President's Photographer: Fifty Years Inside the Oval Office*, Washington, D.C.: National Geographic Society, 2010, pp. 160–161, quoting Michael Evans, 'Memoire', *Digital Journalist*, July 2004, http://digitaljournalist.org/issue0407/evans.html.
7. DeFoore and Walker, "Reagan's Death Returns Photographer to Limelight," p. 24.
8. Lois Romano, "Pictures from Power Central: Photographer Michael Evans and his White House Yearbook," *Washington Post*, Jan. 15, 1985, p. C1.
9. Ibid.
10. Ibid.
11. Schudel, "Reagan Photographer Michael Evans."
12. Geraldine Baum, "Eyewitness to History," *Los Angeles Times*, Sept. 9. 1990, p. E1.
13. Ibid.
14. Ibid.
15. Schudel, "Reagan Photographer Michael Evans."
16. Ibid.
17. Ibid.

18. George Tames, *Eye on Washington: The Presidents Who've Known Me*, New York: HarperCollins Publishers, 1990, p. 142.

19. Frank Donatelli, interview with author, Apr. 7, 2016.

20. Kenneth T. Walsh, *From Mount Vernon to Crawford: A History of the Presidents and their Retreats*, New York: Hyperion, 2005, pp. 216–217.

21. Pete Souza, *Images of Greatness: An Intimate Look at the Presidency of Ronald Reagan*, Chicago: Triumph Books, 2004, p. ix.

22. Ibid., p. 45.

23. Ibid., p. ix.

24. Schudel, "Reagan Photographer Michael Evans."

25. Souza, *Images of Greatness*, p. vii.

26. Ibid.

27. Ibid., p. viii.

28. Ibid., p. x.

29. Ibid., p. 139.

30. Ibid., p. viii.

31. Ibid., p. ix.

32. Ibid., p. x.

33. Ibid., p. 75.

34. Ibid., p. vii.

35. Ibid.

36. Bredar, *The President's Photographer*, p. 161.

37. Souza, *Images of Greatness*, pp. vii–viii.

38. Ibid., p. viii.

39. Ibid., p. 81.

40. Ibid., p. 89.

41. Ibid., p. 137.

42. Ibid., pp. 120–123.

43. Ibid., pp. 126–127.

44. Susan Biddle, interview with author, Sept. 26, 2016.

45. Ibid.

HIGHLIGHTS FROM THE VISUAL HISTORY OF THE PRESIDENCY

Ever since photography became popular in the mid-1800s, the visual history of the presidency has been one of the most important stories in American life. Pictures made the presidents familiar and connected them with everyday Americans, starting with Abraham Lincoln. This photo depicted a frail, exhausted Lincoln at the end of the Civil War and illustrated the awful burden he carried from serving as commander in chief during the bloodiest upheaval in U.S. history. He was assassinated not long after this photo was taken in April 1865.
Source: Alexander Gardner. Courtesy of Library of Congress.

THE STRENUOUS LIFE

Theodore Roosevelt believed in striving as hard as he could both publicly and privately. Pictures of him giving speeches illustrated his commitment to what he called "the strenuous life." A friend called him "a steam engine in trousers"—a dynamic image reflected in the photography.
Source: Underwood & Underwood. Courtesy of Library of Congress.

COMBATIVE AND ENDLESSLY ACTIVE

TR sought to dominate everything and everyone around him and he encouraged photography that portrayed him as an irresistible force. Alice, his daughter, said: "My father always wanted to be the baby at every christening, the bride at every wedding, and the corpse at every funeral."
Source: Library of Congress.

A Presidential Secret, Occasionally Revealed

Franklin D. Roosevelt's legs were paralyzed from polio and he never wanted the country to know the extent of his disability. The reporters and photographers who covered him mostly kept the secret but occasionally a photo like this one was taken— showing FDR struggling to leave his car during a campaign trip to Hollywood, Calif. on September 24, 1932. "No movies of me getting out of the machine, boys," he had announced, but someone snapped this still photo anyway. It was not widely circulated. Source: FDR Library & Presidential Museum.

A Presidential Attitude, Constantly Reinforced

This is the image that Roosevelt promoted—the jaunty, optimistic, vigorous president who inspired confidence and led the country through the Depression and World War II. Source: FDR Library & Presidential Museum.

PRIVATE PALS

Harry Truman, FDR's successor, liked to spend vacations at a military base in Key West, Florida. He could relax in the warm weather, and he socialized with the news photographers who covered him, many of whom he considered friends. They returned his affection, regarding Harry as a hard-working, considerate man who treated everyone with respect and admired the photo corps.
Source: Courtesy of Harry S. Truman Library.

THE PRESIDENTIAL CLUB

Shortly after the Bay of Pigs disaster, which was a failed U.S.-supported invasion of Cuba by exiles in April 1961, John F. Kennedy met with Dwight Eisenhower, his predecessor, at the Camp David presidential retreat. They discussed what had gone wrong and sometimes broke away from their entourages for private conversations such as this one. It's often said that only those who have actually been president can know what the job is like. This photo shows the solitary nature of the office—an incumbent commander in chief and his predecessor talking things over, one on one.
Source: Robert Knudsen. White House Photographs. John F. Kennedy Presidential Library and Museum, Boston.

FAMILY TIES

Photographers said it was nearly impossible to get a bad picture of President John F. Kennedy and his family. Photojournalist Stanley Tretick, one of JFK's favorite lensmen, got this iconic image of the president pretending to do some paperwork on October 15, 1963, while John, Jr., nearly 3 years old, played under his desk. Young John peeked through a small door, which he loved to open suddenly and surprise his father's guests. Adding poignancy to the moment is the fact that President Kennedy was assassinated five weeks after this picture was taken.
Source: Estate of Stanley Tretick LLC. Corbis/Getty Images.

THE LURE OF STARDOM

The president, his lovely wife Jacqueline, and their two children Caroline and John, Jr. attained the status of celebrities. Americans loved to keep track of their activities, and they obliged by posing frequently for flattering photographs, such as this one taken by chief White House photographer Cecil Stoughton at the family estate in Hyannis Port, Massachusetts, on August 4, 1962.
Source: Cecil Stoughton. White House Photographs. John F. Kennedy Presidential Library and Museum, Boston.

President Kennedy had many physical ailments that he kept hidden from the country, following Franklin Roosevelt's secretive pattern. One was severe and chronic back pain which he did his best to conceal so he did not seem weak or vulnerable. Occasionally, a photograph slipped out, such as this one that showed JFK using crutches as he left a speaking engagement in Washington on June 16, 1961.
Source: Abbie Rowe. White House Photographs. John F. Kennedy Presidential Library and Museum, Boston.

THE PICTURE OF CHARISMA

Kennedy loved projecting the image of a young, vigorous, exciting leader. Both his staff photographers and the news photographers helped him to do it. They got plenty of access, and made great pictures, such as this one of JFK surrounded by confetti as he campaigned in Los Angeles on November 1, 1960, as published in the Los Angeles Times. *Source: AP Photo/Dick Strobel.*

JACK AND MARILYN

A closely guarded secret was JFK's private relationship with the movie star Marilyn Monroe. The only known picture of them together was taken at a reception after she sang "Happy Birthday" to him during a huge party for Kennedy at New York's Madison Square Garden in May 1962. Secret Service agents tried to confiscate the photos of them together, taken by Cecil Stoughton, but they missed this one.
Source: Cecil Stoughton. White House Photographs. John F. Kennedy Presidential Library and Museum, Boston.

THAT TERRIBLE DAY

This is probably the most famous photo of any president. It shows Lyndon B. John-son being sworn in after Kennedy's assassination in Dallas on November 22, 1963. Johnson wanted this photo—which was taken aboard Air Force One *by Stoughton—to be distributed immediately around the world as a way to show that the Constitution endured and he would continue the Kennedy legacy. Many people still remember that terrible day, and this picture is etched into their memories.*
Source: LBJ Library. Photo by Cecil Stoughton.

Lyndon Johnson agonized over the Vietnam war during his presidency but he mostly kept it to himself. Here, however, White House staff photographer Jack Kightlinger captured an anguished president in July 1968 listening to a tape of his son-in-law, Marine Captain Charles Robb, telling him about conditions in the war zone. Source: LBJ Library. Photo by Jack Kightlinger.

A Proud Man in Defeat

Richard Nixon never wanted to show weakness. But he let down his guard on August 7, 1974, the night before he announced his resignation rather than face impeachment for the Watergate scandal. Nixon allowed Ollie Atkins, his chief photographer, to drop by the White House residence for some pictures. In this one, Nixon hugged his daughter Julie while his other daughter Tricia, near tears, and her husband stood awkwardly to the side. It was an uncomfortable situation for everyone, especially the photographer.
Source: Oliver F. Atkins, Richard Nixon Presidential Library and Museum.

BEHIND THE SCENES

Nixon, a workaholic, had trouble relaxing, even when he was taking some "vacation" time at his seaside estate in San Clemente, California. Walking on the beach was not a natural thing for him to do, as shown in this picture from January 1971.
Source: Bettmann Archive/Getty Images.

MAKING HISTORY

Jimmy Carter thought that most behind-the-scenes pictures were a waste of time, and he never appointed a chief photographer. But some moments were important for him and for history. Here, Carter talks with Israeli Prime Minister Menachem Begin (right) and Egyptian President Anwar Sadat at Camp David, where Carter brokered a historic peace agreement in 1978. It is one of the few historic photos from behind the scenes during the Carter presidency.
Source: Jimmy Carter Library.

TRAGEDY TO TRIUMPH

On March 30, 1981, about two months after Ronald Reagan took office, he was shot by a would-be assassin as he emerged from a Washington hotel after giving a speech. Associated Press photographer Ron Edmonds took this photo of Reagan at the instant he was hit. Secret Service agents immediately pushed him into his limousine and rushed him to a hospital, quick action that saved the president's life. Edmonds won a 1982 Pulitzer Prize for this picture.
Source: AP Photo/Ron Edmonds.

GIVING CONSERVATISM A HAPPY FACE

This was one of Reagan's favorite pictures. Michael Evans, who later became his chief White House photographer, took the image at Reagan's Santa Barbara, California, ranch in 1976, before Reagan became president. Evans made a remark that caused Reagan to break into a grin, and Reagan felt the resulting photograph captured his affability, charisma, and easygoing nature. The picture was widely used in the media for years.
Source: National Archives.

WHAT REALLY GOES ON

Excitement and concern surrounded the first summit meeting between President Reagan and new Soviet leader Mikhail Gorbachev in Geneva, Switzerland, in 1985. No one knew what to expect between the leaders of two superpowers. In public, each man seemed to be supremely confident and in command, but in private, as illustrated in this picture by the White House photo staff, the senior advisers for each side hung on every word, ready to assist with policy details, or, if possible, keep their leader from wandering too far into uncharted territory or making a blunder.
Source: Ronald Reagan Library.

ORCHESTRATING THE IMAGE

Sometimes the president, his staff, and photojournalists work together to choreograph pictures that capture an important moment. In this case, White House handlers wanted a special image to represent President Reagan's June 6, 1984 trip to the World War II battlefields of Normandy on the 40th anniversary of D-Day. What they arranged, in consultation with the news photographers, was the first couple at a cemetery walking solemnly amid row after row of crosses representing American soldiers who had died in battle. The Secret Service cooperated by staying out of the frame. It was an intimate and emotional moment.
Source: AP Photo/Bob Daugherty.

PRIVATE TIMES

Chief White House photographer David Kennerly was given amazing access to President Gerald Ford and his family, even to the point of photographing the down-to-earth commander in chief wearing pajamas at a meeting.
Source: David Hume Kennerly. Courtesy Gerald R. Ford Library.

Chief photographer David Valdez took this iconic picture of George H.W. Bush and his wife Barbara in bed surrounded by grandchildren at their estate in Kennebunkport, Maine, illustrating the closeness of the Bush family.
Source: George Bush Presidential Library and Museum.

RANGE OF MOODS

President Bill Clinton and Russian President Boris Yeltsin share a laugh during a public appearance, showing that world leaders often enjoy each other's company and there are light moments in diplomacy.
Source: William J. Clinton Presidential Library and Museum.

Presidents don't like to admit it but sometimes they lose their tempers. Here, White House photographer Bob McNeely captured Clinton berating aide George Stephanopoulos about news coverage he disliked. Clinton had a flash-and-fade type of anger, and his fury would disappear as quickly as it exploded.
Source: Robert McNeely/White House Photo Office.

SHARED OUTLOOK

President Bill Clinton and First Lady Hillary Clinton had a real partnership in governing. Here, they both react with similar consternation during a briefing aboard Air Force One.
Source: William J. Clinton Presidential Library and Museum.

THE START OF A WAR

*One of the most dramatic moments of any presidency occurred on September 11, 2001
when terrorists hijacked four airliners. They crashed two of them into the World Trade
Towers in New York City, flew the third plane into the Pentagon, and fought passengers on the fourth, which went down in the Pennsylvania countryside. In this photo,
President George W. Bush looked startled when White House Chief of Staff Andy
Card, at a public event in Florida, whispered into Bush's ear the news that the second
plane had crashed into the towers. This marked the start of what Bush called the global
war on terror. Chief White House photographer Eric Draper's images from that day
recorded the drama and seriousness of the crisis.
Source: Paul J. Richards/Getty Images.*

ICONIC MOMENT

Three days after 9/11, President Bush traveled to New York and visited Ground Zero, the still-smoldering ruins where the twin towers once stood. He grabbed a bullhorn and told firefighters and other first responders that he would make sure the perpetrators were brought to justice, perfectly capturing the nation's angry mood.
Source: Official White House Photo by Eric Draper.

A DARING MISSION

*Chief White House photographer Pete Souza was given extraordinary access, such as
on the day that President Barack Obama ordered a raid that killed terrorist master-
mind Osama bin Laden. One of Souza's historic images was of Obama and his senior
advisers watching live video of the actual mission in Pakistan on May 1, 2011.
Source: Official White House Photo by Pete Souza.*

ROLE MODEL

President Obama took being a role model very seriously, especially his potential to inspire African American young people to strive and emulate his success as the first African American president. When a young black boy, visiting the Oval Office, wondered if the president's hair felt like his own, Obama invited him to see for himself. The picture, taken by Pete Souza, was one of Obama's favorites.
Source: Official White House Photo by Pete Souza.

A WISH COME TRUE

President Obama and First Lady Michelle Obama shared a joyful moment with
106-year-old Virginia McLaurin of Washington, D.C., when McLaurin visited the
White House to mark Black History Month in February 2016. The Obamas took their
African American visitor by surprise, and she broke into a dance with the first lady as
the president watched with delight.
Source: Official White House Photo by Pete Souza.

DEFINING LEADERSHIP

The presidency can be an isolating job, and the toughest decisions are made by the president alone. Here, Souza captured a solitary, contemplative moment for President Obama, replicating a famous image of President Kennedy from a half-century earlier which was entitled "The Loneliest Job."
Source: Official White House photo by Pete Souza.

Promoting A Larger-Than-Life Image

President Donald Trump likes to project dominance, strength and confidence, which he did during this speech, with his own gigantic image projected on a screen behind him. Source: AP Photo/Carolyn Kaster.

Pete Souza, the chief photographer for President Obama who had earlier been a staff photographer for President Reagan, had remarkable access and was instrumental in shaping Obama's image.
Source: Photo by Ben Wirtz Siegel. Courtesy of Ohio University.

Yoichi Okamoto, the chief photographer for President Lyndon Johnson, also enjoyed close-in access and helped explain LBJ to the country.
Source: LBJ Library photo by Yoichi R. Okamoto.

Both Souza and Okamoto saw themselves as photographic historians. They were pace-setters, widely regarded as among the best still photographers ever to cover the White House.

CHAPTER EIGHT
BEHIND THE SCENES WITH GEORGE H.W. BUSH AND DAVID VALDEZ

Dave Valdez quickly figured out the key to his success in the world of George H.W. Bush. It happened in December 1983, during Valdez's first day on the job as the chief photographer for Bush when he was vice president. Son Jeb Bush and daughter-in-law Columba brought their new infant to see grandpa at a Miami Beach hotel. While the proud grandfather was making a fuss over the child, Jeb and Columba had to leave the hotel suddenly and Bush and Valdez found themselves alone with the baby. At that point, the new photographer asked himself, "Now what?"[1]

The vice president took the infant into a back bedroom, and Valdez's first reaction was not to intrude. But he guessed that this situation might make a good picture and he wanted to set the precedent that he would have all the access he wanted in the future, as David Kennerly had during Gerald Ford's presidency. So Valdez followed his boss into the other room, where he took several photos of Bush as the doting grandfather.

Valdez sent prints to Barbara Bush, the vice president's wife, and she sent back a note: "As long as you take pictures of my grandchildren," she wrote, "you can go anywhere and photograph anything." Valdez considered the note a license for access: "That was my opening and I kept that note," the soft-spoken, self-effacing, perpetually polite photographer said. Barbara was his ally after that, strengthening Valdez's bond with Bush and his family.[2]

Valdez also quickly learned that the Bushes prized discretion. "I never spoke up [during official photo shoots] because you weren't there to talk," you were just there to take photos of "what's in front of you." Valdez added: "You don't alter things. You photograph what's there." Valdez said, "The job was to document what the president did" not to shape his thoughts or affect policy.[3]

After Bush was elected president in 1988, the new commander in chief asked Valdez to stay on as the official presidential photographer, and Valdez served the president from January 1989 to January 1993, taking 65,000 rolls of film.[4] He was delighted with the opportunity. Valdez's father had worked on a farm in South Texas and then had a career in the military. Valdez had earned a journalism degree from the University of Maryland and worked for years as a government photographer, never expecting to rise so high in his profession. Now he was the first Latino to be the chief White House photographer. He was immensely proud to serve the commander in chief.

*   *   *

WHAT MATTERED most to President Bush was "family, faith and friends," and he prized loyalty, Valdez learned. This fit perfectly with Valdez's value system, and he grew so close to Bush that he felt part of the president's family.[5]

As Valdez learned, family was most important of all. Bush told his photographer that what he was most proud of in his life was the fact that his children always came home and they wanted to maintain a good relationship with their parents all their lives.[6] (I covered the Bush presidency as White House correspondent for *U.S. News & World Report* since 1986, and Bush told me this, too.)

"You've got to have a personal relationship with these people [on his staff], I think, to make it really good, and that was easy to do with Dave Valdez," former President Bush said years later. "I think that's why his work, at least why Barbara and I loved it. It brought out what was natural, what we were about, what we thought, what we cared about, what we cried about, what we laughed about."[7]

For his part, Valdez said: "The highest honor for me during the nine years of working for . . . George Bush was for him to introduce me as his friend. I would always address him as Mr. President throughout our working relationship and thought of him only in those terms. This became quite evident one morning at Walker's Point in Kennebunkport when Mrs. Bush came out of their bedroom and asked me if I had seen George. George? George? Who was this George? Not a staffer. Not Secret Service. She realized I had no clue who she was talking about and said, "You know, the president of the United States.'"[8]

Bush gave Valdez a valuable insight into his character and values when he told his photographer about an incident from his boyhood. He came home one day and boasted to his mother that his soccer team had just won a key game. His mother didn't like his superior attitude and she asked if the other team had played well. Her advice, which she repeated whenever her son, nicknamed "Poppy," got too egotistical, was "Don't brag on yourself."[9]

Valdez says Bush took this advice to heart as an adult and as president. One could see it clearly when the Soviet Union unraveled while Bush was in the White House. It was finally clear that, after decades of struggle and international tension, the United States had won the Cold War. As millions celebrated the destruction of the Berlin Wall that had kept East and West Germans separate for a generation, Bush declined to gloat or even to express much satisfaction, at least in public. He told Valdez he wouldn't "dance on the Wall" because it might cause too many hard feelings and make reconciliation between East and West more difficult.[10] He was probably correct in this assessment.

"President Bush always struck me as a compassionate man who worked for the underdog but was reluctant to receive praise for his efforts," Valdez recalled.[11] Praising Bush for also having "integrity and class," he added: "I always maintained that if every American could have witnessed what I did, George Bush would have been reelected."[12]

One of Valdez's favorite assignments was visiting Bush's seaside estate in Kennebunkport, Maine, every summer to take an annual picture of the large Bush family, often with the clan's sprawling Walker's Point house as the backdrop. *Life* magazine got the idea of assigning a photographer to capture the Bushes at their estate, but the then-vice president ruled that it would be too intrusive. *Life* decided to use Valdez's pictures, if the family would agree to let Valdez take the shots. He was already planning to be at the estate in Kennebunkport on his annual mission to add to the family portfolio. The vice president and his wife were delighted to give Valdez the access, and Barbara Bush invited Valdez to the main house at 6:00 one morning so he could "see what happens."

What resulted was the famous photo of Bush, his wife, their daughter Doro, and six grandkids in their bedroom. It was Valdez's most iconic picture. The moment happened at 6:00 a.m. when the grandkids burst into "Gampy's" bedroom. They found him and Barbara in bed, looking more than a bit disheveled. Two of the grandkids jumped in bed between them and four others pranced or stood around the room. The Bushes' daughter Doro sat at a window. This was when Valdez, entering the room and recognizing the great picture in front of him, began shooting frames.

In the most celebrated photo, Barbara, wearing a nightgown under a blue robe, seemed camera conscious as she smiled beatifically at a grandchild playing at the foot of the bed, but the president was not so aware of the camera. He looked more than a bit groggy, as if he has just awakened, his hair uncombed and his orange robe wrinkled. A bookcase behind the headboard was crammed with volumes, memorabilia, a few family photos, a white phone and a red phone.

Valdez explains that two of the president's four sons, George W. Bush and Jeb Bush, were sitting in chairs but they were off camera.

Life used the photo as a two-page spread, an accurate depiction of Bush as a family man.[13]

The Bushes were delighted. "We felt comfortable having David there," former President Bush recalled. "It's kind of typical of the way our family operated then, and the way our family operates today. And it wasn't staged. It was just a moment that David captured. He saw them running around and just took some shots. I love that picture."[14]

Life later reprinted the picture in special editions.[15]

Valdez called it "my defining photo," and it has been reproduced widely over the years.[16]

In another revealing snapshot, Valdez captured the president walking across the South Lawn on a rainy day, wrapped in his coat as he hurried indoors from his *Marine One* helicopter. It is a rather gloomy scene, and reflected the commander in chief's mood. This was just after he had given the order to launch the Persian Gulf War to expel Iraq from tiny Kuwait. In a move designed to signal to the Iraqi leaders nothing was afoot, Bush had gone to his Camp David presidential retreat as if he were on a short vacation. Far from it. A massive strike by the United States and its allies was about to hammer the Iraqis. Bush returned to the White House by chopper at the last minute to oversee the operation. Aides later said that he was pondering what was about to unfold, and the lives that would be lost as Bush determined to send hundreds of thousands of Americans into harm's way. The war was viewed as a success, with relatively few U.S. casualties and an impressive international coalition built by Bush that held together remarkably well.

Valdez said in a 1990 interview, about halfway through Bush's four-year term, "Maybe he'll look a little tired. But, really, with George Bush, you don't get dramatic swings. What you see is what you get, a man looking relaxed and in control."[17] Of course, this was the image that Bush wanted to project.

Valdez realized early on that Barbara Bush didn't like being photographed wearing eyeglasses, and she would take them off when he started shooting. When she was ready for the picture-taking to end, she would put the spectacles back on and Valdez would take that as a signal to stop.[18]

He attributed one of his best shots to good luck. In May 1990, Bush and then-Soviet leader Mikhail Gorbachev were meeting at Camp David, in the Maryland mountains, when Gorbachev and his wife Raisa took a break and found themselves at the horseshoe pit that Bush had installed. Valdez accompanied them and showed the Soviet leader how to play. Later, when Bush and Gorbachev had a friendly game, Gorbachev made a ringer and there was jubilation all around. Valdez captured it on film but it wasn't released for nearly two weeks.

"We had to be sensitive to Gorbachev's political problems at home and to show him playing might not have been good," Valdez explained. But after discussions among senior U.S. officials, it was decided to release the picture and there were no negative repercussions. In fact, Valdez said it was one of his most memorable pictures. "To get two world leaders alone enjoying themselves is unusual," he said. "It was a remarkable shot."[19]

*   *   *

SUSAN BIDDLE, the White House photographer who was one of Valdez's deputies after covering Reagan in 1987 and 1988, learned much about Bush during her four years on his staff. She came to like and respect him as a caring, honest person. She holds the distinction of having worked for two modern-day presidents in succession—Ronald Reagan and George H.W. Bush—and then was a photojournalist for the *Washington Post*. Biddle graduated from the University of Colorado with a degree in French and served in the Peace Corps. A photographer gave her a camera to take pictures of a family wedding, and this sparked her interest in photography.[20]

She said her work at the *Washington Post* was "historical" but orchestrated by the White House—too often just a series of photo ops designed to make the president look as good as possible, at least in the minds of his handlers.[21]

She had much more access as a White House staff photographer, but there were self-imposed limits. Biddle said her job was to shoot pictures, not to get into discussions or chitchat with the president, and she often didn't pay much attention to what was going on as she tried to get the best images possible.[22]

She said Bush, former director of central intelligence, was always nervous about keeping things secret. He sometimes asked her to leave meetings when extremely classified matters came up, even though she had a high-level security clearance.

Whenever a touchy subject arose in a discussion that he wanted to keep secret, he would turn to Biddle and announce, "OK, you're history." This was his way of ordering her out of the room. She didn't mind. She felt that Bush was just being super-careful and didn't want any inadvertent leaks or disclosures. This was perfectly understandable.[23]

Biddle, who had been a news photographer before her White House stint, told me later that Bush had nothing to worry about from her. Like many other photographers, she said she was so intent on taking pictures, making sure the f-stop and the lighting and the composition were all optimal, that she didn't listen to what was being said. So she couldn't have disclosed anything secret.

On another occasion, Bush was about to give a big speech and he asked her to listen to a few lines to get her reaction. "Here I was, sitting in a room with the president of the United States and my head was feeling hot," she recalled, because she was so nervous about what she should say.[24] Biddle managed a few positive words that the lines sounded fine to her. She left the incident impressed that the president would reach out and ask a non-expert for a reaction to his ideas.

And being an insider gave her special insights in unusual ways. Biddle was struck by how different the atmosphere was in the White House residence between the Reagans and the Bushes. Ron and Nancy were a very close, romantic couple, and Biddle said the residence always smelled of flowers during their time in the White House. The Bushes were frequently surrounded by their adult children and grandchildren, and in the morning the entire residence floor smelled of bacon and eggs, which the extended family had for breakfast.

Biddle was on a Secret Service vessel while Bush was fishing from his speedboat *Fidelity* near his estate in Kennebunkport, Maine, one blustery August afternoon. The president got a phone call from the Soviet Union but couldn't hear clearly because of the wind and crashing waves.

As it developed, the caller was Soviet leader Mikhail Gorbachev, being held under house arrest in Crimea by coup plotters.

Bush immediately turned his boat around and sped back to his estate, and he took the call in his bedroom. Biddle was there with him, thinking this would be a historic moment she wanted to capture on film. "Mikhail, are you all right?" Bush asked as he sat on the bed. He beckoned for his wife Barbara to come into the room; she had been standing just outside. When she entered, she immediately noticed Biddle taking pictures and was aghast at her husband's appearance. "Why didn't you do anything about his hair?" she chastised Biddle. Biddle thought to herself: Well, I'm not about to touch the president's head. Barbara quickly grabbed a brush and began straightening out her husband's hair, which was looking unkempt from the speedboat ride.[25]

It was another lesson for Biddle—that there was very little vanity or pretense in George Herbert Walker Bush. He had other things on his mind, such as the safety of another world leader whom he admired.

*   *   *

BUSH HAD a good rapport with the news photographers who covered him, even though he didn't grant them the personal access he gave to Valdez. He knew nearly all the photographers and the reporters from the White House press corps by their first names and he often inquired about how their families were doing. He would recognize credit lines and compliment the photographers on their work.

He referred to the news photographers as the "photo dogs," an affectionate term he came up with when he noticed them barking as they humorously protested being herded like a pack of dogs behind ropes to keep them confined and under control at public events.

Early in his administration, he began to drop by the White House media briefing room in the evenings when the reporters had gone home and he was working late. He almost always found some "photo dogs" still on the job, sometimes lounging in the seats or even taking naps after a long day. He would sit with the shooters and chat under the unspoken agreement that everything would be kept off the record. But when reporters found out what the president was doing, they began showing up to ask questions, and this ended the practice.

*   *   *

BUSH WAS resistant to what he called "stagecraft" and being "handled" by advisers. He rejected advice on how to get the best camera angles so he would look his best, and stubbornly insisted on being himself even when this led to less-than-flattering images. Departing Washington, D.C., on *Air Force One* early in the morning, Bush would often visit the press compartment to say hello to reporters and photographers who were accompanying him. And he often looked as if he had just jumped out of bed, with his hair uncombed or still wet from the shower. The resulting photos taken by the news photographers and camera operators while he answered reporters' questions gave him a disheveled, not-ready-for-prime-time look.

On one occasion, Marlin Fitzwater, his press secretary, suggested that he comb his hair before meeting the press, and Bush at first rejected the idea. But after seeing himself in a mirror, the president changed his mind and asked Fitzwater to lend him a comb. The aide produced his own comb which he hadn't cleaned in a while, and Bush thought better of the idea. But he did spruce himself up when similar situations arose later in his presidency, and his press secretary made sure to have clean combs always at the ready.

Fitzwater also tried to discourage Bush from doing things that made him look silly, often to no avail. He repeatedly urged the president not to try on hats because he sometimes looked ridiculous in the headwear and news photographers were only too happy to snap and distribute such images. (In contrast, Kennedy refused to wear hats most of the time, including a top hat at his inauguration, because he didn't think he looked attractive and glamorous in headwear.)

Bush resisted Fitzwater's entreaties. On one occasion, during a meeting with a team from the University of Arkansas, whose nickname was "the Razorbacks," after the wild boar, Bush was presented with a red cap bearing the image of a fierce-looking wild boar with fangs bared. Fitzwater advised his boss not to don the cap. But Bush rebelled, telling his press secretary he would wear whatever he wanted. Bush carried the cap with him throughout the event and finally put it on and turned to the news photographers with the request, "Take a picture." Fitzwater was correct. The resulting pictures made Bush look goofy, not presidential.[26]

Bush endeavored not to be restricted too much by the PR rules under which his White House advisers tried to place him. This became clear on his first trip back to his seaside family retreat in Kennebunkport, Maine, after he was inaugurated as president in 1989. He walked to his big house on Walker's Point with a few aides and suddenly stopped in his tracks and began removing his suit jacket, tie, shirt, shoes, and socks. Then he sprinted to the rocks bordering his property, with the water crashing all around, and dove into the sea. Realizing what Bush was up to, Fitzwater immediately signaled to get the shot, and Valdez snapped a single frame, showing the president from the side as he launched himself into the water.[27]

Afterward, an alarmed Fitzwater warned the president that this was entirely too dangerous and the commander in chief shouldn't be taking such risks. Bush then admonished Fitzwater, noting that he had been jumping or diving into these waters from these same rocks since he was 2 years old, and he wouldn't be told to stop. Fitzwater learned the lesson that Bush could be very stubborn about staying true to himself and refused to forget his roots or what came naturally to him.

Valdez became a strong admirer of his boss. He told me: "Look at all the experience he had before he became president"—in the Texas oil business, in Congress, envoy to China, U.S. ambassador to the United Nations, chairman of the Republican National Committee, director of central intelligence, and vice president. This enabled Bush to develop personal relationships with important people across the United States and around the world, which became important as he conducted his presidency.

Valdez also saw Bush's lighter side, notably his delight in practical jokes which he rarely showed to the public and which he used to relieve stress or escape from his official, ceremonial persona. In the summer of 1984, while Bush was Ronald Reagan's vice president and the Reagan–Bush ticket was running for reelection, Bush and his entourage went to Kennebunkport for a break. As he and Valdez walked to the main house on Walker's Point, a rocky promontory, he pointed out that he had played in the waters here as a boy. It was the same area from where he would dive in the water in front of Fitzwater in 1989. Bush asked Valdez if he'd like to go for a swim, and Valdez replied that he had his work clothes on and was carrying camera equipment. But Bush insisted. They went back to the house changed into bathing suits (the vice president lent one of his to Valdez) and then walked back out to the rocks. Bush said to jump in at the count of three and after shouting "One . . . Two . . . Three," Valdez hurled himself into the cold water but Bush watched silently from shore, smiled, then turned and walked back to the house. Valdez had to clamber back up the rocks and make his way, shivering and embarrassed, to the house to change into his work clothes. Bush didn't mention the incident again.[28]

Valdez never became one of Bush's closest friends, but they had an affinity for one another. Valdez traveled all over the world with Bush and sometimes, at a particularly historic meeting or grand setting, Bush would gently elbow his photographer and whisper, "Can you believe this? Two guys from Texas doing this?" That camaraderie lasted for all nine years that Valdez was Bush's photographer, both when he was vice president and president.[29]

On election night in 1992, after it became clear that Bush had lost his bid for a second term to Democratic challenger Bill Clinton, the defeated president decided it was time to make the customary but always painful phone call to congratulate the victor. Valdez was there to capture the moment with his camera, and as he snapped his pictures, he felt his eyes tearing up. "It was kind of sad," Valdez said with typical understatement.

*   *   *

VALDEZ KEPT in contact with George and Barbara Bush during their years out of office, but the obvious decline in the former president's physical condition was troubling for many in their circle. The man known for his vigor and love of athletics, from jogging to tennis and golf, was confined to a wheelchair with a variety of ailments, When Valdez suggested that he practice fly-casting from the rocks around Walker's Point, which Bush had explored as a boy and felt extremely familiar with all his life, the former commander in chief demurred. "I'm afraid that now I'll fall in there and no one will ever find me" Bush confided sadly.[30]

Notes

1. David Valdez, interview with author, Apr. 25, 2016; see also David Valdez, comments at "White House Photographers," panel discussion at the Lyndon Baines Johnson Presidential Library, Austin, Texas, Jan. 20, 2010, www.c-span.org/video/?291502-1/white-house-photographers.
2. Valdez, interview with author, Apr. 25, 2016; Valdez, comments at "White House Photographers."
3. David Valdez, video interview with Erica Lies, Briscoe Center for American History, University of Texas, Sept. 27, 2013.
4. Valdez, interview with author, Apr. 25, 2016.
5. Ibid.
6. Valdez, video interview with Erica Lies, Sept. 27, 2013.
7. John Bredar, *The President's Photographer: Fifty Years Inside the Oval Office*, Washington, D.C.: National Geographic Society, 2010, p. 164.
8. David Valdez, *George Herbert Walker Bush: A Photographic Profile*, College Station: Texas A&M University Press, 1997, p. ix.

9. Valdez, interview with author, Apr. 25, 2016.
10. Ibid.
11. Valdez, *George Herbert Walker Bush*, p. xiii.
12. Ibid., p. xiv.
13. Valdez, interview with author, Apr. 25, 2016; Valdez, comments at "White House Photographers."
14. Bredar, *The President's Photographer*, p. 167.
15. Juan Castillo, "Eyes on History: David Valdez, Only Latino White House Photographer," *NBC News*, Dec. 25, 2014, www.nbcnews.com/news/latino/eyes-history-david-valdez-only-latino-white-house-photographer/12/25/2014.
16. Valdez, interview with author, Apr. 25, 2016.
17. Geraldine Baum, "Eyewitness to History", *Los Angeles Times*, Sept. 9. 1990, p. E1.
18. Ibid.
19. Ibid.
20. Jennifer Dryden, "Photographer gets Personal Side of Presidents," *CBS News*, Oct. 16, 2008, cbsnews.com/news/photographer-get-personal-side-of-presidents.
21. Ibid.
22. Ibid.
23. Susan Biddle, interview with author, Sept. 26, 2016.
24. Ibid.
25. Ibid.
26. Marlin Fitzwater, interview with author, May 22, 2016.
27. Marlin Fitzwater, interview with author, Apr. 9, 2016.
28. Valdez, interview with author, Apr. 25, 2016.
29. Valdez, video interview with Erica Lies, Sept. 27, 2013.
30. Ibid.

Chapter Nine
Behind the Scenes with Bill Clinton, Bob McNeely, and Sharon Farmer

Bob McNeely vividly remembers taking his first photographs in the Oval Office. It was during the administration of President Jimmy Carter, and McNeely was working for Vice President Walter Mondale, who asked McNeely to accompany him to a meeting with the president.

"I walked in there and it was like my hands were shaking, the first time. I can literally still remember it, knees knocking, hands shaking, you know, trying to take the pictures but obviously that goes away after a couple [of times]," McNeely recalled.[1]

Sixteen years later, McNeely was given the top job of chief White House photographer under Bill Clinton, and he made the most of it. It helped that McNeely had worked for Vice President Mondale but also that he had served in the Vietnam War and was accustomed to extreme situations. He had to deal with many of them at the White House. But in the end, the reason he was hired was simple: good chemistry between him and Bill and Hillary Clinton: "They hired me because they trusted me and liked me," McNeely says.[2]

McNeely learned much about Clinton over the years. He was impressed with Clinton's ability to focus on an objective or a task even when there was chaos all around him, which happened often. In February 1993, within a month of his inauguration, Clinton was about to

make his first televised speech to the nation and there were a dozen people, including Vice President Al Gore, gathered in the small dining room
adjacent to the Oval Office, working on the final version or watching the
proceedings with only a few minutes to go. Clinton, seeming cool and
calm, sat in shirtsleeves at a round table centered with a floral arrangement, focused on the speech text in front of him as he considered the
final edits. McNeely, assessing the photo later, said: "In the back corner
you have the steward, sort of looking in there, like, 'Jesus, look at all
those people . . . it's just chaos.' . . . What made it good was he was very
able to be involved in the moment and let it happen around him, let
things happen around him, and we see that in pictures where there's a lot
of people on the periphery, but he's focused on what he's doing. He'd
forget you were there, which is great."[3]

McNeely added that, unlike the way the White House is often
depicted on TV or in the movies, the staff always plays a secondary role.
"The president is always the center of attention," he said. "There's only
one important person in the real White House and that's the president."[4]

Other pictures in McNeely's archive are reminders of Clinton's talent for personal diplomacy. Two shots stand out. One, taken during a
Clinton visit to Northern Ireland, showed the president with hard-line
Protestant leader Ian Paisley. Another showed Clinton with insurgent
Catholic leader Gerry Adams. The two Irish activists would not meet
with each other, but Clinton got them to sit down in the same chair in
sequential meetings with the U.S. president, who was serving as a peace
maker. It was a gamble, but it helped build trust in Clinton from both
sides, and eventually he did broker a peace agreement.

Another McNeely picture became a key public-relations tool for the
White House in its ongoing battle with majority Republicans in Con-
gress over the budget.[5] Israeli Prime Minister Yitzhak Rabin was assassi-
nated in Israel during the 1995 budget negotiations in Washington and a
U.S. delegation led by Clinton flew aboard *Air Force One* to the funeral.
The delegation included House Speaker Newt Gingrich (R-Ga.), and
Senate Majority Leader Bob Dole (R-Kan.). After the journey home,
Gingrich complained he had been snubbed on the plane and that Clin-
ton wouldn't discuss the budget impasse. Therefore, he felt justified in
shutting down the government in retaliation.

As the furor grew in Washington over who was at fault and who was
more stubborn, McNeely recalled that he had taken pictures of Clinton,
Gingrich, and other members of Congress sitting together aboard *Air*

Force One on the return home. This suggested there had been no snub, and, even if Clinton didn't raise the budget issue, Gingrich could easily have done so. McNeely showed the pictures to White House Press Secretary Mike McCurry, who immediately realized their value in outmaneuvering Gingrich. McNeely made scores of prints and brought a stack of the photos to the media briefing room in the West Wing, the congregation point for the White House press corps. And the prints were immediately snapped up by the journalists.[6]

Gingrich was widely criticized for falsely claiming he had been snubbed, and McNeely's photos were a big reason the speaker lost the PR war over the budget and was blamed for the stalemate.

Throughout his presidency, Clinton puzzled the journalists and news photographers who covered him and were frequently unsure whether the mood Clinton was conveying publicly was genuine or an act. Among the skeptics was Pete Souza, who had been one of Ronald Reagan's staff photographers and during the Clinton years was a shooter for the *Chicago Tribune* based in Washington.

Souza said of covering Clinton as a photojournalist: "With Clinton, he's a guy on stage. This is the way I look at it. He could show you five different faces during any one appearance. I transmit my photos digitally to Chicago every day, and the most difficult thing I do is figure out which one to send because I don't know which one is the true moment. I can make him look any way you want to match a story of the day. Do you send the pensive look? Which look do you send?"

"Towards the end of the year [1998], when it looked like he was going to get impeached, he sort of changed his game face. When he appeared publicly it was more showing that his staff is behind him. It's the happy face, kind of a little smirk, almost. But whether it's a true moment, I don't know. It's so hard to tell."[7]

*   *   *

THE PHOTO GAME began to change in a fundamental way under McNeely and Bill Clinton. "Although the official White House photographers had occasionally made their work available to the media in the past, the Clinton press office recognized the public relations value of the White House photo office work" more than its immediate predecessors, writes news photographer Dennis Brack. "These releases were the beginning of a cascade of White House photos over the next two presidential administrations. The White House-released photographs were the source of many disagreements with the news photographers and the White House press office. The bond between the news photographers and the official photographers that had been made by David Hume Kennerly, Michael Evans, and David Valdez began to fade."[8]

* * *

MCNEELY HAD A DIVERSE and interesting background. Born in Bath, New York, he was drafted into the Army at age 21 in November 1967 and spent 14 months in Vietnam, where he served in combat and earned a Bronze Star Medal. Then he was assigned to run an Army photo lab, bought his first Nikon camera and grew fascinated with photography.

After his stint in the military, he moved to Aspen, Colorado, where he studied photography at a workshop with professional photographers and became friends with counter-cultural journalist Hunter Thompson, who called McNeely "a wild boy." He loved his camera so much that "he carried it around with him everywhere," Thompson observed.[9]

He moved to San Francisco to make his way as a photographer there, and in 1972 became a supporter of liberal Senator George McGovern (D-SD), because of McGovern's opposition to the Vietnam War. For a while McNeely took pictures on the campaign trail. After McGovern's loss, McNeely moved to Washington, D.C., where he pursued his interest in a career as a photojournalist.

He eventually came to the attention of Vice President Walter Mondale and his wife Joan and they hired him in 1977 to be the new vice president's official photographer. When Mondale and President Jimmy Carter lost to Republican Ronald Reagan and vice-presidential running mate George H.W. Bush in 1980, McNeely went into the private sector as a photographer, worked as a freelance for several prestigious publications including *Time* and *Newsweek*, and opened a portrait studio in Washington.

* * *

MCNEELY GOT the job of chief White House photographer after serving as Bill Clinton's campaign photographer in 1992. He grew to know the Clintons well, developing bonds of trust, and they liked his work. McNeely was also a Democrat, as were the Clintons, which helped build the relationship. In all, McNeely took 20,000 rolls of film during his five and a half years at the White House.[10]

One of his most revealing photos of the long-shot 1992 presidential candidate was a picture of Clinton sitting alone on an NBC-TV set prior to a Democratic debate during the primary campaign on December 15, 1991. Clinton, wearing his hair closely cropped and looking impossibly young, sat in his chair alone and straightened his tie. Five empty chairs to his left held headshots of each of his competitors, so they knew where to sit when they arrived. Clinton looked confident and ready for the encounter to start.[11]

There were some awkward moments while he worked for the Clintons. During his first few days at the White House, the new president got annoyed that McNeely was always at his side, snapping pictures. This was much more intrusive than on the campaign, and Clinton wanted more separation. Clinton took McNeely aside and asked how much longer this would go on. McNeely said he understood the president's concern but added: "I just worry about missing something." Clinton agreed that it was important for his photographer to capture history, and he didn't question McNeely's proximity again.

McNeely says he always called Clinton "Boss" or "Sir," and they never developed a close friendship. Yet other Executive Branch officials complained that McNeely was having an undue influence on policymaking. McNeely said: "My unrestricted access caused an incredible amount of resentment. At a certain point I became a target because people feared, due to Clinton's gregarious nature, that I was impacting policy, that I tried to talk policy with him. It's complete nonsense. We talked about sports or television or the weather and we swapped jokes about people, but we basically never talked policy."[12]

McNeely wrote in *The Clinton Years*: "The job of White House photographer entailed long hours spent going to an event, waiting for an event to begin, or waiting to leave when it was over. I would always have my camera at the ready, even when nothing momentous was happening. In these moments people let their guard down, giving me some revealing character insights. Such a shot happened just after the president gave his first State of the Union address, when he and First Lady Hillary Rodham Clinton met in an anteroom and spontaneously hugged. There in their faces is the obvious joy they feel in his success—in which she played no small part. But, as you can see in the reflection in the mirror behind them, they were rarely alone."[13] What is revealed in the mirror is a room full of people. McNeely had carefully framed his shot to show the Clintons a bit off to the side, looking into each other's eyes, Bill with a flirtatious look on his face and Hillary smiling with delight. But as McNeely wrote, it was not really a situation that allowed privacy.

McNeely's day started at 7:00 a.m. and often ended after midnight. "There were scheduled events to cover, a staff to manage, and travel plans to make; about a third of the time was spent on the road," he wrote. "But even within that rigid timetable, I found time to wander around looking for candid shots. Periodically throughout the day, with my camera preset and ready, I would roam the West Wing, look out on the lawn and stick my head into offices, including the Oval Office. That's how I came upon the image on page 136 [of *The Clinton Years*] of Clinton's secretary, Betty Currie, and her office draped with portrait rugs sent by the president of Azerbaijan. Found shots like these were gems after all the handshake photo-ops with dignitaries and visitors."[14]

The photo, dated August 1, 1997, showed Currie seated at her desk, on the phone, while two huge rugs leaned against a wall and her desk, one showing Bill and Hillary and the other showing daughter Chelsea. The likenesses, woven into the rugs, came relatively close to showing what the family members actually looked like, although it must have been a challenge to figure out what to do with the items.

Over time, McNeely produced some memorable images that showed the inner workings of the Clinton White House and his often chaotic management style, as with the February 1993 speech-writing flurry, and his flash-and-fade temper. McNeely released many of those photos to the public in consultation with the White House press secretary.[15]

"He'd get himself worked up quickly and he'd cool off quickly," McNeely recalled.[16] One of McNeely's photos showed the president berating key adviser George Stephanopoulos as Clinton, eyes wide, towered over the short, slight aide, glaring at him and pointing to the side with his right arm, his face contorted in rage. McNeely says Clinton really wasn't angry with Stephanopoulos: he was furious at the news media (which happened often) and was pointing toward the briefing room where news conferences and official briefings were held, and where the reporters and news photographers had their work spaces. McNeely made the picture with a small 35mm Leica, which was silent and enabled McNeely to be unobtrusive and let the angry scene play out as if he weren't there.[17]

"I was very, very careful taking that picture," McNeely recalled in an interview, "and I wouldn't have made that with anything but a Leica. He was off on one of his upsets with George, about the press. He would always start slow, and . . . after our first couple times you knew where he was going. So I'm standing over George's shoulder. It's not personal, you know, he's pointing to the press room, 'Those guys out there,' so as he's in the middle of a very slow boil [At this point in the interview, McNeely pretended to put a camera to his eye and snap a frame]. I put it back down, it was like, phew. He never noticed. I think that's important imagery. A hundred years from now, that picture tells historians . . . about Bill Clinton."[18]

McNeely added that Clinton was actually a very empathetic individual. And this is reflected in the body of the photographer's work, such as the many pictures of Clinton mingling with everyday people in crowds, which he loved to do, dropping into a fast-food restaurant to chat with patrons over coffee, and consoling victims of tragedies such as natural disasters.

McNeely's access to President Clinton was so unfettered that he snapped photos other presidents would have nixed because they showed a certain degree of vulnerability. One was a shot, taken with a Leica, of the Clintons resting aboard *Air Force One* on a flight from Uganda to Rwanda during their 1998 tour of six African countries. The picture shows the president leaning back behind his desk in shirtsleeves with his right arm propping up his head, exhausted, as if he had sat down to do the paperwork that was in front of him and tucked in a bulging carry-on bag at his feet, but fell asleep. On the other side of the cabin, Hillary Clinton sat stiffly on a couch under a lamp with her legs extended on the sofa and her shoes and hat still on, her arms folded across her lap. Bill looked natural in repose; Hillary seemed coiled like a spring, ready to suddenly take action.[19]

Bill was easier to get along with than his wife. Hillary had a penchant for letting everyone know she wanted things done her way, in no uncertain terms, "She's a control freak," McNeely said. "She's in charge. You tell her where to stand at your peril. . . . I really like her but I could never work directly for her. She is so tough and so hard on everybody and on herself."[20]

David Kennerly, who was Ford's photographer, gave his usual blunt appraisal: "Bob produced excellent, dramatic, and insightful photos of the Clinton presidency. A problem Bob encountered that I hadn't experienced was the virtual DMZ between the East and West Wings. For him, there was no transgressing the boundary between 'upstairs, downstairs.' First Lady Hillary Rodham Clinton had her own staff and agenda and the president had his. Unfortunately for Bob, he wasn't able to move between those worlds without difficulty."[21]

* * *

MCNEELY HAD three other staff photographers working for him: Sharon Farmer (who became chief White House photographer after McNeely's departure), Barbara Kinney (who later became Hillary Clinton's chief campaign photographer in 2016), and Ralph Alswang.

Alswang, a former staffer at *National Geographic* and *Newsweek* who worked for McNeely and served as one of four White House staff photographers for all eight years of the Clinton presidency, embodied the work ethic and goals of all the modern White House shooters. "I always felt my job was to document the president," Alswang told me. "How our photographs were used [including whether they were released to the media] was not up to us."[22]

He quickly found that the day-to-day, minute-to-minute demands were inexorable because the media wanted endless information, in words and pictures, about the most powerful person in the world. "It's an insatiable media machine," Alswang says. But President Clinton was a full participant in his own visual documentation. "He gave all four of us unparalleled access," adds Alswang. Each photographer had top-secret security clearance, Alswang says, in case something sensitive was discussed at a meeting. Not that the shooters were indiscreet. "The unspoken rule about being a White House photographer is, what happened behind those doors stayed there," he told me.[23]

The photographers had a pattern of separating the president's day into 15-minute segments: this helped them organize their own time and enabled them to more easily hand off the coverage in bite-sized chunks to colleagues when they needed to. The four shooters assigned themselves to three or four shifts per day, starting at 6:30 a.m. and ending after social events in the evening. Each photographer's work day lasted 8 to 10 hours.

They learned to accommodate each other. Alswang, being single and Jewish, volunteered to be on duty over the Christmas holidays when his married Christian colleagues wanted to spend time with their families. This gave him an interesting perch to observe President Clinton, First Lady Hillary Clinton, and their daughter Chelsea in private family moments. He photographed the president, wearing a bathrobe in the White House residence, wrapping a gift for his wife; Bill liked to do the wrapping himself as a personal tradition rather than leave it to a store or his staff.

Each photographer shot 10 to 20 rolls of film per day, depending on what was going on. At 36 images per roll, that amounts to 360 to 720 frames per shooter per day for a grand total of up to about 3,000 images daily for the entire four-person photo staff.

This number has increased dramatically with the prevalence of digital and other technologies. Under Pete Souza, President Barack Obama's chief photographer, the total could easily reach 10,000 images per day.

*   *   *

THE PHOTOGRAPHERS saw essentially the same version of Clinton that the public saw, only in more detail and up close. There was no difference between the private Clinton and the public one: he was gregarious, engaged, and energized by people.

Sometimes Clinton would let news photographers and visitors get too close when they took his picture, and often wasn't happy with the results. Often, the president thought his nose looked too big and bulbous. He asked Alswang how to tell when the photographers were getting too close, and the veteran shooter replied that if he extended his arm and could touch a lens, it was too close. This became Clinton's guideline,

Alswang said Clinton was more religious than the public and his critics thought. He read the Bible, knew much of it by heart, and could recite long passages from Scripture. He also attended a religious service on most Sundays.

Clinton also had empathy. On one occasion, a 12-year-old girl, bald, frail, and afflicted with a fatal disease, visited the president in the Oval Office with her parents. Clinton immediately put her at ease by beckoning to the chair behind his big desk and saying: "If you sit in that chair you have the same chance as any president to get it right—a 50–50 chance to get it right." The girl then asked to see the president privately and the room cleared. They read the Bible together and a tear rolled down the president's cheek.

Afterward, the girl seemed serene when she told her father, "It's all going to be OK. I talked to the president." She died a few days later.[24]

The photographers also witnessed many private moments showing Clinton's intellectual curiosity and command of facts. At a meeting with Agriculture Department officials, Clinton regaled the staff with his knowledge of the market and prices for tomatoes, even to the extent that he knew McDonald's was placing more tomatoes on a Big Mac than other burgers.

Summing up his experience, Alswang said, "I was 27 when I started and left at 35. Everybody's young. Everybody's beautiful. Everybody's strong. It was the best high ever."[25]

*   *   *

AFTER FIVE AND A HALF YEARS, McNeely was ready to move on. The pressure, the work load and the sheer repetitiveness of the job took their toll, but the larger reason for his departure was Clinton's admission that he lied about his affair with former White House intern Monica Lewinsky.

McNeely left the White House in September 1998 amid the disappointment in Clinton that many White House staffers felt during the president's sex-and-lies scandal. This resulted in Clinton being impeached by the House of Representatives in December 1998 for lying under oath about his sexual relationship with Lewinsky. The Senate declined to remove him from office, but the year-long scandal featured one sensational and salacious revelation after another. And all this made life at the White House miserable and in the end undermined trust between the president and his staff.[26]

McNeely at one point was sitting with his two preadolescent daughters, watching TV coverage of the scandal after it became clear that Clinton had mislead everyone about the affair. One of the girls exclaimed that Clinton must be telling the truth. McNeely had to tell her she was wrong. "I had to explain to my children that the president was a liar," he told me.[27]

McNeely realized that he had been witness to a small part of the Lewinsky episode without realizing what was going on. During a government shutdown, the president was meeting with staff members under crisis conditions when he motioned to a young, dark-haired woman, gestured to McNeely, and said: "Take my picture with the intern." McNeely shot two frames, showing Clinton with his arms at his sides and Lewinsky next to him wearing a big smile. McNeely later surmised, after additional information became known, that Lewinsky had performed oral sex on the president earlier that day.

McNeely never sent the pictures to Lewinsky. She made requests for the photos, but still he refused. Even before he knew about the affair, McNeely was skeptical of Lewinsky's intentions, calling her "flirtatious" and a devotee of tight clothing that he and other staffers considered inappropriate.

Kenneth Starr, the lawyer conducting an official investigation of the scandal, eventually subpoenaed the pictures.

Because of the sex-and-lies scandal, McNeely's access to Clinton was drying up, as the besieged president's lawyers kept staff members including the chief photographer away from him. The lawyers seemed to fear that some detail of the case might somehow emerge from Clinton, and they didn't want anything new revealed unless they cleared it in advance.

After observing him nearly every day for more than five and a half years, during the start of the Lewinsky scandal and under many other circumstances, McNeely found President Clinton immature. "Boys make mistakes," McNeely once told a public forum, "and Bill was still a boy."[28]

McNeely was asked during the forum to describe the relationship between Bill and Hillary Clinton, the subject of rampant speculation and puzzlement during the Clintons' eight years in the White House. The photographer contended that many people mistakenly believed the couple had only a "working relationship," but it was much more complicated than that.

McNeely often saw "an extraordinary amount of affection" between them but he said their relationship could seem icy and there would be an "edge" between them at times. This came through in photos that McNeely took during the worst of the Lewinsky scandal when it became clear that the president had lied about his improper relationship. In one image, Bill was looking out a window in the White House while Hillary stood stiffly beside him with a cold look on her face, what McNeely called a "thousand-yard stare." At this moment, they seemed to be ordinary people under very difficult circumstances, a couple struggling to patch things up after one partner got caught in adultery.

The photographer went on to say that Hillary, and many others in Bill's orbit, also felt "an extraordinary amount of disappointment" because of his conduct in the Lewinsky affair. On the other hand, both Clintons were "so brilliant" and "so hard working" that they remained widely admired as public leaders, if only for their work ethic and commitment to public service and improving the lives of everyday Americans.[29]

Sharon Farmer, one of McNeely's deputies, was eventually promoted to director of White House photography in 1999.

*   *   *

SHARON FARMER was unique. Not only was she the only African American woman ever to hold the job of chief White House photographer, she also didn't define herself only as someone who took pictures. She was outspoken in promoting civil rights and was a strong anti-war advocate and communitarian. She retained an interest in music and the arts and has continued to define herself in very diverse ways since she left the White House in January 2001.

Farmer was born in 1951, the daughter of two public-school principals in the Washington suburb of Prince George's County, Maryland. She never forgot her roots and tried to bring a black sensibility to her work. She says: "I have been a professional photojournalist and have exhibited photography for more than forty years, shooting news stories, political campaigns, cultural events, conferences, portraits and my neighborhoods."[30]

She attended Ohio State University, where she studied music and received a B.A. degree in 1974. She also studied photography and contributed pictures to *Makio*, the student yearbook, and *Our Choking Times*, the black student newspaper. She attended protests for racial justice, participating in sit-ins and taking photos of incidents and situations that illustrated the racial climate and other aspects of campus life. She looks back fondly on her days of student activism. "Once you make a coalition with people whose values are the same as yours, change occurs," she told an interviewer in 2015, 14 years after her White House stint.[31] She worked as an intern for the Associated Press during her senior year in college.

After graduation, she returned to Washington, D.C., and was a freelance photographer, working for the Smithsonian Institution, the *Washington Post*, and the American Association for the Advancement of Science, taking photos of cultural events and political campaigns and shooting portraits. She also taught at American University, Mount Vernon College and Indiana University.[32]

* * *

IN 1993, McNeely hired Farmer as a White House photographer. From 1999 to 2001, she served as director of White House photography. She traveled the world with President Bill Clinton and First Lady Hillary Clinton.

She was always outspoken. "I was never a shrinking violet," she said. And she described her experience as a photographer this way: "I'm of color. I have to be really good." Explaining why she wasn't hired as a *Washington Post* staff photographer before her White House stint, but instead worked at the newspaper as a freelance, she said, "I never kissed enough butt to get a full-time job."[33]

While working for the president, life wasn't any easier. "At the White House, you're up against a lot of people who don't think you belong there," she recalled. She remains loyal to the Clintons but notes that others gave her trouble. A local sheriff in Montana questioned her access when he noticed her standing on a railing to get good shots of the president. She kept taking photos and the sheriff backed off.[34]

With her outfits of bold colors and glowing smile, Farmer could light up a room, and she stood out amid the endless stream of men in business suits and patterned ties who surrounded the president as advisers, heads of state, members of Congress, civic leaders, and lobbyists. On foreign trips, it wasn't unusual for a security officer or dignitary to attempt to exclude Farmer from official events because she didn't "look like" she belonged there, At that point, U.S. officials would need to intervene, and sometimes President Clinton did so himself to make sure she was allowed into events.

Her distinctive appearance made it difficult sometimes to fade into the background, which was her goal as it had been for her predecessors and successor. She wanted to photograph people naturally and get as many truly candid shots as possible, and she mostly succeeded.

Farmer's tactic was the same as the one used by every other White House photographer who wanted good pictures: Remain as unobtrusive as possible—like a familiar "piece of furniture"—so your subjects don't get self-conscious or nervous about how they might look and perhaps ask you to leave. "I was quiet," she recalled. "We would come into a room and I'd try to be like a fly on the wall." She would position herself in an out-of-the-way spot but would manage to move around the room during the course of a meeting, snapping pictures all the while. Her theory was if she stayed in one place and didn't reposition herself several times, she wouldn't get the best shots. She also made sure to listen carefully to what was being said so she knew the news and historical significance or anecdotal value of what she was witnessing.

*   *   *

OVER THE YEARS, she developed a strong admiration for Bill and Hillary Clinton and felt their guiding principle was to do as much as they could to improve life for as many Americans as possible, and Farmer told me she felt they lived up to that standard very well.[35]

Farmer remains a fan of both Clintons, a feeling apparently undiminished by the improper relationship that Bill Clinton eventually admitted having with Lewinsky.

Farmer says that in their public roles, both Clintons believed in the Golden Rule: "Do unto others as you would have them do unto you."[36] And she always admired that.

Farmer learned a lot about Bill and Hillary from those years of close observation. She says of Bill Clinton: "The guy was a nighthawk. . . . He was a history buff, too. . . . Bill is more gregarious, and you could see that in his meetings. She wanted to get the meeting over with and move on." Bill also liked meetings with lots of people in attendance, and he liked to bat around ideas; he enjoyed the intellectual byplay. Not Hillary. She preferred small, efficient sessions. "Her meetings were to the point," Farmer recalls, "We did not dawdle."[37]

"I don't think people understood all the good they were trying to get done," Farmer adds. "They knew they had limited time. The president was on a mission about what he could accomplish. . . . And they were friendly. People have no idea how genuinely nice these folks are."[38]

Regarding Bill and Monica Lewinsky, Farmer says: "You make mistakes. . . . That was just off limits. I wasn't there. I didn't want to be there. . . . People's private lives have a right to be private." She said she wasn't sure what the truth was about Clinton's affair, and she stayed as far away from that story as she could.[39]

*　*　*

IN 1998, Farmer recalled two moments as particular high points both for her and for a global audience. "I accompanied the President and Mrs. Clinton to Ghana," Farmer says. "There was a huge rally in the stadium in Accra. There must have been over 250,000 people cheering the President and First Lady. What a moment in time! Never in my wildest dreams did I ever imagine that an American President would visit an African country and be received so wonderfully. That moment, to me, is only second to watching and photographing Nelson Mandela being sworn in as President of South Africa. I attended the event with Mrs. Clinton and the delegation that Vice President Gore led. Every day I pinch myself to see if I'm dreaming that I have this job here, in this time, in this world."[40]

Farmer took some famous pictures. Among them was an image of Israeli Prime Minister Yitzhak Rabin and Palestinian leader Yasser Arafat shaking hands on September 13, 1993, after reaching a peace agreement. A grinning President Clinton is shown standing between them with his arms open wide in a welcoming gesture. It captured a rare moment of optimism in the strife-torn Middle East.

She also captured an image of President and Mrs. Clinton at the Kennedy Space Center in Florida delightedly watching the October 29, 1998 launch of the space shuttle *Discovery*, with famous astronaut John Glenn, a pioneer from the original space program, on board. It reflected America's pride in the space program and its historic achievements.

Farmer said recently, "Creativity is still the key for my enjoyment of life as the good goes hand in hand with the bad. Passivity is not my nature. . . . My camera is pro-active."[41] Of her own career, Farmer told me: "I'm a local yokel from D.C. The last place I thought I'd be was inside the White House."[42]

Notes

1. John Bredar, *The President's Photographer: Fifty Years Inside the Oval Office*, Washington, D.C.: National Geographic Society, 2010, p. 89.
2. Robert McNeely, interview with author, Apr. 26, 2016.
3. Bredar, *The President's Photographer*, p. 207; see also Robert McNeely, comments at "White House Photographers," panel discussion at the Lyndon Baines Johnson Presidential Library, Austin, Texas, Jan. 20, 2010, www.c-span.org/video/?291502-1/white-house-photographers.
4. McNeely, comments at "White House Photographers."
5. Ibid.; see also Bredar, *The President's Photographer*, pp. 210–211.
6. McNeely, interview with author, Apr. 26, 2016.
7. "How the Real Story gets Told in Pictures," *Nieman Reports*, Fall 1999, pp. 13–14.
8. Dennis Brack, *Presidential Picture Stories: Behind the Cameras at the White House*, Washington, D.C.: Dennis Brack, Inc., 2013, pp. 137–138.
9. Robert McNeely, *The Clinton Years: The Photographs of Robert McNeely*, New York: Callaway, 2000, p. 25.
10. Ibid., p. 33.
11. Ibid., pp 34–35.
12. Ibid., p. 25.
13. Ibid., p. 244.
14. Ibid., p. 235.
15. McNeely, interview with author, Apr. 26, 2016.
16. McNeely, comments at "White House Photographers."

17. Bredar, *The President's Photographer*, p. 210.
18. Ibid.
19. McNeely, *The Clinton Years*, pp. 218–219.
20. McNeely, interview with author, Apr. 26, 2016.
21. David Hume Kennerly, *Extraordinary Circumstances: The Presidency of Gerald R. Ford*, Austin: Briscoe Center for American History, 2007, p. 16.
22. Ralph Alswang, interview with author, Mar. 1, 2016.
23. Ibid.
24. Robert McNeely, telephone interview with author, Apr. 22, 2016.
25. Alswang, interview with author, Mar. 1, 2016.
26. McNeely, telephone interview with author, Apr. 22, 2016.
27. Ibid.
28. Robert McNeely, comments at "White House Photographers."
29. Ibid.
30. Charles Henry Rowell, "Sharon Farmer", *Callaloo: A Journal of African Diaspora Arts and Letters*, vol. 38, no 4 (2016), p. 823.
31. Nathalie Baptiste, "Breaking Barriers," *American Prospect*, Mar. 30, 2015, http://prospect.org/article/how-campus-radical-became-first-woman-run-white-house-photography-operation.
32. Sharon Farmer, interview, *History Makers*, Apr. 29, 2008, www.thehistorymakers.com/biography/sharon-farmer-41.
33. Baptiste, "Breaking Barriers."
34. Sharon Farmer, interview with author, Aug. 19, 2016.
35. Ibid.
36. Ibid.
37. Ibid.
38. Ibid.
39. Ibid.
40. Rowell, "Sharon Farmer,", p. 822.
41. Quoted ibid., pp. 822–823.
42. Farmer, interview with author, Aug. 19, 2016.

CHAPTER TEN
BEHIND THE SCENES WITH GEORGE W. BUSH
AND ERIC DRAPER

Eric Draper never forgot the advice he got from White House Chief of Staff Andy Card when he took the job of chief photographer for President George W. Bush. "Andy said working at the White House was like trying to drink water from a fire hose," Draper recalled. "And he was right."[1]

Draper held the job for the entire Bush presidency, from January 2001 to January 2009, and the pace never slowed.[2] In the process, he made a million images, including hundreds of thousands of digital photos, which have become the standard photographic technology today.[3] When the work of his deputies was included, the number of pictures taken by the photo office went up to four million.[4]

Draper had been an Associated Press photographer who covered Bush's successful 2000 presidential campaign for 18 months. On election night, the outcome was so close that no one could be sure whether Bush or Democratic Vice President Al Gore had won. Draper returned home to Albuquerque, New Mexico to wait it out.

After Bush was declared the winner, Draper thought back on the friendly relationship he had developed with the president-elect and his family, and, "I realized I had a shot at the White House job," he said.[5]

He wondered, "Could a black kid from South-Central Los Angeles be the photographer for the President of the United States?"[6] (Actually, as noted earlier, a black woman, Sharon Farmer, had held that position for Bill Clinton during Clinton's second term.)

Draper put a portfolio of his campaign photos together and wrote a cover letter, then flew with his wife from his home in Albuquerque to Austin, Texas, for a Christmas party that Bush was arranging. "I pulled a page out of his political playbook," Draper told me. "I remembered how Bush said (at campaign appearances), 'I'm going to look you in the eye and ask to be your president.'" So Draper took the same approach.

He went up to the president-elect at the party and announced, "I want to be your presidential photographer." Bush looked surprised, as if he hasn't thought about naming a chief photographer before. He gave Draper a sustained and very warm handshake and said, "I really appreciate that. I'll get back to you." Draper gave his portfolio and cover letter to a Bush aide, enjoyed the party and went home to Albuquerque.

A week later, he got a call from a Bush aide and was told that Andy Card, who would become Bush's White House chief of staff, wanted to interview him for the chief photographer's job. The interview turned out to be very brief. Card's main concern was not whether Draper could take good pictures—that wasn't in doubt—but whether he could manage the photo office, which included having Draper and his deputies cover scores of events and presidential activities each day, process the pictures, and send the appropriate ones where they needed to go, such as to members of Congress, who were always eager for prints. Draper made his case and got the job of personal photographer of the president and director of the White House photo office.

It took a while for Draper to win Bush's full confidence but eventually it happened. "Slowly we were able to have this non-verbal communication," Draper said. He could sense when Bush wanted him to stop taking pictures and leave a room, and he came to understand how to be unobtrusive and do his job without "stepping on anyone's toes or interrupting the flow of a meeting."

*   *   *

"I DIDN'T KNOW exactly what I was getting into, but I knew it would be an experience [and] I did like [Bush] personally," he recalled. And he got the chance to document history during tumultuous times.[7]

Bush was impressed with Draper from the start. "His discretion and knack for blending in gave him unprecedented access and therefore a truly unique perspective on my Administration," the former president said later. "It helped that he was never far from the action. His office, a former White House barbershop in the West Wing [dating back to President Lyndon B. Johnson's administration], was right under the Oval Office."[8]

Draper said: "I chose an extremely talented team of photographers, editors, and support staff to help me get the job done. Covering the president 24/7 can never be a job for one person. It takes many confident and trusted people to do it well. I tasked dedicated photographers to cover Mrs. Bush and Vice President Cheney and still others to focus on historic staff happenings around the White House. We couldn't miss a thing."[9]

As the Bush presidency entered its final months in 2008, Draper summed up: "There's never a typical day. There's a lot of built-in repetitiveness, in terms of scheduling. The President starts his day at 7 a.m., like clockwork, and there are certain meetings at certain times of the day; but then it varies depending upon other events during the day. . . . There's a lot of waiting. Within that framework there's the challenge of making images that communicate on different levels. There's the official level and the historic level; there's a personal side that nobody else sees, and every day follows a different story line."[10]

The approval process for releasing pictures from Draper's office, including the many requests from the media, started with him, but the final decision was made by the White House communications staff.[11]

Of course some gatherings were more sensitive than others. At the daily intelligence meetings, where national security issues were discussed, Draper would take a few pictures at the start and then leave. One reason for allowing photography at such sessions was to visually document who actually attended, and this was an advantage for Draper when he asked to be there.

In general, Bush would signal Draper when to depart. "Usually it's a 'thank you,'" Draper said, "That usually means 'leave.' There's a lot of non-verbal communication. I can't stop things and say, 'Hey what's going on? Should I stay? Should I go?' I have to be very intuitive. I know the President's moods: when he's upset, when he's in a good mood, when he's tense."[12]

Draper cleverly devised a method to stay in tune with Bush's preferences. He compiled a "photos of the week book," which he would leave for the president at the Oval Office every seven days. Bush and his wife Laura enjoyed seeing the pictures arranged together and the first lady would comment on his work, giving Draper a good idea what the first couple liked and what they didn't. As for Bush, Draper said that in reviewing the "photos of the week" Bush made clear that, "any time he can touch a person emotionally or give them a little joy by meeting with them, and being able to give that person a photo, is really important to him. He likes to personalize pictures from those moments."[13]

Draper used other techniques to showcase his work internally. "During the first term, on the way back from our first trip to Asia, I began a tradition of presenting slide shows for President and Mrs. Bush and their staffs on the final leg home of every foreign swing," Draper said. "We would all gather for the show in the conference room of *Air Force One* in jeans and sweats and stocking feet. I raised the bar after every foreign trip, adding title slides and indigenous music to the production. It was a lot of extra work for my staff and me, but the joy and laughter the presentations provided made it well worth the effort."[14]

"When I would return from trips abroad with President Bush," Draper added, "my staff would have worked miracles to put giant photos of the trip on the White House walls for the president to see. I believe it gave him a chance to reflect, in a very real way, on his role in the world."[15]

Draper was following a tried-and-true pattern. Posting jumbo photos around the White House every few days was something White House photographers had done for years. It showcased their work, documented what was going on, and made the photographers an important part of life at the White House for the president, the first family and staff.

"The job is never stale," Draper observed. "There is always something going on in the world that the President has to react to that always makes the job very interesting."[16]

Draper recalled that it took him only 10 to 12 seconds to sprint from his desk in the basement to the Oval Office, and this proximity helped him cover things as they happened.

He wrote in his memoir: "Working inside the White House was a constant learning experience. At times, it was surreal. I always expected someone to tap me on the shoulder and ask me to leave the room. But when the president is comfortable with your role, everyone else is, too."[17]

"During my time at the White House, I made nearly one million pictures," Draper said. "They included major events like 9/11, the wars in Afghanistan and Iraq, the space shuttle *Columbia* disaster, and the funerals of two U.S. presidents and a pope. I recorded the president through another close election, during Hurricane Katrina, and during the worst economic crisis since the Great Depression. . . . But I photographed the president during small moments, too; in the White House residence with Mrs. Bush, in Kennebunkport, Maine, with his parents, in quiet moments at Camp David with his daughters, and at his beloved ranch in Crawford, Texas. These moments included the absolute quiet of him fishing on a lake, sipping coffee while reading, and even praying."[18] Draper said he came to know Bush as few others did, as "a leader, a husband, a father, a sportsman, a dog lover."[19]

One of his main achievements in improving the White House photo office was to shift from film to digital. Starting on inauguration day in January 2005, he directed his staff "to begin a digital workflow for the first time in White House history." This means better technology to make the pictures sharper and enable the shooters to take vastly more photos than they could with film.[20]

Draper admitted that he made his share of mistakes: "On inauguration day, January 20, 2001—my first full official day on the job—President Bush and First Lady Laura Bush escorted President Bill Clinton and First Lady Hillary Clinton down the south steps of the Capitol to their waiting motorcade. I jumped in a nearby minivan, thinking it was time to return to the White House. I didn't recognize anyone in the van. Turned out, I was in the Clinton motorcade. Behind me, I heard Clinton photographer Ralph Alswang say dryly, 'Uh, Eric Your guy is staying,' I jumped out of the van and ran to meet the right president."[21]

Draper also told of another embarrassing moment: "In the spring of 2007, Queen Elizabeth II and Prince Philip, the Duke of Edinburgh, visited the White House. After the South Lawn arrival ceremony President and Mrs. Bush led their royal guests on a tour of the private residence. The first stop was the Queen's Bedroom, named for the many royal guests it has hosted. Mrs. Bush and the Queen disappeared into the bedroom alone. I didn't want to miss anything so I followed quickly on their heels. Unfortunately, I missed the fact that Mrs. Bush was showing the Queen to the adjacent restroom. When I realized my mistake, I made a quick about-face. Standing before me was Prince Philip. 'Are you following them to the loo?' he asked with a straight face. I stood there stunned with embarrassment. Thank goodness, we all burst out in laughter."[22]

On another occasion, Draper witnessed and photographed Bush's lighter side when Prime Minister Lee Hsien Loong of Singapore gave the president a fold-up bicycle. After the two leaders' meeting ended and the staff except for Draper left the Oval Office, Bush took the bike for a spin. He pedaled through the Oval Office, down the main hall of the West Wing, and into an office where he found Karl Rove, his chief political strategist. Bush rang the bike's bell on his arrival.[23]

Also on the lighter side was a photo of Bush and his wife Laura in their limousine heading to the White House after attending several balls and parties on the night of his inauguration in January 2001. Both were obviously exhausted, and the new president couldn't suppress a huge yawn.

"I also witnessed stunning emotional moments," Draper said, "such as when Coretta Scott King and her family, with plans for the Martin Luther King memorial in hand, entered the Oval Office. I shot the beginning of the meeting and expected to walk out to give them privacy. But Mrs. King then asked the president to join hands to pray. I turned around, lifted my camera, and made one of my most memorable images."[24]

* * *

DRAPER'S MOST CHALLENGING and most historically important task was to document the aftermath of the terrorist attacks of September 11, 2001, in which 3,000 people were killed when terrorists hijacked two commercial airliners which they crashed into New York's World Trade Center. The terrorists hijacked a third plane which crashed into the Pentagon, and took over a fourth airliner which was destroyed in the Pennsylvania countryside when passengers put up a fight and tried unsuccessfully to gain control of the aircraft.[25]

"I didn't want to miss a thing," he recalled. "It was almost like a nightmare playing out in front of me."[26]

It became a severe test of Draper's ability to serve as a "visual story teller," which is the way he defined his role.[27]

Later, Bush would recall, "9/11 is a good example of why there is a White House photographer." And Draper said, "I knew it was going to be a very historic day so I tried to document every moment."[28]

President Bush was publicizing his education agenda at an elementary school in Sarasota, Florida, when the first plane struck. In a holding room, an aide told him about the crash and at first everyone though it was an accident. But after the second plane struck at 9:14 a.m., it became clear that this was no accident. Bush was sitting in a classroom ready to give a brief talk when Andy Card, his chief of staff, whispered in his ear that a second plane had hit the towers and "America is under attack." Bush looked stunned.

Draper effectively captured the reactions of Bush and his top aides during these first moments of crisis. In one picture, White House Communications Director Dan Bartlett was shown pointing to a TV in a private room of the Sarasota school as smoke rose ominously from the trade towers.

Amid the growing crisis, President Bush and his entourage sped back to *Air Force One* as he tried to decide whether to return immediately to the White House.[29]

Bush decided against it because his security advisers told him it was too dangerous. No one could be sure where the terrorists would strike next, and the White House might be a target. There were rumors, Draper recalled, that a car bomb had gone off at the State Department, that a "fast-moving object" had been spotted heading for Bush's ranch in Texas. Bush emerged from his personal cabin in the front of the plane and announced to the staff, "I just heard that 'Angel' is the next target." This was the military's code name for *Air Force One*. It turned out to be a false report, but no one at the time could be sure what was really going on. Draper's initial photos of the president aboard the plane showed a man who seemed more than a bit dazed and shaken.

Bush flew to Barksdale Air Force Base in Louisiana, a secure location. He taped a message to the country, broadcast a bit later in the day, calling for calm and pledging that the perpetrators would be found and punished. He then flew to Offutt Air Force Base in Nebraska, where he received more briefings on what happened and what might be next.

At one point during this horrible day, Draper took an iconic picture of President Bush looking out a window of *Air Force One* as he talked on the phone to Vice President Dick Cheney, a former defense secretary who was in Washington coordinating parts of the intelligence gathering and crisis management. Bush looked calm and decisive by this point, apparently having righted himself from the first chaotic and shocking moments of the crisis. He held an old-fashioned phone to his left ear with the cord extending to the desk below and he gestured upward with his open right hand. This photo was released to the media and was widely seen by the public in the United States and abroad, showing the commander in chief confident and taking charge. It was an image designed to reassure everyone that the country was in good hands, and it worked.

The moment occurred after *Air Force One* had left Offutt AFB in Nebraska. Bush was heading back to Washington. The worst appeared to be over, for that day, as a feared second wave of terrorist attacks never materialized. Bush and his war cabinet were plotting retaliation and taking steps to wage what the president called a global war on terror that would last for the remaining seven years of his administration.

"That was a day that I truly felt invisible," Draper recalled. "I could stand just inches from the President and make pictures, and he would look right through me. It was almost like I wasn't even there."[30]

Draper captured another vivid image as *Air Force One* flew into Washington, D.C., later that day. It's a photo of one of the Air Force F-16 fighter jets escorting the president's plane back home, a rare occurrence, as seen through a window in the front of *Air Force One*. "This scene made you feel that we were truly at war," Draper recalled.[31]

On September 14, three days after the calamity, Bush gave a powerful speech, consoling and resolute, at the National Cathedral during what he declared as a national day of prayer. Draper captured the moment of solidarity when he photographed President Bush with his father the former President George H.W. Bush and their families sitting in the front pew after Bush had given his speech. The elderly president was shown reaching over and touching his son's hand, demonstrating pride and admiration.

Later that day, Bush flew to New York to visit first responders and fire fighters. They were still searching for victims and bodies at the site of the 9/11 attack on the trade towers, which had been reduced to smoldering rubble. I traveled to New York with Bush in a small group of reporters chosen to stay by his side for much of the day. I watched him jump atop a burned-out fire truck, bring an elderly volunteer fire fighter named Bob Beckwith to his side and listen as the fire fighters chanted "USA! USA! USA!" at the commander in chief. He grabbed a bullhorn and told them that he heard them, the world heard them, and the terrorists who brought down the buildings would be hearing from all Americans very soon as U.S. forces sought retribution. The fire fighters cheered as Bush told the country exactly what it wanted to hear—a message of resolve, strength and determination—at that moment of national tragedy. Draper recalled, "I got chills when he said that line—"I can hear you.' It was the culmination of all the emotion that had been building among the fire fighters." They immediately gathered around Bush after his exhortation, hugged him and shook his hand. Several shouted, "Go get 'em, George."

Draper captured the "bullhorn" moment with his camera, then sent the image around the world. Bush recalled: "The destruction was incredible. It was like entering the gates of hell."[32]

There was another event that day that went mostly unrecorded although it left a deep impression on Draper and everyone else who was there. This was President Bush's private meeting in New York with the families of the dead and missing. For three hours, Bush walked from one family group to another, commiserating, praising their loved ones, embracing one person at a time, and sometimes engulfed in group hugs. Many showed the president photos of their lost family members; some had signs asking plaintively if anyone had seen their husbands, wives, mothers and children who were not accounted for.

The scene was heartbreaking, and many attendees shed tears. Draper was so moved that he only took "two or three" photos, not wanting to intrude on the immense grief he was witnessing. "It was very, very hard to lift a camera," he recalled. One photo he did get showed Bush and two family members in a group hug as seen from a discreet distance behind them, with their faces not visible to the camera, keeping private the most intimate view of their grief and pain. Draper said it was the most difficult situation he has ever dealt with as a photographer.

Some time later, Draper realized that Bush was carrying with him the law-enforcement badge owned by George Howard, a New York Port Authority officer killed on 9/11. Howard's mother gave the badge to the president during his meeting with the families on September 14 and asked him to keep it. He carried this in his pocket wherever he went, as a way to honor those who were lost and to keep them at the forefront of his presidency. Draper asked Bush if he could take a picture, and the president produced the worn silver-colored badge—Number 1012—from his pocket. Draper photographed the badge in the president's hand, and it remains one of the photographer's most telling pictures.[33]

*　*　*

LOOKING BACK on his time as chief White House photographer, Draper said he always felt his first obligation was to serve the president who hired him. But Draper said the experience showed him how much the news photographers miss in covering the president, compared to the access he got from the inside. "It's two different worlds," he said. And for the insider/photographer, "it's almost overwhelming at times because there's so much. . . . There's so much access. It's great."[34]

Draper learned two things above all from his close access to George W. Bush as the president's chief photographer: how disciplined his boss was, and how he had a talent for establishing personal links with people, one on one.

"He was very disciplined, very organized, didn't want to waste time," Draper told me. "He really lived every moment to the point where he would leave meetings early if he felt the session wasn't achieving anything productive. He would do whatever was in front of him 110 percent."[35]

Bush was also very engaging. "What didn't come across was, he was able to make a connection with people, from a janitor in the hall to the king of Saudi Arabia. He was a people person," able to find something in common with virtually everyone, Draper said.[36]

Notes

1. Eric Draper, interview with author, Jan. 17, 2017.
2. Eric Draper, comments at "White House Photographers," panel discussion at the Lyndon Baines Johnson Presidential Library, Austin, Texas, Jan. 20, 2010, www.c-span.org/video/?291502-1/white-house-photographers; Draper, interview with author, Jan. 17, 2017.
3. Eric Draper, video interview with Erin Purdy, Briscoe Center for American History, University of Texas, Feb. 15, 2013.
4. Ibid.
5. Draper, interview with author, Jan. 17, 2017; Draper, video interview with Erin Purdy, Feb. 15, 2013.
6. Eric Draper, *Front Row Seat: A Photographic Portrait of the Presidency of George W. Bush*, Austin: University of Texas Press, 2013, p. 4.
7. David Walker, "Q&A: Eric Draper, Chief White House Photographer," *Photo District News*, vol. 28, no. 12 (Dec. 2008), pp. 14, 16 18.
8. Draper, *Front Row Seat*, p. xiv.
9. Ibid., p. 5.
10. Walker, "Q&A: Eric Draper," p. 18.
11. Ibid.; Draper, interview with author, Jan. 17, 2017.
12. Walker, "Q&A: Eric Draper," pp. 14, 16, 18.
13. Ibid.
14. Draper, *Front Row Seat*, p. 172.
15. Ibid., p. 5.
16. Walker, "Q&A: Eric Draper," p. 14.
17. Draper, *Front Row Seat*, p. 5.
18. Ibid., pp. 4–5.

19. Ibid., p. 5.

20. Ibid.

21. Ibid., p. 8.

22. Ibid., p. 26.

23. Ibid.

24. Ibid.

25. John Bredar, *The President's Photographer: Fifty Years Inside the Oval Office*, Washington, D.C.: National Geographic Society, 2010, p. 173.

26. Draper, video interview with Erin Purdy, Feb. 15, 2013.

27. Draper, comments at "White House Photographers."

28. Bredar, *The President's Photographer*, p. 157.

29. Draper, comments at "White House Photographers."

30. Bredar, *The President's Photographer*, p. 171.

31. Draper, comments at "White House Photographers."

32. Bredar, *The President's Photographer*, p. 174; Draper interview with author, Jan. 17, 2017.

33. Draper, comments at "White House Photographers."

34. Draper, video interview with Erin Purdy, Feb. 15, 2013; Draper, interview with author, Jan. 17, 2017.

35. Draper, interview with author, Jan. 17, 2017.

36. Ibid.

Chapter Eleven
Behind the Scenes with Barack Obama and Pete Souza

Pete Souza played the key role in creating a positive, everyman image for President Barack Obama. In the process, Souza revolutionized White House image-making. He used modern technology more effectively than his predecessors, most of whom didn't have the advantage of making instantaneous and high-quality digital photos and transmitting them faster, more widely, and more easily than ever.

Souza had the distinction of serving as a full-time, paid White House staff photographer for two presidents of different parties, different ideologies, and different eras—Republican Ronald Reagan during the 1980s and Democrat Barack Obama two decades later. It was during the Obama period, from January 20, 2009, when he was inaugurated, to January 20, 2017, the date he left office, that Souza truly made his mark as the alpha White House photographer.[1]

Souza was very aggressive about disseminating his photographs through the White House website, and through social media such as Flickr, Facebook, Instagram, and other internet sites, in addition to the mainstream media. This aggressive campaign to promote President Obama through photographs and videos went considerably beyond what Souza's predecessors did.

Souza was listed by the White House as both "the Chief Official White House Photographer for President Obama," and "Director of the White

House photo office." This gave him broad control of the image-making operation in the official West Wing and the family quarters of the East Wing.[2]

Souza proudly declared that his access to President Obama was unrivaled. "I don't think there's really anyone in the White House that has that kind of exposure to him," Souza said in September 2016 during his final year as the chief White House photographer. "I mean, they may know him, the national security team. They know him from the Situation Room, and the tense meetings in the Oval Office. But they don't see him interact with his daughter after work, or on a Saturday. From a documentary standpoint, I'm the only person that sees him in all these different roles."[3] Souza said in another interview: "The one thing that's unique about my job more so than anybody else who works at the White House or with him, is that I see all the different compartments of his life. Certainly the National Security advisor is in all the National Security meetings. Well, so am I. And certainly you know his personal aide is present when all these kids come in the room. Well, so am I. The point being that I'm sort of like the only person who crosses all those boundaries. I'm with him and his family on Christmas Day. I'm in the Situation Room for all the security meetings. I'm on every trip on *Air Force One*. So I see all these compartments of his life."[4]

For his part, President Obama said he found Souza's photos "evocative, accurate, creative" and he said Souza was "a great friend and someone I trust." They became so close that Obama allowed Souza to hold his wedding to Patti Lease in the White House Rose Garden during October 2013, a ceremony which the president attended.[5]

Souza certainly had as much or more access than any other White House photographer in history, not only to private family moments but also to important decisions and presidential reactions to crises. In this way, he was in the same stellar league as other ultimate insiders including Okamoto during the LBJ years and Kennerly under Gerald Ford.

Souza said in November 2010: "There are no ground rules, per se. I have full access to every meeting. . . . If it's a one-on-one meeting, I tend to leave the room after I've got the pictures I need. . . . President Obama has grown comfortable in front of the camera. I say that in the sense that after the initial first couple of months, both he and the staff got used to me being around all the time. I try to work in a way so I'm not distracting to what is taking place. Sometimes. I'm pretty sure he even forgets I'm in the room."[6]

Comparing covering Ronald Reagan as a staff photographer with covering Obama as the chief photographer, Souza said in 2010: "President Reagan was in his 70s. President Obama is not yet 50. That accounts for a big difference. I have much better access as the president's photographer than I did [with] Reagan as a 'junior' photographer. Plus, President Obama is just a better subject because he is so engaged and because he is the father of two young girls."[7]

Souza said Obama was very open to him: "This administration has made more behind-the-scenes photographs available to the public than any ever before. My pictures have thus given people a real-time look inside this presidency. I don't think there has been any time when I've put my camera down, but there are private moments with the girls that we don't release."

Souza noted that until George W. Bush's administration from 2001 to 2009, every picture taken by the White House photographers was made on film. Eric Draper, Bush's chief photographer, converted to a digital system halfway through, which was a breakthrough that allowed the photo staff to take many more pictures of very high quality, a system that still exists today.[8]

Robert Gibbs, Obama's press secretary during his first term, called Souza Obama's "most important illustrator."[9] Anita Dunn, former White House communications adviser, observed: "If a picture is worth a thousand words, then Pete Souza has written the comprehensive story of the Obama presidency with his images that help foster the direct connection the people of America feel with their President."[10] Columnist Chris Cellizza wrote in the *Washington Post*: "No president before Obama and no presidential photographer before Souza has had access to Flickr, Twitter and the variety of other social networking and sharing sites. Those sites allow any image of the president that the White House wants people to see to be seen, a massive distribution channel simply not available to past presidents."[11]

Souza agreed. "I happened to be the person in this job when all these social media tools came into existence," he said. "I mean, Instagram did not exist before this administration." He added that the new media platforms gave him "a chance [to show] some of my documentary photos to the public now, instead of waiting post-presidency." The White House Instagram account had 2.6 million followers and the executive Flickr account posted more than 6,000 images from Souza and other White House photographers during the eight Obama years.[12]

It was, in effect, a photo stream that went directly from Pete Souza to the public, an advantage that no other White House photographer had enjoyed in the past.

Souza's body of work and his personal observations in various interviews over the years depicted Obama as a likable family man devoted to his wife and children; a smart policy maker who tried to take a long view and not just rush into decisions for the moment; unflappable in a crisis; and able to control his anger and his emotions nearly all the time.

Flickr was particularly important and ground-breaking for Obama and Souza. Created in 2004, it is a public photo website that let Souza and his staff upload as many photos as they wanted and make them immediately accessible to people around the world. Often they were behind-the-scenes images that provided personal insights into Obama, the first lady, their two daughters, and their advisers and events of the day. Page views of the White House Flickr pages ranged from 30,000 to 1 million per day. Obama rarely signed off on the photos in advance (a big contrast to Lyndon Johnson, for example, who would rule on the public release of nearly every photo of himself). The approval process was run by Souza and his staff and the White House press secretary or a deputy press secretary.[13] Souza estimated that he took 2 million photos during Obama's eight-year presidency.[14]

Another pioneering aspect of the Souza regime was the use of video, not just still photography. Under Souza, White House staffers took video of many aspects of the president's life and posted it on the White House website and in social media. It was effective in promoting the likeability of the president and first lady.

Obama had an instinctive understanding of the importance of storytelling for modern presidents as a way to get people interested in them personally and in their ideas. "You have to leverage different platforms because a fireside chat just gets lost in the noise today," he said. "People aren't part of one conversation; they're part of a million. . . . Part of what I've always been interested in as president, and what I will continue to be interested in as an ex-president, is telling better stories about how we can work together."[15] And visual storytelling was essential to Obama's objectives, including the positive tone he wanted to set.

One of the most successful examples of the White House's PR deftness through imagery came in February 2016 when Barack and Michelle Obama hosted a Black History Month celebration. One of the attendees was Virginia McLaurin, an African American woman from Washington,

D.C., who was 106 years old. When the president and the first lady approached her as a surprise, Virginia whooped and did a joyful dance, shaking her cane with delight at meeting the first African American president and first lady. The Obamas quickly joined in the dance and said the diminutive senior citizen made their day. Michelle complimented her on her blue dress and blue nail polish, and the president said they were very happy that she could come to the event. It was a delightful moment that showed the Obamas at their most accessible and charming. The White House video went viral, and it had 64,481,174 views on Facebook a month later.[16]

Souza had a gift for recognizing larger significance in what seemed to be small moments in the president's day. One of his best images—and one of my favorites—showed Obama bending at the waist so a young African American boy could touch his hair. The 5-year-old, Jacob Philadelphia of Columbia, Maryland, visited the Oval Office in the spring of 2009, when his father, a former marine, was leaving the White House staff, and Obama had the family in for a group photo. As the family was preparing to leave, the father told Obama that Jacob had a question. "I want to know if my hair is just like yours," the boy asked, so softly that Obama couldn't hear him at first. After he repeated his question, Obama said, "Why don't you touch it and see for yourself?" Obama bowed and Jacob hesitated. The commander in chief urged him, "Touch it, dude." After Jacob patted Obama's head, the president asked, "So, what do you think?" Jacob replied, "Yes, it does feel the same." Jacob, wearing a neat shirt and tie, was shown in Souza's picture with his arm outstretched touching the top of the president's head as Obama bowed to his diminutive visitor.[17]

It was an endearing moment with powerful resonance for African Americans, driving home how important Obama's election as the first African American president was to many black people and especially to children who saw themselves in him. Souza recalled: "As a photographer, you know when you have a unique moment. But I didn't realize the extent to which this one would take on a life of its own." The photo was enlarged, framed and prominently displayed for years on a wall of the West Wing, and it has also been widely distributed in the media. David Axelrod, one of Obama's longtime advisers, said of Jacob: "Really, what he was saying is, 'Gee, you're just like me.' And it doesn't take a big leap to think that child could be thinking, 'Maybe I could be here some day.' This can be such a cynical business, and then there are moments like that that just remind you that it's worth it." [18]

Souza was able to take many pictures of this softer side of presidential life. In one, Obama ran into his two teenage daughters, Malia and Sasha, in the colonnade outside the Oval Office as they returned home from school. The girls were shown walking their dad back to work as they enjoyed a group hug. In another, President Obama was on the basketball court blocking a shot by his personal assistant Reggie Love, who was a member of the 2001 NCAA champion Duke basketball team. It was one of Obama's favorite pictures, all the more so after the Secret Service persuaded him, then in his 50s, to give up the game he loved because of the possibility of injury.

*   *   *

AMONG SOUZA'S most famous photos was a picture of Obama, surrounded by advisers, in the White House Situation Room on May 1, 2011 watching video in real time of a daring military operation. Obama had ordered the raid to capture or kill terrorist leader Osama bin Laden, and it ended with Bin Laden's being shot to death. The photo was distributed by the White House via its Flickr feed and showed Obama as a hands-on commander in chief looking somberly at the engagement as it proceeded. He showed no emotion but intently watched a video screen on which the raid was being shown. Obama was surrounded by worried-looking advisers including then-Secretary of State Hillary Clinton. The photo has been viewed on Flickr millions of times and has been widely disseminated in other media.

Souza said it became an unforgettable moment. "I was in that room for 40 minutes," he recalled. "It was very tense. You can see it in the faces of those people. And I can't say I knew that singular image would get as much attention as it did."[19]

Another memorable image, from 2012, was Obama cavorting with a child dressed as Spiderman for Halloween, with the president, hands up, "caught" in an imaginary spider web. This showed Obama as a man who didn't take himself too seriously.

Just before New Year's Eve 2015, Souza as chief White House photographer released his 111 favorite images, taken by him and his staff, of Obama and the White House on the website Medium.[20] Obama was shown admiring babies, meeting with other world leaders, and sharing private moments with his wife Michelle. One poignant image was when the couple held hands discreetly at a ceremony marking the 50th anniversary of the March 7, 1965 Selma to Montgomery civil-rights march in Alabama. This frame showed how profoundly impressed they were by the civil-rights activists' courage and persistence as they paved the way for a black man and woman to become president and first lady of the United States.

Other Souza photos took simple moments and used them to depict Obama as a normal person who hadn't let the office of president go to his head. No one wins the presidency without a huge ego. But the image that Souza successfully projected was of a down-to-earth family man who would make a wonderful next-door neighbor, who understood the many currents in popular culture and tried to stay in touch.

This was the case with a photo Souza took and released on October 30, 2015. It showed the president, wearing an immaculate dark blue suit with black shoes shined to a high gloss, flat on his back behind a sofa in the Oval Office, holding a child in the air over his head. Souza's caption, as printed on the Medium website, read: "The president lifts Ella Rhodes, daughter of Deputy National Security Adviser Ben Rhodes, dressed in an elephant costume for a Halloween event at the White House."[21]

Souza captured a charming moment on October 11, 2015 in still another photo and caption posted on Medium: "The president was playing golf at Torrey Pines Golf Course in San Diego, California. As he was finishing his round, he began to shake hands with guests waiting for a wedding ceremony about to begin. The bride and groom were waiting inside but when they looked out the window and saw the president, they decided to make their way outside. I made a grab shot as the bride, Stephanie Tobe, and her soon-to-be husband, Brian Tobe, came running to greet the president. I made sure to send a copy to the happy couple and both wrote back to me that they were extremely grateful to have the President 'crash' their wedding."[22] The photo shows the shocked and delighted bride, resplendent in her white gown, rushing toward the president with her soon-to-be husband a few paces behind her as Obama, wearing a white short-sleeve shirt and baseball cap, moves forward to extend his congratulations.

A picture taken by Souza on December 7, 2015, prearranged with the Secret Service, shows comedian Jerry Seinfeld tapping on a window of the Oval Office while standing in some bushes outside while Obama does paperwork at his desk. Souza wrote, "Comedian Jerry Seinfeld knocks on the Oval Office window to begin a segment for his series, 'Comedians in Cars Getting Coffee,'" in which he interviewed Obama to show the lighter side of life in the White House.[23]

On March 27, Souza's assistant photographer Amanda Lucidon captured the image of the president and first lady enjoying a private moment in a public area of the White House. "The first lady snuggled against the president during a videotaping for the 2015 World Expo, recorded in the Diplomatic Reception Room of the White House," Souza wrote in the caption on Medium.[24] The president looked serious and his hands were clasped behind his back in a show of reserve; the first lady's hands were folded demurely in front of her as she smiled with delight. Adding to the unusual nature of the image, George Washington, in a portrait hanging over the fireplace, looked on somberly.

On March 10, Souza took a photo of Obama in shirtsleeves taking a jump shot alone on a basketball court as a few Secret Service agents and aides watched from the sideline. Souza wrote: "Although he doesn't play competitive basketball anymore, basketball is still a big part of his life. He had just given a speech on education and college affordability at Georgia Tech in Atlanta, and when we passed through the gym on the way back to the motorcade, he took a few minutes to try and drain some three-point shots."[25] Souza, ever discreet, didn't say how many shots the president sank, an indication that Obama wasn't on his game that day.

Obama's desire to allow access was so great that he permitted Souza to capture special private moments. One was on the night of Obama's inauguration in January 2009. The new president and his wife Michelle were in a freight elevator leaving an inaugural ball by a quick and secret route, and Obama had lent his wife his tuxedo jacket. They were sharing a private, almost intimate moment, smiling and looking into each other's eyes, as they stood in the middle of the large elevator while a dozen members of their entourage stood apart, looking down at papers, peering at the walls, inspecting the floor, all to give the first couple a modicum of privacy in a very awkward situation. It also had a larger meaning, illustrating how abnormal the life of the president and first lady could be.

* * *

SOUZA'S DAY began at 8:00 a.m. when he arrived at his office in what was formerly a barbershop in the West Wing basement. He sat at his computer and, using a mouse pad bearing the presidential seal, searched the website for the Executive Office of the President. He downloaded the president's schedule, printed it at one-third its full size, stapled the pages together into a pocket-sized pamphlet and used it as his own schedule for the day. He said he got to decide what to cover. He and his three-person photo staff took an average of 20,000 pictures a week.[26]

One possibility that he always looked for was an "OTR," the initials for an "off the record" movement by the president. These tend to be more unpredictable and more interesting than the normal run of official and utterly routine events. To better protect the president, the chief photographer and his staff, and nearly all other White House aides, aren't privy to the advance details, by order of the Secret Service. The Secret Service and a handful of top aides will have two or three possible venues in mind, which agents will tour in advance. The decision on precisely where to go is often not made until an hour or two before the OTR happens.

Souza worked 12 to 15 hours every weekday and on most weekends, although his hours were shorter on Saturdays and Sundays because that's when the president had shorter hours. Souza stayed on the job, often seemingly glued to Obama, even when the events seemed tedious because he never wanted to miss anything.

Souza told an interviewer in late July 2016, with six months left in his stint at the Obama White House: "I have not much of a personal life. It's very difficult on my family. I'm kind of on-call all the time. I'm pretty much with [President Obama] all day long, until he goes up to the residence for dinner. And then on weekends, it depends on what's happening in the world. I have this Blackberry with me 24/7, and I'm looking forward to not having that with me after January 20 [when Obama left office]. I think that will be quite a relief."[27]

During Souza's eight years at the White House working for Obama, his photographs were placed in large frames all around the work areas of the West Wing, sometimes on the day they were taken, a tradition that started before Souza. There were several reasons: the photographers liked to show off their work, and staffers liked to see themselves in pictures with the president and the first lady or in famous places around the premises such as in the Cabinet Room or Rose Garden. It was also thought to be inspirational and motivational to have a figure of history, the president, as a constant, visible presence in photographs everywhere one turned.

Souza said: "I feel like I'm the luckiest SOB photographer in the world. You know not only did I have a chance to do this once before, but now I'm getting a second chance and I have tried to make the most of that. I have got this incredible access to this historic Presidency. I'm not going to let these years go by without . . . really pushing the envelope as much as I can in terms of creating this visual archive."[28] He succeeded in achieving his goal.

It's striking how much more access the White House photographer gets that the news photographers don't. Often, the news photographers are admitted to the Oval Office or some other venue at the White House for just a minute or two at the start of a meeting, then ordered out. Not Souza. "As usual, the best pictures are just before the meeting starts and just as it breaks up," Souza said.[29] This is a time for informality and sometimes expansive gestures and comment, which can result in excellent pictures.

Souza, as mentioned, was the first chief White House photographer to use social media in a sustained way. And he not only built up a huge following of Obama fans and photography aficionados on Twitter, Facebook, Flickr, and Instagram, he also constructed a personal following. Souza used the White House website—www.whitehouse.gov—not only to send out photos in a huge and steady steam. Like his own official photo agency, he maintained a continuous dialogue with millions of Americans who clicked on the website. This relationship between a White House photographer and the public had never been cultivated before, and it marked one of Souza's biggest successes.

In weekly and sometimes more frequent messages to web viewers, Souza was ingratiating, conversational, and informative, providing insights into how he did his job and into the life of the first family. He also posted a "Photo of the Day" on the White House website to get more attention for his work and add to the aura around the first family as likeable, hard-working, decent people.

"When people ask me how I do what I do, I often recite the words of Bob Dylan," Souza wrote on the White House website on December 9, 2015. "'I was just doing what I could with what I had where I was.' That kind of sums up my approach to my job as the President's photographer.

"Every once in a while, you also just get very lucky," he added. "Such was the case last week, when a rainbow came along just as the President's helicopter was arriving at the airport in Kingston, Jamaica, where he would board *Air Force One* for the flight to Panama. Fortunately, I was manifested aboard the second helicopter—which always arrives before *Marine One*—giving me a few minutes to prepare for photographing the rainbow."

A colleague, staff photographer Amanda Lucidon, got several good pictures of the president with the rainbow in the background, but Souza explained that he "ran under the wing of the plane to try and line up where the President would be when he waved goodbye at the top of the stairs." The result was a striking photo released to the public of Obama waving, with a rainbow appearing to emanate from his right hand and streak across the sky.[30]

*   *   *

SOUZA, WHO WAS raised in Massachusetts and attended Boston University, was unassuming in person but very proud of his work and his place in history. When he was 9 years old, his parents took him and his sister on a family vacation to Washington, D.C., and they went on a tour of the White House. He bought a book entitled *The Living White House* published by the National Geographic Society and the White House Historical Association, and he was inspired.[31]

Souza recalled admiring the photographs of various rooms such as the Oval Office where presidents have made so many important decisions and the Cabinet Room where so many historic meetings have taken place. Beyond this, Souza loved the photos of then-President Lyndon Johnson and some of his famous predecessors "at work and play" which he felt were candid and fascinating. "At the time, I thought these were the coolest photographs I'd ever seen, and I wore that book out looking at those historic photographs again and again for the rest of my childhood," he recalled.[32]

Prior to his first White House stint, Souza had worked as a photographer for newspapers including the *Chicago Sun-Times*, and the *Chanute Tribune*, and the *Hutchison News*, both in Kansas. After his work in the Reagan White House he shot photo essays for *National Geographic* magazine and worked for the *Chicago Tribune*, covering the wars in Afghanistan and Kosovo. Prior to working for the Obama White House, he taught photojournalism at the School of Visual Communication at Ohio University.[33]

He got to know Obama when the promising young politician was a U.S. senator from Illinois and Souza was assigned by the *Chicago Tribune* to cover him photographically starting with his first day in office in January 2005. "I met Obama's communications director over lunch," Souza recalled, "and told him what we at the *Tribune* wanted to do. Once we resolved our differences about access, it was just a matter of staying in contact with them. Subsequently, the day Obama was going to be sworn into the U.S. Senate, I had my first conversation with him. It took a month or two for Obama to be comfortable with me. The access didn't come right away, but it did come."[34] Souza published a book in 2008 called *The Rise of Barack Obama* and the senator liked it, strengthening their bond. Souza also covered Obama's successful presidential campaign in 2008, for the *Chicago Tribune*. Souza was hired after the election as the official White House photographer.

One aspect of Souza's work that Obama particularly appreciated was his photography of Sasha and Malia, Obama's two daughters. This ability to take good pictures of presidential families has always been an important way to ingratiate a White House photographer to a president and a first lady.

"I usually tell my friends that, following in the footsteps of those who came before me, I am trying to make timeless photographs that people can look back upon in 50 years," Souza explained before he left the White House. "But I recently listened to a long-ago presentation by Okamoto [LBJ's photographer] when, essentially making the same point, he said not 50 years but 500 years. Wow! I thought. Imagine someone combing through my photographs of President Obama in 2510. That really makes me realize that this is visual history I am recording with my camera. I will do my best to take that to heart every day."[35]

Souza adopted Okamoto's philosophy about being invisible to the president and the first lady while he was on the job. "I think they have become so used to my presence that they don't even pay attention," Souza said in 2016 as the administration entered its final year.

President Obama agreed. "You know it is actually a very difficult thing for anybody who occupies this office to be under that kind of constant observation," he once said. "That's one of the hardest things to get used to in being president. But when you have somebody like Pete Souza who you trust, who is a friend and who is able to purposely fade into the background so that at a certain point you don't notice he's there, then it makes it a little bit easier." Added Souza: "There are images we don't release. But not many things that we don't shoot." Among the moments that are generally kept under wraps photographically are those involving very sensitive national security issues, private moments with the presidential families, when a president is having makeup applied before a television appearance, and when the president is firing someone, to prevent embarrassment. When Obama was interviewing possible Supreme

Court nominees to replace the retiring Associate Justice David Souter, Souza was allowed to take pictures of the meetings but not share the contents of his camera's memory card with anyone else on the photo staff. When Obama announced that he had chosen Sonia Sotomayor, the White House released the photo of her meeting with the president.[36]

* * *

SOUZA TANGLED repeatedly with news photographers who covered the White House. These photojournalists argued that Souza and other Obama White House officials were too restrictive in granting access to them and this hindered the photojournalists in doing their jobs. The news photographers were especially angry that Souza and his colleagues excluded them from important events and presidential moments to which Souza got exclusive access and then released his own pictures. The journalists argued that this amounted to photographic propaganda.

The irony was that Souza had agreed with them when he was one of them, during the years when he was a newspaper photographer for the *Chicago Tribune*. In that capacity, he told an interviewer: "My pictures don't suffer because of my limited access, but I think if a politician isn't letting me in to capture those [candid] moments, then they essentially suffer, because it presents them in a more town hall, staged format that seems contrived and less honest."[37]

In November and December 2013, hard feelings toward the Obama White House from journalists spilled over, and Souza found himself at the center of a media furor.[38]

The episode illustrated the fact that the chief White House photographer had become a central figure in shaping public perceptions of the president through aggressive use of social media and the internet, bypassing the mainstream media far more than had ever been done before.

What bothered news photographers and their allies among White House reporters was that the news photographers didn't have much close access to President Obama. In November 2013, the White House Correspondents' Association and 37 news organizations sent White House Press Secretary Jay Carney a letter arguing that White House officials were denying the public an "independent view of important functions of the executive branch of government" by limiting news photographers' access to the president and important meetings and distributing Souza's photos instead.

Reporters were also frustrated by what they considered other attempts by the White House to limit media access, such as holding relatively few presidential news conferences and channeling reporters' questions through press-office staffers instead of letting reporters talk to the actual policy makers, which had happened in the past.

Carney met with media representatives but the journalists complained that there was little change.

And in December, relations took another turn for the worse. The reason was the refusal of White House officials to let news photographers take pictures of President Obama with former President George W. Bush and former Secretary of State Hillary Clinton aboard *Air Force One* en route to the funeral of former South African President Nelson Mandela. Journalists argued that it was a historic moment that news photographers should have been allowed to document.

In response, Santiago Lyon, director of photography at the Associated Press, published an op-ed essay in the *New York Times* arguing that the administration was going too far in disseminating visual "propaganda": "Manifestly undemocratic . . . is the way Mr. Obama's administration—in hypocritical defiance of the principles of openness and transparency he campaigned on—has systematically tried to bypass the media by releasing a sanitized visual record of his activities through official photographs and videos, at the expense of independent journalistic access," Lyon wrote. He added: "The official photographs the White House hands out are but visual news releases. Taken by government employees (mostly former photojournalists), they are well composed, compelling and even intimate glimpses of presidential life. They show the president in the best possible light, as you'd expect from an administration highly conscious of the power of the image at a time of instant sharing of photos and visuals. By no stretch of the imagination are these images journalism. Rather, they propagate an idealized portrayal of events on Pennsylvania Avenue."[39]

Carney, a former White House correspondent for *Time*, countered that he had been meeting with representatives of the correspondents' association to discuss the access questions. "I can commit to you that we are working and have been working on expanding access where we can," Carney said. "Let me be clear: That is the view from the very top."[40] But the journalists said that while Carney claimed to be listening, he still hadn't changed the system very much.

Souza was offended by the controversy. He didn't consider himself a propagandist, and he resented being labeled that way. He considered himself a chronicler of the Obama presidency through photographs, he told associates.

But he had placed himself in an awkward position. As Kennerly wrote in 2007, a year before Obama's election: "I've always felt that photojournalists covering the president should be able to take their own pictures and make their own observations rather than have their publications rely on White House handouts. The American people shouldn't have to depend on spoon-fed official photographs to judge their leaders. Certainly matters of secrecy and other considerations sometimes prevent outsiders from being in the room with the president, but in many instances that isn't an issue. The editors of newspapers, wire services, and television networks who accept and use a constant stream of official White House photographs as part of their daily coverage are doing their readers and viewers a great disservice and are failing to provide true and objective journalism."[41]

Doug Mills, a photographer for the *New York Times* who has covered the White House since 1984, was a strong behind-the-scenes advocate for the photographers as a member of the White House Correspondents' Association's governing board. He said the "friction between the still photographers and the White House was growing worse in 2013. The White House photo office under Souza was operating what amounted to a photo wire service on its own, circumventing the photojournalists and dispensing propaganda."[42]

After Carney resigned and Josh Earnest replaced him as White House press secretary in 2014, the news photographers did notice some improvement. Working with White House Communications Director Jennifer Palmieri, Earnest helped to expand access for the photojournalists. But Souza was still reluctant to do so, Mills and other news photographers said.

Michael Martinez, a photojournalism professor at the University of Tennessee who has studied White House photography, says Souza became in large part a PR man for Obama, starting on Obama's first day as president. "When Chief Justice [John] Roberts screwed up the swearing-in on Inauguration Day, there was a re-do private ceremony," Martinez observed. "Media were not allowed in. It was a handout from the White House Press Office." Martinez adds that such media limitations are not healthy for the country because presidential photography "becomes a PR function, not a documentary function."[43]

Notes

1. "Time for Your Closeup, Mr. President: Pete Souza Gains Access by Building Trust," *Imaging Info*, Jan. 12, 2011, www.imaginginfo.com/online/printer. jsp?id=2781.imaginginfo.com/online/printer.jsp?id=2781.

2. Diane Smyth, "Pete Souza on Eight Years as Chief White House Photographer," *British Journal of Photography*, Jan. 19, 2017, bjp-online.com/2017/01/pete-souza.

3. Mimi Schiffman, "Capturing Unguarded Moments with Obama," *CNN*, Sept. 28, 2016, http://edition.cnn.com/2016/09/22/arts/pixel-pete-souza.

4. Mike Hofman and Alex Reside, "Pete Souza, Obama's Chief White House Photographer, on Making Pictures for History," *GQ*, Jan. 19, 2017, www.gq.com/story/pete-souza-obamas-chief-white-house-photographer-interview.

5. Schiffman, "Capturing Unguarded Moments with Obama"; see also Hofman and Reside, "Pete Souza." For Obama's praise of Souza, see "Former WH Photog Pete Souza Trolls Trump with Contrasting Obama Pics," *CBS News*, Feb. 15, 2017, www.cbsnews.com/news/pete-souzas-instagram-photo-commentary-on-trump; see also Justin Sink, "White House Photographer Weds in Rose Garden," *The Hill*, Oct. 20, 2013, http://thehill.com/blogs/blog-briefing-room/news/329521-white-house-photographer-weds-in-rose-garden.

6. Aamer Madhani, "Shooting History as White House Photographer," *National Journal*, Nov. 13, 2010.

7. Ibid.

8. Ibid.

9. Quoted in Chris Cillizza, "How Pete Souza became President Obama's Secret Weapon," *Washington Post*, Dec. 19, 2012, www.washingtonpost.com/news/the-fix/wp/2012/12/19/pete-souza-president-obamas-secret-weapon/?utm_term=.4e620fe317e2.

10. Quoted ibid.

11. Ibid.

12. Schiffman, "Capturing Unguarded Moments with Obama."

13. John Bredar, *The President's Photographer: Fifty Years Inside the Oval Office*, Washington, D.C.: National Geographic Society, 2010, pp. 241–242.

14. Schiffman, "Capturing Unguarded Moments with Obama."

15. Philip Galanes, "The Role of a Lifetime," *New York Times: Sunday Styles*, May 8, 2016, p. 14.

16. "This 106-Year-Old Woman Dancing for Joy as She Meets Barack Obama will Warm your Heart", *BuzzFeed*, Feb. 22, 2016, www.buzzfeed.com/aliciamelvillesmith/this-106-year-old-woman-dancing-for-joy-as-she-meets-barack#.rjXK2Gv5Y.

17. Jackie Calmes, "When a Boy Found a Familiar Feel in a Pat of the Head of State," *New York Times*, May 23, 2012, www.nytimes.com/2012/05/24/us/politics/indelible-image-of-a-boys-pat-on-obamas-head-hangs-in-white-house.html.

18. Ibid.

19. Chris Jansing and Corky Siemaszko, "What Pete Souza Learned after 2 Million Photos of Obama," *NBC News*, Nov. 16, 2016, www.nbcnews.com/news/us-news/pete-souza-white-house-photographer-keeps-focus.

20. Pete Souza, "Behind the Lens: 2015 Year in Photographs," *Medium*, Dec. 30, 2015, https://medium.com/@ObamaWhiteHouse/behind-the-lens-2015-year-in-photographs-b5064a44df4a.

21. Ibid.

22. Ibid.; see also Obama White House, "Year in Photos 2015 by Peter Souza," *Flickr*, Oct. 11, 2015, www.flickr.com/photos/obamawhitehouse/24154936811.

23. Souza, "Behind the Lens: 2015 Year in Photographs."

24. Ibid.; see also Chelsea Matiash, "A Love Story," *Time*, Aug. 25, 2016, time.com/barack-michelle-obama-love-story-photos.

25. Souza, "Behind the Lens: 2015 Year in Photographs"; Obama White House, "Year in Photos 2015 by Peter Souza," *Flickr*, Mar. 10, 2015, www.flickr.com/photos/obamawhitehouse/24237480915.

26. Bredar, *The President's Photographer*, pp. 21, 179.

27. Raghu Manavalan, "White House Photographer Peter Souza takes the Marketplace Quiz," *Marketplace*, July 29, 2016, www.marketplace.org/2016/07/29/life/marketplace-quiz/white-house-photographer-pete-souza-takes-marketplace-quiz.

28. Bredar, *The President's Photographer*, pp. 145–146.

29. Ibid., p. 152.

30. Pete Souza, "Behind the Lens: Somewhere Under the Rainbow," *White House*, Apr. 13, 2015, www.whitehouse.gov/blog/2015/04/13/behind-lens-somewhere-under-rainbow.

31. Pete Souza, 'Foreword', in Bredar, *The President's Photographer*, p. 13.

32. Ibid., p. 13.

33. Bredar, *The President's Photographer*, p. 30.

34. "Time For Your Closeup, Mr. President."

35. Bredar, *The President's Photographer*, p. 14.

36. Ibid., pp. 120, 122.

37. "Time For Your Closeup, Mr. President."

38. Kenneth T. Walsh, "Ken Walsh's Washington: Media Miffed at White House Access," *U.S. News & World Report*, Dec. 13, 2013, www.usnews.com/news/blogs/ken-walshs-washington/2013/12/13/media-miffed-at-white-house-access.

39. Santiago Lyon, "Obama's Orwellian Image Control," *New York Times*, Dec. 11, 2013, www.nytimes.com/2013/12/12/opinion/obamas-orwellian-image-control.html.

40. Jose Delreal, "W.H. Press Hits Carney over Access," *Politico*, 12 Dec. 2013, politico.com/story/2013/12/white-house-press-briefing-press-access-101090.

41. David Hume Kennerly, *Extraordinary Circumstances: The Presidency of Gerald R. Ford*, Austin: Briscoe Center for American History, 2007, p. 16.
42. Doug Mills, telephone interview with author, Feb. 22, 2017.
43. Benjamin Freed, "A Brief History of Presidents and Their Official Photographers," *Washingtonian*, Feb. 13, 2015, www.washingtonian.com/2015/02/13/54-years-of-official-white-house-photographs.

Chapter Twelve
Behind the Scenes with Donald Trump and His Commanding Style of Image Making

Donald Trump, the 45th president, shocked the political world with his victory over Democratic nominee Hillary Clinton in November 2016. He was propelled by his personal celebrity, public anger toward the establishment, and his pledge to represent Americans who felt left behind and ignored by the ruling elites.

His success as the Republican candidate was also due to his brilliant instincts as a showman with an uncanny knack for creating powerful perceptions of himself through the media. Trump had spent years developing his brand as a tough, strong, flamboyant real estate developer. And he persuaded millions of Americans that he was one of the most successful businessmen in U.S. history with a larger-than-life personality.

Photography was a key element in Trump's image-making, both in his business and political lives. As a PR-oriented businessman in New York, he hired some of the best photographers of the time to construct his image. As a real-estate mogul, Trump also welcomed top photographers on assignment for various news organizations, but only if he admired their work and could exert a large degree of control over the pictures they made. He continued these tendencies in his presidential campaign.

This reluctance to trust photographers, especially news photographers whom he couldn't fully control, explains why there were so few revealing pictures of Trump distributed during his campaign, and why keeping a visual record of his presidency will be so challenging. As explained by photojournalist Damon Winter of the *New York Times*: "No matter how restrictive the campaign, there are usually some opportunities to capture the small and revealing moments that occur in back rooms at rallies and during the grueling, cross-country trips as the candidates court voters. These, traditionally, have been vital elements of campaign coverage, allowing us to produce a richer, more nuanced account. In the Trump campaign, there have been almost none."[1]

Winter added that for almost the entirety of the 2016 campaign, "the only vantage point from which we could photograph him was the 'press pen,' an enclosure in the back of the room at his events, which offers only a head-on view. Mr. Trump doesn't like to be photographed from behind, from the side or from below and, as a result, we have had little access to the areas closest to the stage."[2]

Winter said Trump events could "at times feel dark, both visually and in tone. At rallies, the press [was] routinely harassed by supporters and insulted by the candidate himself." The photographer said he often heard "racist and violent comments" and saw "young children chanting, 'Lock her up! Lock her up!'—referring to Hillary Clinton—alongside their parents."[3]

Still, Winter found Trump to be "a fascinating visual subject. He is instantly recognizable from almost any angle and any distance. His signature hair reflects more light than anything around him, making him stand out in any scene. . . . He is also very expressive when he speaks, which can present a challenge: He makes grand gestures so often that they begin to lose any meaning or significance." Winter observed that while Trump would be cordial on the few occasions when Winter got close to him for photos, "he had very firm ideas about how he wanted to be shown. My biggest challenge was getting past his standard repertoire of poses and the near-scowl that he seems to favor the most."[4]

Winter recounted what it was like to take Trump's picture for a *New York Times* magazine story in late 2015.[5] They were at a Trump-owned golf course in Palos Verdes, California, and the candidate decided to drive the photographer around in a golf cart. "Photograph me here in front of the ocean," Trump said. "It's a great place. Wait, why are you shooting from such a low angle?" Trump continued giving directions throughout the shoot. Winter observed: "He's very aware of what he thinks are his good angles and his bad angles and what he wants to do and doesn't want to do. He always wants to have his chin down and be forward facing, and he wants to represent himself in a strong way. He's agreeable but very image conscious, and he wants to be portrayed the way he wants to be portrayed."

Photos of the private Trump were rare and none became iconic. "Photographs have had, in past elections, a tremendous impact on people's perception of presidential candidates," wrote independent photojournalist Ed Kashi in November 2016, shortly after Trump's victory over Democratic nominee Clinton. "The election of Barack Obama in 2008 is a good example. Damon Winter won a Pulitzer Prize for his coverage, which included so many unique and iconic pictures. But when I think back over the past year-and-a-half of political coverage, no particular photograph or photographer stands out."[6]

"Images seemed less significant in this election cycle," Kashi added. "Social media is what people reacted to. Tweets mattered, not pictures. Almost every day would begin with something about or by Donald Trump, which would then set the agenda. It was as if there was less time to absorb imagery because there were so many distractions. There are the images of Trump angrily shouting into a microphone, but all of those pictures are really the same picture. Not one stands out."[7]

Winter added: "We're looking for those pictures that you can't find anywhere else: these quiet, contemplative, behind-the-scenes pictures of him before he takes the stage. We're looking for those pictures because we haven't seen them anywhere. But, at least from what I was allowed to see, those moments don't seem to exist on Trump's campaign. He's mobbed from the moment he steps out of the vehicle at these events. There's no quiet time. There's no Donald Trump reflection. It's just a series of chaotic scenes one after another, even backstage."[8]

But compelling images of Donald Trump behind the scenes do exist, illustrating what might be possible if he loosens his grip on photographers during his presidency. These pictures were taken before his entry into politics.

*   *   *

HARRY BENSON, the renowned Scottish photographer, was among the best at visually chronicling "The Donald," as the brash businessman was nicknamed in New York. Benson said he always tried to encourage his subjects to work with him in arranging the photo sessions so they would be comfortable with him. He also flattered his subjects to lubricate the relationship. And both techniques succeeded with Trump.

Regarding a Trump photo shoot he did for *Time*'s July 25, 2013 issue, Benson said the first thing he mentioned when he walked into the room was that he thought Trump might run for president some day. Trump loved the reference.[9] And there was plenty of feedback. Benson added: "He'll tell you afterwards: 'That was a good picture, and give you a thumbs-up.'"[10]

As *Time* wrote later, after Trump had entered the 2016 presidential campaign: "On their own, Benson's pictures show a camera-ready mogul surrounded by his favorite things: his buildings, limos and helicopters, his wives and even a million dollars in cash. Seen together, this is an album of Trump's one of-a-kind rise."[11]

After meeting Trump at his Taj Majal Hotel in Atlantic City, New Jersey, for *People* in 1990, Benson said what had happened: "I was there to photograph Donald Trump. He told me there was over a million dollars in the 'cage' in the casino where the money is kept. I told him I had never seen a million dollars. Donald proceeded to walk right in and pick up exactly a million dollars to hold for the photograph, which caused quite a stir as it was totally against the rules of the casino. When some of the money started to fall off his lap, I found it was the most interesting photograph of the day." The picture showed a youthful Trump struggling awkwardly to balance the huge stacks of bills which he held with both hands against his chest.[12]

In September 1999, photographer Tomo Muscionico took a picture of an arrogant-looking Trump, sitting in the back seat of his limousine, his legs spread wide as he looked smugly into the camera. "Looking back, I think it's a powerful portrait of a mogul whose body language shows his privilege, sexuality and arrogance," Muscionico said.[13]

Photographer "Platon" (born Platon Antoniou) shot Trump in New York for *Fortune* on August 21, 2003, and one of his images captured Trump's face from slightly to the side, in a cold stare, with a squinting look of suspicion, even menace, in his eyes and his lips pressed into a grimace. "I photographed Mr. Trump at Trump Tower in Manhattan," Photon recalled in 2016. "It was a cathedral to gaudy, postmodern excess. I asked him to look straight into the camera, trying get his head as symmetrical as possible. With a glint in his eye, he looked at me and said, 'No—this is my best side.' He turned to his right cheek, as if to present me with Trump Inc. on his terms. I thought about this moment many times since the picture, and to me, it says something fascinating about the character of this extraordinary, disrupting figure. For me, he understands the media. He's comfortable within his own skin. He's happy to play with the process of photography . . . and consequently is able to project his own brand of authenticity. I believe he has singlehandedly transformed the political and media landscape this year [2016, when Trump won the presidency]. Our presidential election has essentially been turned into a reality TV show. All media pundits and political opponents have been forced to play on Donald's terms."[14]

Other photographers shot similarly harsh images of Trump over the years. Portraitist Nigel Parry photographed Trump for *Esquire* in November 2015, five months after he announced the start of his presidential campaign in June. "After being unable to fulfill the brief due to Mr. Trump insisting that I couldn't photograph his profile, I decided the only route was a confrontational photograph for a confrontational subject," Parry said. He added that one particular picture filled the bill. It showed an even more hostile-looking Trump than the image Platon produced, a full head shot of a glowering, pugnacious man who seemed to be eager for a fight. That, of course, was the persona that won him the election.

Occasionally, the original idea for a photo session didn't work out well. One was a photo of Trump seated at his desk looking up from some paperwork. To his left was a bald eagle, not a stuffed bird but the real thing. Martin Schoeller shot the image in New York for *Time* in August 2015 and he recalled: "I wanted to play on this idea that he thinks of himself as a great leader and savior of the American people. I thought what could be better than our national bird. It's the perfect symbol. Having worked with birds of prey in the past, I knew that wouldn't be easy and there would be a lot of room for surprise; I thought those two attitudes colliding was the perfect match."[15] But the picture seemed contrived, and Trump appeared uncomfortable with the situation as it turned out.

Trump wasn't bashful about letting his arrogance and narcissism show on other occasions, just as they were evident in his willingness to pose with the eagle. One such case was his posing as "The Thinker," the famous sculpture by Auguste Rodin, while sitting on a gold-plated tree stump. Photographer Peter Yang got the shot of Trump at his New York penthouse for *Rolling Stone* in 2011. Yang recalled, "When I was commissioned to photograph Donald Trump in 2011, the first thing that came to mind was this gold-plated tree stump I'd been eyeing at a ritzy furniture store down the street from me. I had been to Trump's house before (to photograph wife Melania Trump) and noted the bevy of things gold. Gold leafing on all the walls, a gold front door, even a golden toilet. With the log in mind, the idea of Trump being The Thinker came next, and while I loved the idea, I was pretty sure he would nix it."

"On the day of the shoot," Yang added, "I was told to work fast, real fast. . . . I had three setups ready to go when Mr. Trump got there. There were two safe shots, then The Thinker. The first shot was Trump in front of the Manhattan skyline. Pretty standard stuff and it only took a minute. Trump was way more understated that I imagined he'd be, almost soft spoken. I'd mostly seen him firing people on *The Apprentice*, and I was glad I didn't get that guy. The second shot was a close-up portrait of him. It's always interesting to see famous folks up close, and when he, unprompted, pointed and yelled into the camera, I knew I got the shot."

"We then walked over to the gold log. I took a deep breath and showed him a picture of The Thinker. Before I could say anything, he grabbed the paper out of my hand, studied it for a moment, and hit his mark on the log. I snapped a few frames, he shook my hand, and was quickly out the door."[16] Yet the photo looked more than a bit silly, and Trump appeared to be thinking, why am I doing this?

*   *   *

OVERALL, it's clear that for many years Trump has sought to create and enhance an image of being a larger-than-life leader. This is a major goal of his presidency, and he is likely to use carefully managed photography to help him achieve it. He started doing so almost from his first day in office by allowing news photographers to take pictures of him in orchestrated settings such as signing executive orders, talking to aides, giving speeches from the grand surroundings of the West Wing, and sitting in shirtsleeves at his big desk aboard *Air Force One*, apparently hard at work. He also had aides choreograph his appearances as much as possible to minimize photos of him from the front at a low angle or from the sides, because he thought his double chin became too obvious.

Even so, says Doug Mills, longtime White House photographer for the *New York Times*, "Donald Trump loves having his picture taken. He's not camera shy."[17]

And his reluctance to show a kinder, gentler side slowly began to fade within a few weeks of his inauguration in January 2017, as many Americans became concerned that he was too pugnacious. Shealah Craighead, his chief White House photographer, and Sean Spicer, the

White House press secretary, began allowing news photographers to take pictures of Trump in more personal settings, such as walking across the South Lawn holding hands with his grandchildren. Trump had clearly decided to soften his image somewhat. He concluded, as had so many of his predecessors, that presidential photography should be a part of the White House propaganda machine, although he remained deeply distrustful of what he called the "fake" mainstream news media, including the photojournalists.

Notes

1. Damon Winter, "In Sight, yet Elusive: A Year of Photographing Donald Trump," *New York Times*, Nov. 8, 2016, p. P9, www.nytimes.com/2016/11/09/us/politics/donald-trump-presidential-campaign.html?_r=0. Winter won the Pulitzer Prize for feature photography for his *New York Times* coverage of Barack Obama's campaign in 2008.
2. Ibid.
3. Ibid.
4. Ibid.
5. James Estrin, "Photographing Donald Trump on the Campaign Trail," *New York Times*, Oct. 1, 2015, https://lens.blogs.nytimes.com/2015/10/01/photographing-donald-trump-on-the-campaign-trail/?
6. Ed Kashi with Gabriel Ellison-Scowcroft, "Lightbox Opinion: What Trump's Win Says about the State of Photography in America," *Time*, Nov. 21, 2016, www.time.com/4578752/trump-America-photojournalism.
7. Ibid.
8. Estrin, "Photographing Donald Trump on the Campaign Trail."
9. Tara Johnson, Chelsea Matiash, and Paul Moakley, "I've Photographed Donald Trump more than Anyone Else," *Time*, July 14, 2016, www.time.com/4404431/harry-benson-donald-trump.
10. Ibid.
11. Ibid.
12. Ibid.
13. Ibid.
14. Ibid.
15. Ibid.
16. Ibid.
17. Doug Mills, telephone interview with author, Feb. 22, 2017.

CHAPTER THIRTEEN
THE VITAL ROLE OF THE "PHOTODOGS"

An important dimension of the presidency's visual history is the role played by news photographers, the men and women who work for news organizations such as wire services, magazines, and newspapers and who have taken millions of pictures of presidents over the years.

They don't have the access that the official White House photographers have, and much of what they do involves visually recording events staged by White House media advisers who simply want to make the president look as good as possible.

But the news shooters, as they are called in the West Wing, do observe the president closely and learn much about him as the focal point of their cameras. During more than 31 years covering the White House for *U.S. News & World Report*, I've learned that the news photographers have a special insight into the presidents, their personalities and their moods, since they keep them in their lenses for hours each day.

Hugh Sidey, a longtime White House correspondent for *Time* and *Life* magazines, has called them "the foot soldiers of history."[1] Reporters and historians can and mostly do quote others on the events they are writing about; they often don't see the scenes or hear the words spoken by the principals first-hand. Photographers, of course, need to be on the spot to take their pictures.[2]

Former *Time* photographer Dirck Halstead has said: "If you want to try and figure out what sort of president a person is going to be, the best people to ask early on are the photographers. We don't get the handouts. We don't get the spin sessions. All we know is what we see. We are looking into the soul of that president. And we're highly trained to do that. That's our job. And so, as a result, these pictures can have tremendous consequences. That is one of the reasons why I feel as a photographer, I have an enormous responsibility."[3]

The daily routine tends to be tedious. "When you're covering the White House, it is boring beyond belief," says Halstead. "You spend most of your time sitting in a pressroom, dozing. And then you have 20 or 30 seconds in which to take a picture. And that picture could turn out to be the most important picture of your career."[4]

White House photojournalist Dennis Brack adds: "The photographers covering the White House have always had the close-in views of presidential administrations that no one else in the media can get. And they have their own stories to tell. Generally their stories have never been recorded, but they are told and retold in the White House press work area over the years."[5] This chapter will retell many of them.

*   *   *

PHOTOGRAPHERS have often used their wiles to get access. In 1919 and 1920, amid rumors that President Woodrow Wilson was in bad health (he had suffered a stroke in October 1919, but this was kept secret), the photographers were desperate to get pictures of the president.[6]

One lensman, H.M. Van Tine, and a colleague tried a dramatic ploy. They knew that every morning workmen rolled a wagonload of hay through the White House gates to feed a flock of resident sheep grazing on the South Lawn. Early one morning, Tine and his sidekick hid themselves under the hay hoping to get a photo of Wilson in a wheelchair. But a Secret Service agent noticed the hay didn't look right and began poking a stick into it. He discovered the two men and made them leave the White House grounds immediately.[7]

*   *   *

NEWS PHOTOGRAPHERS have always had an up-and-down relationship with presidents. On the positive side, in 1861 Mathew Brady wanted to take pictures of the battles between the North and South in the Civil War and was concerned about being detained by Union troops. Brady walked from his Washington studio to the White House and told

President Lincoln of his concerns. Lincoln, respectful of Brady's work and the photos that Brady and his assistants had taken of Lincoln in the past, wrote on a card, "Pass Brady. A. Lincoln." It was in effect a special press pass that made Brady's movement around Union lines much easier.[8]

But the history of news photographers at the White House also contains many examples of tension between the photojournalists and the commander in chief and his aides—part of the normal give-and-take between the press and the president. The situation was so strained by June 1921, that 24 movie and still photographers in Washington met in the office of the National Photo Company and formed the White House News Photographers Association, to promote their access as a group. Among the organizations represented were International Newsreel, Associated Screen News, the *Washington Post*, and the *Washington Star*.[9]

President Warren G. Harding, publisher of the *Marion Daily Star* in Marion, Ohio, decided to recognize the photographers as journalists just like reporters. Up until then, the "picturemen" were not allowed inside the White House except on special occasions. Harding noticed them standing at the gates waiting for admission each day and became sympathetic to their plight. He had a small wooden shed built near the West Wing door for the photographers to gather and store their equipment. It made their life a lot easier and they were grateful to the president for his consideration.[10]

Harding had a soft spot for human-interest stories, especially tales about himself. He knew they would add to his image as a likable, engaging fellow. When he accepted an Airedale as a gift and the dog arrived at the White House, he stopped a cabinet meeting and went outside to greet the animal, named "Laddie Boy." They took a walk around the White House grounds and posed for pictures. This started a series of "first dog" stories that continued through the Harding administration and helped to popularize both Laddie Boy and the president.[11]

Harding also made himself available to the photographers both for pictures and personal interaction. When a group of photographers accompanied the president to Virginia for a reenactment of the Civil War Battle of the Wilderness, several of the lensmen were sitting in a tent playing poker one evening when they were interrupted. The tent flap opened and Harding stuck his head in, asking if anyone had a chew of tobacco. The photographers asked him to play a few hands of poker but he declined politely, saying he'd like to but needed to get back to his own tent.[12]

Calvin Coolidge, a vice president who succeeded to the presidency when Harding died suddenly in 1923, liked to have his picture taken.

He especially liked newsreels, which would play along with most feature films in movie theaters across the country.

Cal had one serious run-in with a still photographer. It happened on June 4, 1927, when he was reviewing Navy ships at Hampton Roads, Virginia. He had spent hours standing at the railing of the presidential yacht, the USS *Mayflower* and saluting the ships as they passed by. At one point, a weary Coolidge sat down and saluted the ships from a comfortable sofa on deck. Photographer Buck May took a picture of the president leisurely saluting while seated, looking more than a bit lackadaisical about the review. Coolidge sternly asked May why he would take such a picture and then turned back to the ships. But May distributed the photo and it was played prominently in many newspapers, including the *Washington Star*, to Coolidge's embarrassment.[13]

This didn't sour Coolidge's relationship with the lensmen. In fact, his wife Grace was an admirer of photography and photographers, and they liked her. On one occasion, the president and first lady were leaving a church service but one photographer, Johnny Di Joseph, missed the shot. Mrs. Coolidge noticed his distress and asked what was wrong. When he told her, she said, "Don't worry, we'll just do it again." She persuaded her husband to walk back up the church steps and come down again, and this time Di Joseph got his picture.[14]

*   *   *

VERY MUCH on the negative side, the news photographers had a strained relationship with President Herbert Hoover and his wife Lou from 1929 to 1933. President Hoover didn't like cameras and thought photographers were looking for ways to embarrass him, a common complaint of presidents over the years. "He had a rather square face with small features," photographer George Harris remembered, "and he was not sufficiently interested in showing [himself] to good advantage to be helpful to the man behind the lens."

Hoover lacked charisma, and his speeches often landed with a thud. J.C. Brown, an MGM movie cameraman, remembered that when Hoover made appearances, the crowds were passive. To liven things up and make for better crowd pictures, Brown would shout at the audiences, "Wave, smile, cheer—do something besides stare." It didn't work.[15]

Photographer Johnny Di Joseph, who had benefited from the graciousness of Grace Coolidge, blamed the first lady. "He was okay," Di Joseph recalled. "It was his wife." First Lady Lou Henry Hoover was made an honorary member of the White House News Photographers Association, too, but it didn't matter. "Mrs. Hoover imposed a rule that no photographer could come within fifteen feet of her husband to make a picture," writes Brack. "The president wore two-inch high collars with his shirts—Di Joseph called them 'horse collars.' Mrs. Hoover did not like the way the president's double chins fell over his collar, and she thought that keeping the photographers at a distance would prevent them from making close-up photographs emphasizing his weight."[16]

Eventually the restrictions became so severe that few news pictures of Hoover made their way into the public domain during his presidency, adding to his image of being isolated from the public and hurting his standing.

The battle extended to Hoover's favorite way to relax, fishing. After a run-in with the media during a fishing trip to Oregon while he was a presidential candidate in 1928, he banned photographers and reporters from a retreat he had built in rural Virginia, a three-and-a-half hour drive south of Washington, called Camp Rapidan. He built dams, creating pools in the river to lure trout, and loved fishing there. But he banned the press, explaining that "fish will not bite in the presence of the representatives of the press."[17]

Hoover refused to pose for photographs with African Americans, apparently fearing a white backlash. He relented when he was up for reelection in 1932. Late in the campaign, he had his picture taken at the White House with several black leaders.[18] It was a futile gesture. He lost the 1932 election to Franklin D. Roosevelt by a landslide, doing poorly with African American voters.

Roosevelt totally changed the relationship between the photojournalists and the president, adding a larger degree of manipulation to the relationship.

* * *

UNDER FDR, the news photographers were subject to more specific restrictions than ever and they "played by rules that today's photojournalists find difficult to understand," writes Brack. "Yet those rules came with access to the White House that news photographers had never enjoyed before.

"When Roosevelt replaced Herbert Hoover in March 1933, only fifteen or so news photographers—both 'the stills' and 'the reels'—covered the White House." Roosevelt's press secretary, Steve Early, brought them together for a meeting. George Tames, a young photographer at the time for the New York Times, recalled Early telling them, "President Roosevelt is crippled. There's nothing secret about that. And he has a favor to ask of his friends in the media, his photographer friends, and that is not to photograph him when he's being carried, or when he is in some of the more compromising positions. In return, the president pledges to make himself more available to the photographers."[19]

The rules were specific and extensive: no pictures of Roosevelt in a wheelchair, on crutches, or in leg braces; no photographs of FDR getting into or out of a vehicle which would have revealed the extent of his disability and showed that his legs were paralyzed. On a few occasions, a veteran White House photographer would slap another's camera to the ground or block a shot in order to protect FDR from a picture showing his disability. There were occasional objections, but in nearly all cases, the White House news photographers obeyed the rules.[20]

There were other restrictions. FDR was bothered by flashbulbs, which could temporarily blind him. Early ordered that photographs could be shot only when the press secretary said, "Shoot." This gave FDR a moment to look away so he wasn't troubled by the flashes.[21]

There also were outright deceptions designed to fool the press. One of the most egregious was when Secret Service agents told journalists in 1945 that Roosevelt had been driven to the presidential retreat in rural Maryland called Shangri-La, now Camp David. Actually, this was a cover story to hide the reality that Roosevelt had flown to Yalta for a conference with Soviet leader Josef Stalin and British Prime Minister Winston Churchill.[22]

The news photographers largely swallowed whatever objections they had because Roosevelt did give them more photo opportunities—and good ones—than any of his predecessors. He liked being photographed, as long as the pictures were flattering or made the point he wanted. If he felt one pose didn't work well, he would suggest trying another one, and would sometimes accept the photographers' suggestions. He was also very genial and seemed pleased when the photographers showed up, greeting some by name or nickname. A fan of horse racing, he would occasionally ask which horse the photographers liked at the Pimlico race track in Baltimore that day.[23]

*   *   *

HARRY TRUMAN had an excellent relationship with the lensmen. He got to know many news photographers while he was a U.S. senator from Missouri, and he developed a real liking for them. He felt that they didn't have axes to grind, and were often interesting personalities. The photographers returned Truman's affection. Woody Wilson, a photojournalist who covered Truman, recalled: "He was the sort of guy you would like to be your uncle."[24]

A key moment came during Truman's brief stint as Franklin Roosevelt's vice president. After a speech at the National Press Club, Truman was persuaded to play the piano and as he did so, a young actress named Lauren Bacall, who would soon become a famous starlet, jumped on top of the piano to get some publicity. United Press International photographer Charlie Corte snapped the pictures, which showed Bacall with her long legs just in front of Harry's face and Truman unsure where to look. These photos were widely used by the newspapers, and Truman's wife Bess thought he looked goofy and seemed entirely too interested in the provocative actress.[25] But Truman didn't blame the photographer or the newspapers; he realized they had a job to do and didn't hold a grudge against them.

On the day he was sworn in after Franklin Roosevelt's death during April 1945, Truman allowed photographers into the Oval Office but reporters were prohibited. For the actual swearing-in, photographers swarmed around the Cabinet Room to get the best shot and some asked for "just one more." Truman obliged, and took the oath a second time so the cameraman could get better shots.[26]

Shortly after taking over, Truman toured the press areas of the White House and saw only reporters. "Where are the photographers?" he asked. He was told they weren't allowed in the main press room but were kept in a 6-by-25-foot shed-like room outside the West Wing, which they called "the dog house." The photographers spent endless hours waiting there for FDR's visitors to come in and out of the West Wing doorway, visible from their windows, or to be summoned for some official event involving the president. "I want them in here," Truman said, referring to the main press room.[27] They were admitted immediately.

The news photographers had such access to Truman that they got to see his earthy side more than almost anyone else. Once, AP photographer Henry Burroughs recalled, Truman visited Defense Secretary Louis

Johnson for a meeting at the Pentagon. Burroughs was one of a small group of photographers assigned to a "pool" that accompanied Truman, but he told them there would be "no pictures." Burroughs, thinking he could take a break, went to the men's room and suddenly realized that the man at the next urinal was none other than the president. Burroughs, nonplussed, mumbled, "Hello, Mr. President." Truman smiled and replied, "This is the only place over here where anyone knows what they are doing."[28]

Truman once heard that a news photographer was running low on cash during a presidential vacation to Key West, Florida. This was a serious problem because credit cards weren't in widespread use then. The president noticed the man during a picture-taking session, reached into his pocket and pulled out a $100 bill, which he gave to the photographer. "Remember," Truman said, "this is a loan, not a gimme." The photographer immediately wired to his office for more money.[29]

Photographers accompanied Truman and his Secret Service bodyguards on his early morning 2-mile walks around Washington to get some exercise. Truman would pass street cleaners doing their jobs. They would wish him good morning and he would give a hearty hello. He would sometimes drop personal letters into local mailboxes along the way.

Truman was very considerate of the lensmen, also known as "stills." During his morning walks, AP photographer Johnny Rouse, who was overweight, couldn't keep up Truman's 120-step-a-minute pace and he would fall behind. Truman would stop and wait for Rouse to catch up.[30]

Explaining his consideration for the stills, Truman once said: "Photographers have to make a living, too." He called them "the hardest working men in town."[31]

There was occasionally friction. During a Truman vacation to Key West in March 1949, presidential press secretary Charles Ross got upset when movie and still photographers took pictures of Truman and Chief Justice Fred Vinson from a Navy blimp. The two officials were sunning themselves on the president's private beach. When the blimp landed, Ross and a Secret Service agent demanded the film. The still photographers exposed the film to light, ruining it, rather than turn it over to the authorities, while the movie photographers did turn over their film magazines. White House photographers called it censorship. Ross said he was just trying to protect the president's "right of privacy."[32]

The incident didn't cause any lasting rift. In fact, the relationship between Truman and the stills remained very close—too close by today's standards. "It was a feeling that we had with Truman that we've never had with any other President," observed George Tames of the *New York Times*. "It was a family; we were family, more than we were adversaries the way the press is today. We didn't have any adversarial relationship. It was a very close personal relationship."[33] Truman gave the news photographers an affectionate nickname—"The One More Club"—a reference to their regular plea for Truman to let them take "one more" picture at his events—and he declared himself president of the club.[34]

Truman allowed the photographers to take his picture in the White House without reporters present. "We heard many, many secrets; many, many good stories," recalled Tames, "and we never reported them when we came out because there was an unwritten rule that anything said in there was privileged, so we never said anything."[35]

On a quiet afternoon in November 1950, the moment every White House newsman and photographer fears came to pass: an assassination attempt on the president.

Two Puerto Rican nationalists tried to shoot Truman while he was quartered at Blair House, a government guest complex across the street from the White House, which was under extensive renovation (as captured by government photographer Abbie Rowe.) One would-be assassin was shot dead, the other seriously wounded, and a White House policeman was killed.

Nearby on Pennsylvania Avenue a car full of news photographers, a few of the 130 then covering the White House, including *New York Times* lensman Bruce Hoertel, heard the gunshots and ran to the scene in time to capture the immediate aftermath. Hoertel's picture of a guard sheathing his pistol over the body of one assailant on the steps of Blair House won a first-place award in the White House News Photographers Association annual contest that year. As it happened, in July 1948 Hoertel had almost lost his press credentials when he photographed Democratic convention acceptance speech notes that Truman had written down on a pad during a portrait shoot. Breaking with news photographer etiquette, Hoertel reported them to *Times* editors who used them in an exclusive story.[36]

In 1952, when Truman wasn't seeking reelection, he was riding an elevator with Democratic presidential nominee Adlai Stevenson, along with three photographers. The incumbent told Stevenson: "These are the best friends you'll ever have. They see everything. They know everything. And they say nothing."[37]

This description applies today only to the White House staff photographers, not the outside photographers, who no longer feel like part of the presidential "family"

* * *

DWIGHT EISENHOWER, the former military commander who succeeded Truman in the White House, never had much rapport with the news photographers. Ike didn't feel a need to orchestrate pictures of himself or even be very cooperative with the photographers. He didn't believe he had anything to prove. As a result of his ambivalence, there are few memorable pictures of Ike as president. He was a bit vain, sensitive about the size of his earlobes, but didn't think he could do much about it. Overall, he didn't have a lot of patience with or interest in photographers or photo sessions.[38]

* * *

THE RELATIONSHIP between photographers and the presidency warmed greatly under John F. Kennedy, but there was still a sense among some Kennedy aides that the photographers were a bit of a rabble. Letitia Baldrige, the White House social secretary, once complained to a White House press aide who wanted to bring some photographers to the East Wing residence on a winter day. Baldrige said the lensmen would "muddy the rugs." The press aide felt it would be insulting for her to tell the photographers to "clean their feet before they came in," and she said nothing to them.[39]

Kennedy didn't seem to share Baldrige's sense of superiority in dealing with the photographers. And in at least one case, President Kennedy was a profile in courage. At a news conference in April 1961, a reporter for *Jet*, an African American-oriented magazine, criticized Kennedy for planning to attend an annual awards banquet scheduled for May and sponsored by the all-white White House Photographers Association. Kennedy was thrown off balance and promised to look into the situation. His aides then said he might not attend unless the group added a black photographer to its membership immediately. The association hastily granted membership to Maurice Sorrell, a photographer for the Afro-American Newpapers group in Washington.[40]

First Lady Jacqueline Kennedy was very protective of her children and was eager to shield them from the media. She imposed a rule that there should be no photos of Caroline and John Jr. unless she approved them in advance. But the president believed the kids could give him a public-relations boost and he found ways around his wife's edict, notably by having their pictures taken when she was out of town.

The most memorable photo from Kennedy's funeral was taken by a news photographer. It was the heartbreaking picture of John Jr. saluting his father's caisson, which contained the president's casket, as it left St. Matthew's Cathedral in Washington and headed for Arlington National Cemetery. The only photographer who captured the image was Stan Stearns of UPI, and he knew immediately that it was the photo of his career. It was used on the front pages of newspapers around the country, and has since become one of the most recognized images of the Kennedy presidency.[41]

*   *   *

LYNDON B. JOHNSON, who succeeded Kennedy, was another micro-manager of the photographers, as FDR had been. As mentioned in Chapter Three, he thought his best side was his left, and he and his aides always tried to position photographers so they would take pictures of him from this vantage point. He was worried that TV lights would cause the creases in his face to appear as deep unflattering shadows, so a canopy was placed around his podium at news conferences in the East Room and the lights were dimmed for a more pleasing look. LBJ found the noise of Nikon motor drives on cameras distracting during his news conferences so he ordered that the photographers be allowed only one minute at the beginning to take pictures. There were lapses, and news photographers were chastised for them when they snapped pictures at unauthorized times, but mostly the rules were obeyed.[42]

Johnson would let photographers know if he didn't like their work. In 1964, photographer Charles Gory of the Associated Press made a picture of the president lifting one of his pet beagles by the ears while a group of visitors to the White House stood by awkwardly. The photograph appeared in newspapers across the country and many dog lovers were upset. The next time Johnson saw Gory, he admonished him. "Charlie," he said sternly, "why did you take a picture like that?" He added: "That picture got me in a heap of trouble. Don't ever take a picture like that again!"[43]

Sometimes, Johnson used the photographers to unwittingly help him make a political point. This happened with the famous photograph in which LBJ showed his scar from gall-bladder surgery. He had called in several reporters and photographers and, to their surprise, after one of them asked how he was recovering, the president raised his shirt and gestured to the scar. Many people considered the resulting pictures vulgar, but he had another objective. An aide later explained that the president suspected many Americans thought he was very sick and had gone to the hospital for cancer treatment. He felt that pictures of the scar, while somewhat embarrassing, would end these rumors, and they did.[44]

* * *

RICHARD NIXON had little interest in what the news photographers did. He felt it wasn't really vital to his success as president. More important than still photography, he believed, was his coverage on television and in the printed stories of newspapers and magazines. He delegated dealing with the "stills" to aides. He hired some competent people to wrangle the photographers and, for a while, allowed them to get acceptable pictures of him and the first family in official settings. The system worked relatively smoothly during his first term in office, from 1969 to 1973, and the news photographers were for the most part satisfied with the Nixon system. They weren't pals with the president, but he tolerated them.

Nixon even authorized an expansion and improvement of the media work space in the West Wing. The indoor swimming pool installed by Franklin Roosevelt was covered over, and a new White House briefing room was installed in its place. It resembled a hotel lobby, with couches (on which some photographers would take naps during the many hours of down time), comfortable chairs, and table lamps. The space is still used today for media briefings but has been redesigned with theater-style rows of seats, a podium in the front and a platform for photographers in the back.[45]

Things didn't go so well after Nixon's reelection. As the Watergate scandal grew, Nixon withdrew. He became more distant from the news photographers, apparently feeling that they would embarrass him with their pictures if they could.

Nixon's final day as president gave the photographers a poignant opportunity to record history. He was, after all, the only president in U.S. history to resign. After a reception in the East Room to say goodbye to his staff, he was scheduled to walk to the South Lawn and board his *Marine One* helicopter. Each photographer knew in advance that he or she wouldn't have time to do both events—it was either cover the reception or cover the walk to the helicopter, not both. It turned out that the moment at the chopper was the shot of the day.

Each photographer's camera held 36 exposures on a roll of film, and there would be no time to change rolls, so the photographers had to decide how to pace their shots. "Everything was fine until Nixon walked up the ramp to the helicopter and turned to face the crowd on the lawn," photojournalist Brack wrote in a memoir. "First, there was a wave, almost a salute—better get that, it might be all there is. Then he continued with his right arm, bringing it across his face and holding his hand high above—certainly want that. The photographers' prayers started: 'Lord, please let me be on frame thirty-one and not frame thirty-five.' Finally, the classic Nixon Double Whammy, his arms straight out and both hands making the 'V' sign. The Nikon motor drives were zinging away. Some photographers got the picture and were happy, some did not and were not so happy. But all wanted Nixon to just get in the helicopter so that they could rewind and reload."[46]

* * *

GERALD FORD WAS everything Richard Nixon was not—open, accessible and friendly. In August 1974, with Nixon preparing to resign amid the Watergate scandal, the news photographers noticed a change immediately when they staked out Ford's home in Alexandria, Virginia. "From time to time the vice president's wife, Betty Ford, or their daughter Susan would appear while leaving the house or coming home; they would yell a greeting," Brack recalled. "If photographers needed a special picture, the Fords invited them inside and they were welcome to stay and talk for a bit after the pictures were made."[47]

Ford and several Washington photographers got to know each other while he was a member of the House from Michigan starting in 1949 and when he became House minority leader. Nixon had chosen him to be vice president after Spiro Agnew resigned in 1973. "He had a style; he had an honesty; he had a demeanor that is not typical of presidents," recalled photographer Fred Ward, who became acquainted with Ford while he was vice president. "Normally they are difficult to be around at close range—they don't like it; they're apprehensive. And he had none of those characteristics."[48]

David Kennerly helped keep the relationship friendly and respectful when he became Ford's personal photographer. A former *Time* shooter who was named Ford's chief photographer as soon as he became president, Kennerly helped former news colleagues arrange many photos and photo projects, and the photojournalists were grateful.

Ford endeared himself to his photographic press corps by being accessible and gracious as part of his routine, a welcome change from the Nixon approach of stonewalling and complaining. When the photographers clamored to take pictures of Ford in the White House swimming pool, where he did laps every morning, Ford decided to let them all in at once. Ford arrived at the outdoor pool wearing a white terrycloth robe, a simple one with no presidential seal or monogram. The photographers snapped their pictures as he took off the robe and proceeded with his swim. Afterward, he stood and chatted with the photographers, typically amiable and low-key.[49]

Ford was widely mocked by comedians and commentators for being clumsy and an intellectual lightweight because of several incidents captured by the news photographers. One was when Ford fell down the rain-slick stairs of *Air Force One* upon his arrival at Salzburg, Austria. He was also photographed hitting his head on the doorway of the presidential helicopter, taking spills during ski runs at Vail, Colorado, and beaning bystanders at golf tournaments. But Ford didn't apportion blame. "Ford could have considered the photographers his enemy," Brack writes, "but he did not. He knew that they were only doing their jobs."[50] Through it all, he continued to treat the photojournalists with respect and no small degree of affection. They shared these same sentiments about Ford.

* * *

JIMMY CARTER had a poor relationship with the media. Contrary to his public image as a down-to-earth man who was devoted to helping people and doing the right thing, as president he largely ignored many of the people around him, including the household staff at the White House and his Secret Service agents. "The lowest on his list of little people were the photographers," writes Brack. "For some reason, he never acknowledged the existence of photographers and never called to the 'regulars' by name as many other presidents had. Carter's top staff had about as much interest in photographers as their boss."[51] This included Press Secretary Jody Powell, who had no desire to allow the photographers to develop a comprehensive visual record of the Carter years.

The coverage started badly from Carter's point of view. "On his first day in office the photographers were positioned at the presidential limousine to photograph a confident new president on his way to tell various government agencies about the new 'Carter era' in Washington," Brack says. "He slipped. It was just a tiny patch of ice, but he hit it just right. His arms went up and his briefcase went flying. The photographs were on the front page of every newspaper the next day and the Carter honeymoon with the press was over. The feud began and kept growing. . . . Carter's lack of interest in still photographs continued to the very end of his presidency."[52]

When Carter decided not to name a chief White House photographer to his staff, it was a clear indication that he had little or no understanding of the role of photography in establishing a president's persona for the public. He granted very little behind-the-scenes access, which helps to explain why the photographic record of the Carter presidency seems so stilted and boring, offering little sense of a real human being behind the big desk in the Oval Office.

*   *   *

RONALD REAGAN and his wife Nancy, both former movie stars who understood the need for favorable publicity, had an affectionate relationship with the news photographers. And the camera people quickly concluded that despite their reputation as elitists who were close to the rich and powerful, the Reagans were actually affable, gracious people. The Reagan administration, because of its historical nature, turned out to be a bonanza for photography on matters both positive and negative.

Veteran photographer Ron Edmonds was newly hired by the AP, covering the White House for his second day on March 30, 1981, when Reagan was shot as he left a speech at the Washington Hilton Hotel. Edmonds was lucky to be standing at the presidential limousine after the speech, ready to take pictures of the president heading back to the White House, when he heard the gunfire. "When the first shot rang out, I saw the president's eyes flinch," Edmunds recalled. "I pushed the shutter down on my camera, which shoots six frames a second. Even at that speed, the Secret Service agents reacted so quickly that Reagan is only visible in three frames." But this was enough. Edmonds earned a Pulitzer Prize for his pictures, some of the most historic ever taken of a president in crisis. They were used on front pages and magazine covers around the world.[53]

Reagan could not easily recall the names of individual photographers, even most of those on his own staff. But the photographers forgave him. Unlike Carter, who seemed to actively disdain the photographers,

Reagan's problem was a general failure to recognize people. So it was considered nothing personal with the photographers. He even referred to Bill Fitzpatrick, a White House staff photographer for many years, as "the tall fellow."

One reason Reagan was so popular among the news photographers was the counsel he took from Michael Deaver, his media adviser, and Steve Studdert, a top advance man who set up logistics for speeches and trips. Deaver and Studdert knew how to create great photo opportunities: they listened to photographers' suggestions and understood their needs. Another factor was that Michael Evans, Reagan's chief White House photographer during his first term, didn't hog all the best photo opportunities for himself, as other chief photographers had done and still do. He welcomed advice from the news professionals and created many excellent photo moments with their cooperation.

The Reagan team, with full consultation with news photographers, began planning the president's visit to Normandy five months prior to the June 6, 1984 anniversary of the D-Day invasion during World War II. The president's wreath-laying at a massive cemetery was a natural high point, but it had been repeated many times with presidents and other dignitaries. A second option was considered—having the president and first lady walk amid the seemingly endless rows of white crosses at the cemetery to lay a second wreath at another location. This was added to the schedule, and it proved to be a brilliant scene. The Reagans somberly walked amid the neatly arranged rows of crosses at the graves of thousands of U.S. soldiers who had helped liberate Europe. Even the Secret Service cooperated, with the president's bodyguards agreeing to step out of the frame for a few seconds rather than appear in the photos. It was a powerful image and would not have occurred if all the parties involved, including the White House staff and the media, hadn't worked together.

This symbiotic relationship was troubling to media critics who felt that newsmen and newswomen shouldn't have such a cozy and cooperative relationship with the White House. But it did produce great pictures, which was the first priority of the photographers.

*   *   *

GEORGE H.W. BUSH was popular among the photographers, as well as the White House reporters. He was kind and considerate to the news people, many of whom had known him from his past jobs in Washington, such as being member of the U.S. House of Representatives from Texas, director of central intelligence, chairman of the Republican National Committee, and Reagan's vice president for eight years.

Bush took the time to learn a bit about each photographer and reporter in his press corps, and he knew their names. He came up with a nickname for the news photographers—"photodogs." It may have occurred to him when he noticed them barking like pet dogs as a light-hearted protest when they were being herded from one location to another. They loved the nickname. Bush also held a barbeque for the photodogs and their spouses on the South Lawn of the White House each year, which solidified their relationship even more. Some critics would argue that he co-opted them.

Bush also respected the news photographers for refusing to brief reporters on what they heard during meetings involving the president. This was a tacit agreement—Bush didn't want to keep up his guard when the photographers were present without reporters. The photographers knew that if they spoke out of school their access would be severely limited. When reporters, even colleagues from their own organizations, asked the photographers what happened at various photo-only events, the photographers would often say they weren't paying attention because they were so focused on getting the pictures. It was largely an excuse, with the result that the president was protected by the photodogs. But the system, while tilted in Bush's favor, resulted in the news photographers getting many good photos and they liked the arrangement.

Since that time, reporters have pushed to always be included with the photographers in media events involving the president. Sometimes it happens and sometimes it doesn't. The collegial atmosphere under Bush no longer exists, and the White House calls the shots no matter what the media want to do.

*   *   *

BILL CLINTON was transformed negatively by political success, at least in the view of many news photographers. When he was running for the White House in 1992, he seemed to be best buddies with the shooters. He gave them lots of access, such as allowing them to take behind-the-scenes pictures of him preparing for debates and talking with advisers. He even played Pinochle with photographers on the campaign bus and seemed to enjoy himself. But as Clinton continued on to win the Democratic nomination, he became less friendly with the photographers.

Perhaps he felt he didn't need them for favorable publicity as he had before.[54]

The photodogs were satisfied with the situation. "The lack of behind-the-scenes access was not a major concern for the news photographers because there was much to see when Clinton and the first lady were before the lenses," Brack recalls. "Photographing the Clintons was like watching the characters in a Shakespearean play. The emotions [such as when they were miffed at each other] were captured by alert and skillful photographers. Some of these story-telling photographs could have been a reason that the Clintons kept the photographers at a distance."[55]

Bill Clinton's curiosity also benefited the photographers. He insisted that his schedulers include historical sites and other interesting places in his itineraries, rather than sequester him constantly in official meetings. He would take photographers and reporters along on his excursions, and this generated great pictures. "Everywhere he went, he wanted to act like a tourist," said Charlie Archambault, the former chief photographer for *U.S. News & World Report* who covered many Clinton trips. Among the locations were a wildlife preserve in Botswana and the Hermitage art museum in St. Petersburg, Russia.[56]

*   *   *

GEORGE W. BUSH tried to get along with the photodogs, at least at the start of his presidency, but the relationship wasn't close. "In the 'Bush 43' years, the photographers were treated like reporters," Brack says. "They were people to be humored but kept at a distance. An attitude of arrogance by the head of the press advance contributed to the friction between the photographers and the presidential staff. The man was not very good at his job and quickly became the butt of the photographers' jokes."[57]

Despite the problems, the news photographers learned a lot about Bush and his lifestyle. "There were two things about Bush that the photographers dearly loved," Brack reports. "He did not go out in the evenings. The lid came over the White House intercom system right about five o'clock, meaning there would be no travel by the president. If there was an evening event you could count on it being over by seven. And, second, he was always on time."[58]

*   *   *

BARACK OBAMA didn't have much of an affinity for the news photographers and didn't get to know them well. He relied on his official staff photographer, Pete Souza, to portray him visually, and as discussed in Chapter Eleven this resulted in considerable friction with the photodogs. They felt that their access was far too limited and they were excluded from events that they normally would have covered.

One area of cooperation was in protecting Malia and Sasha Obama, the president's young daughters, from public attention. The president and first lady wanted their daughters to have as much of a normal life as possible and didn't want them to be constantly dodging the cameras.

A special ground rule was established: The girls would not be photographed unless they were in the company of their parents. The photographers accepted the rule and there were few violations of the protocol. Mostly, Malia and Sasha were left alone.

But overall the rift widened between the news photographers and the official White House photographers led by Souza. Official photos taken by the in-house staff were released and distributed more widely than ever, especially through social media such as Flickr, and the news photographers felt marginalized.

The problem for the photodogs and their news organizations was that the photos released by the White House were often excellent and difficult for the news outlets to pass up. An added problem was that the "photo wranglers"—the White House staffers who had the job of supervising the news photographers—were often overbearing and tried to dictate what pictures should be taken. This left the photodogs in a regular state of agitation and resentment.

Their long-range worry was that the Obama–Souza pattern would also become the norm with the next administration. Their concern was justified. When any White House seizes control of an aspect of image-making and the technique proves effective, it rarely lets go, and its successor follows suit.

Notes

1. Dennis Brack, *Presidential Picture Stories: Behind the Cameras at the White House*, Washington, D.C.: Dennis Brack, Inc., 2013, p. 2.
2. Ibid.
3. Dirck Halstead, "Looking into the Souls of Presidents: Transcript," Briscoe Center for American History, *Photojournalism and the American Presidency: Reading America's Photos*, www.cah.utexas.edu/photojournalism/transcript.php?media_id=5.
4. Ibid.

5. Brack, *Presidential Picture Stories*, pp. 3–4.

6. Ibid., pp. 5–6.

7. Ibid., pp. 6–7.

8. Ibid., p. 2.

9. Ibid., p. 10.

10. Ibid., pp. 10–11.

11. Ibid., p. 11.

12. Ibid., pp. 12–13.

13. Ibid., pp. 13–14.

14. Ibid., pp. 14–15.

15. Ibid., p. 15.

16. Ibid., p. 16.

17. Ibid., pp. 16–17.

18. Kenneth T. Walsh, *Family of Freedom: Presidents and African Americans in the White House*, Colo.: Routledge, 2011, pp. 80–81.

19. Brack, *Presidential Picture Stories*, pp. 21–22.

20. Ibid., pp. 22–23.

21. Ibid., p. 23.

22. Ibid., p. 24.

23. Ibid., p. 25.

24. Ibid., p. 36.

25. Ibid., p. 187.

26. Ibid., p. 39.

27. Ibid., p. 36.

28. Ibid., p. 41.

29. Ibid., p. 46.

30. Ibid., pp, 37–38.

31. Ibid., pp. 38–39.

32. Marshall Andrews, "At Key West: Truman Aide Bars Photos from Air," *Washington Post*, Mar. 15, 1949, p. 2.

33. Benedict K. Zobrist, "Oral History Interview with George Tames," June 11, 1980, Harry S. Truman Library and Museum, www.trumanlibrary.org/oralhist/tamesg1.htm.

34. " 'One More Club' President is on the Job," *The Express* (Lock Haven, Pa.), Mar. 6, 1952, p. 1.

35. Zobrist, "Oral History Interview with George Tames."

36. Bruce G. Hoertel, "Headaches of a White House Photographer," *Popular Photography*, vol. 29, no. 5 (Nov. 1951), p. 73.

37. Brack, *Presidential Picture Stories*, p. 40.

38. Ibid., p. 51.

39. Barbara J. Coleman, oral history interview JFK #2, Oct. 24, 1969, p. 50, John F. Kennedy Library Oral History Program, www.jfklibrary.org/Asset-Viewer/Archives/JFKOH-BJC-02.aspx.

40. Walsh, *Family of Freedom*, p. 121.

41. Brack, *Presidential Picture Stories*, pp. 66–67.

42. Ibid., p. 70.

43. Ibid., p. 72.

44. Ibid., pp. 73–74.

45. Ibid., pp. 83–84.

46. Ibid., pp. 97–98.

47. Ibid., p. 100.

48. Ibid.

49. Ibid., p. 101.

50. Ibid., p. 105.

51. Ibid., p. 107.

52. Ibid., pp. 108, 116.

53. Ron Edmonds, video interview with Associated Press, Mar. 30, 2011; see also Brack, *Presidential Picture Stories*, p. 122.

54. Brack, *Presidential Picture Stories*, pp. 135–136.

55. Ibid., p. 139.

56. Charlie Archambault, telephone interview with author, Jan. 27, 2017.

57. Brack, *Presidential Picture Stories*, p. 143.

58. Ibid., p. 145.

CHAPTER FOURTEEN
MASTER PHOTOJOURNALISTS WHO MADE
THEIR MARK ON HISTORY

Despite their problems with access compared with the official staff photographers, news photographers have managed to get some historic and memorable images over the years, such as Stan Stearns' photo of John Kennedy Jr. saluting his father's casket. They also have provided insights into the lives, character and personalities of the presidents and first ladies.

* * *

GEORGE TAMES of the *New York Times* had his share of these pictures. He was one of the best photographers ever to cover the White House.

Tames took one of the most iconic pictures ever captured of a president with his photograph of President Kennedy standing alone at an Oval Office window with his head bowed as if the weight of the world was on his shoulders. Actually, Kennedy wasn't really under serious pressure at that moment. He was just reading the newspaper and some documents while standing at a table in front of a window. Tames was doing a major pictorial on Kennedy and happened to be just outside the Oval Office and noticed the scene through an open door, thought it was interesting, and stepped into the office where he snapped the picture. When the *Times* published it later, it took on a life of its own as an example of the president as a solitary decision maker. The picture became known as

"The Loneliest Job," although this was a misinterpretation. First Lady Jacqueline Kennedy later said that regardless of what was really happening, the picture "depicted the awful weight of the presidency" and told Tames it was one of her favorites.[1]

Tames explained it this way:

"I was doing 'A Day With The President.' President Kennedy operated differently than any other president that I have been acquainted with, in that his personal office, the Oval Office, was open. . . . Very few times did they close the door. . . . I'd make a request to see him, and he always was very gracious about giving me some time. One of the things about Kennedy was he appreciated the power of the media, and to my mind was the first president who really knew how to use us. He used us. We thought we were using him but he was using us as much as we were using him.

"President Kennedy's back was broken during the war, when that torpedo boat of his was hit by the Japanese destroyer. As a result of that injury, he wore a brace on his back most of his life. Quite a few people didn't realize that. Also, he could never sit for any length of time, more than thirty or forty minutes in a chair, without having to get up and walk around. Particularly when it felt bad, he had a habit, in the House and the Senate and into the presidency, of carrying his weight on his shoulders, literally, by leaning over a desk, putting down his palms out flat, and leaning over and carrying the weight of his upper body by his shoulder muscles, and sort of stretching or easing his back. He would read and work that way, which was something I had seen him do many times. When I saw him doing that, I walked in, stood by his rocking chair, and then I looked down and framed him between the two windows, and I shot that picture. I only made two exposures on it—we were very conservative with our film. Then I walked out of the room and stood there for a while, then I saw him straighten up. I went in again and I photographed him straight up, for a different shot, from the back, then I walked around to the side and photographed him profile, right and left.

"He had a copy of the *New York Times*. He was reading the editorial page."[2]

During the key frames, Kennedy glanced over at Tames and said: "I wonder where Mr. [Arthur] Krock gets all the crap he puts in this horseshit column of his."[3]

In person, Tames, with his perpetual smile, balding pate, bow tie, and dark sports coats, cut a distinctive figure. He was a charming raconteur and a history buff, full of jokes, rumors, and chatter, who was very savvy about cultivating Kennedy and his aides. In addition to covering the White House, he also covered Congress and he would freely spread gossip and funny stories about members of the House and Senate, which the president and his advisers were always eager to hear. Tames was also able to learn quite a lot about how the White House operated.

Today, relations between the president and the media are so strained by distrust and cynicism that it's hard to imagine allowing a news photographer to spend hours around the Oval Office with the door open, poking his head inside and wandering into the room when a photo opportunity presented itself. As Tames told the story, Kennedy was so oblivious to his presence that he didn't even realize Tames was in the Oval Office when he snapped the soon-to-be-famous picture.

Just before Tames' pictorial and the accompanying story entitled "A Day With the President," ran in the *Times Magazine*, Tames brought the layouts to the White House to show Kennedy. The president browsed through them and liked what he saw. On the cover was a picture of Kennedy and an aide in the Oval Office, taken from the outside through a window. "Very nice," Kennedy said, and then he started perusing the rest of the layout. On the third page, he noticed a small version of "The Loneliest Job." picture and put his finger on it. "This should have been on the cover," he told Tames.[4] In this case, the president's judgment of fine photography was better than the journalists'.

* * *

TAMES CAME from a poor Greek–Albanian family in Washington, D.C. His father was a pushcart peddler. Tames dropped out of high school after the tenth grade to work as a courier in the Washington bureau of *Time–Life*. In 1940, he started accompanying *Time–Life* photographers on assignments to Congress as a helper, and he eventually began taking his own pictures of legislators and events on Capitol Hill. Various publications used his work. He left *Time* in 1945 after six years to work at the *New York Times*.[5]

One attribute that distinguished him was his ingratiating personality and ability to befriend his subjects, advantages he exploited throughout his long career.[6]

He was even able to get Richard Nixon to open up. Tames recalled leaving the Drake Hotel in Chicago, where the Republican National Convention was choosing its 1952 national ticket, when a cab pulled up and out jumped then-Senator Nixon of California. Dwight Eisenhower by this point had locked up the presidential nomination, and the question everyone was asking was: Who would Ike pick as his vice-presidential running mate? Nixon, showing his genial side, said to Tames, "Come on and have breakfast with me." He wanted to hear what Tames was learning about the vice-presidential possibilities.[7]

Tames had a "long breakfast" with Nixon during which the senator quizzed him about whom Ike would choose. Nixon, it turned out, had more than a passing interest in the topic. He wanted the job and in short order he got it. His breakfast with Tames was actually an intelligence-gathering mission.

Tames got along well with Nixon, at least when he was a senator. "Personally, he was very likable, always willing to stop and have a cup of coffee and inquire about us, [members of Tames' family]," the photographer said.[8]

Tames recalled: "By and large, I have no personal complaints about Nixon. . . . Of course, his was a face that cartoonists had a field day with. It was those jowls and that sloping nose. He was conscious of that, and the very fact that he sweated so profusely. You could get pictures of him with the long lens with the water just rolling off of him. I wonder sometimes if he had the same type of mind that I have, in the sense that it races so that your mouth cannot keep up. As a result, you stumble. And you have that detached look in your eye, where you are actually hearing your mind, which is way ahead of your mouth. That's what I thought he was doing. As a result, you could see that he was hesitant. It's a good way to study the people, through that lens."[9]

Beyond assessing individual presidents, Tames revealed an essential fact of the photographer's work, but one rarely discussed: "You're supposed to be neutral: Shoot and observe what you see. But it's practically impossible not to try to improve on situations when there's someone you favor, and not take a person who you disfavor and make him look bad, but only shoot what they're doing at that moment without trying to editorialize a little bit and improve situations. The light may not be as flattering as it would be if you move him fifteen feet away, but you just don't bother to move, you just shoot it the way it is."[10]

"I'm not a great photographer," he said. "I've been a lucky one. . . . If there was one thing that distinguished me from my colleagues, and I do consider about fifteen of them in this city to be my equal—none my better, but my equal—that none of those fifteen have the sense of history that I bring to this business, and the views that I have. That makes a difference. It's one thing to shoot something by blind luck, and another thing to shoot something knowing that what you are doing is a footnote—and sometimes a big, big step—in the notes of history."[11]

Tames died in Washington in February 1994 at the age of 75 while undergoing heart surgery. His career spanned not only a wide range of presidents but also huge advances in technology. He started with bulky Speed Graphic cameras, for which a film holder had to be changed after each picture. He retired a half-century later, when he and his colleagues were using 35mm cameras. These had high-speed shutters, sophisticated lenses, and the ability to shoot many frames with a single roll of film without the need to change rolls very often. Today's photographers have even more options for making great pictures with digital cameras.

Documentary filmmaker Ken Burns praised Tames as "posterity's spy—a mole—penetrating farther and much deeper into our political landscape and psyche than any reporter who hangs on words has."[12]

*   *   *

STANLEY TRETICK was both a visual storyteller and a master at gaining access to the president.

Tretick was born poor in Baltimore and grew up in Washington, D.C., the son of a salesman and a homemaker. He had a rough childhood and was raised for part of his youth by his mother's parents. He served in the Marines during World War II as a staff sergeant and photographer. He later worked for the Acme News Service and rose to become one of the star photographers of UPI, covering the Korean War, the White House, Congress, and presidential campaigns from 1952 to 1960, including JFK's campaign. He became even more famous as a photographer for *Look* magazine during Kennedy's presidency.

He got to know the 1960 Democratic candidate well. Kennedy and his family liked Tretick's pictures and enjoyed his sense of humor, strengthening their bond. As with other successful White House photographers, the key to Tretick's success was getting the president and first lady to trust him.[13]

Tretick was extremely persistent and creative in doing his job. One of his techniques for getting private photos of the Kennedy family was to secretly give cameras loaded with film to the children and ask them to snap pictures when they were with their parents, aunts, uncles, or siblings and then return the camera to Tretick. He made it seem like a game to the kids.

On one occasion, he gave a small Brownie to Caroline, the president's daughter, and she took many pictures while the family was vacationing at their estate in Hyannis Port, Massachusetts. She returned the camera to Tretick, who was staying nearby. But White House Press Secretary Pierre Salinger immediately found out and demanded that Tretick give him the film or Salinger would void Tretick's White House press credentials. These family moments were supposed to be off limits. Tretick handed over the Brownie. The next day, President Kennedy saw Tretick and said pleasantly, "Nice try." He admired the photographer's enterprising spirit and perseverance.[14]

Tretick was always walking a tightrope between his editors at *Look*, who were demanding "insider" photos of the popular president and his family, and the first lady, who was trying to limit access, especially to the children.

Tretick made it clear to Kennedy that he wanted to make the president look as good as possible, a departure from journalistic standards of detachment and objectivity. In a letter to JFK during the summer of 1962, Tretick wrote: "Mr. President, you've known me a long time and I have never once personally broken my word to you. I have great respect for your feeling of good photographs and am attuned to your desire of creating an image of dignity, grace, and warm human qualities in photographs. My great desire is to pictorially record your term in a series of intimate studies which would be beneficial to both you and my magazine."[15]

In a letter to Jackie Kennedy on July 12, 1964, he owned up to the complete loss of his journalistic detachment. Tretick was requesting photo access to her and her children for a special memorial issue of *Look* to mark President Kennedy's life a year after his assassination. Tretick wrote: "As for myself, I am selfish enough to want to do the photographing because there is no photographer who is as sensitive to the Kennedys as I am. No photographer who has felt them the way I have. No photographer who has loved them the way I have." He got the access, and the special memorial issue of *Look* was a big success, with lovely photos of Jackie walking in the wind on Cape Cod, dressed in a yellow t-shirt with white pants and looking confident and strong.[16]

He was an astute observer of JFK. Tretick once described him in a diary-like memo as "extremely polite, great sense of humor, quick as a rapier on the uptake, hard to top, cannot stand posing for pictures, expresses displeasure if he knows you caught him off guard in a photo that might not be to his liking and will ask you please not to use it, absolutely rebels at any photo that shows him eating or drinking." Eating and drinking pictures made him look undignified, he thought, and he hated this image. Like so many men of his generation, Jack avoided public displays of affection, including kisses and hugs with his wife. He felt they made him look too vulnerable.[17]

Kennedy didn't want any pictures taken of him playing golf. He felt that many Americans considered it a rich man's game and he might appear to be goofing off. He refused to allow many photographs aboard *Air Force One*, because it might look like a rich man's plane. He also vetoed photos of his children sitting in the chair behind his big desk in the Oval Office, contending that it would appear that he and his family were too playful and didn't show enough respect for the presidency.[18]

Both Tretick and Kennedy shared an understanding that image had become all-important to the presidency in America's increasingly visual culture. Both were intent on projecting a Kennedy image of youth, vigor, and strength.[19]

Kennedy inspected the picture credits in newspapers and magazines so he could keep track of the photographers who made him look good and those whose pictures he didn't like. He would reward the former with access and punish the latter with being left out. Tretick was constantly rewarded.[20]

Tretick also saw first-hand some of JFK's severe physical ailments, especially his back pain. It became clear to Tretick that the pain grew so severe during Kennedy's presidency that he could no longer pick up his children and he had great difficulty bending at the waist. But Tretick was sympathetic to the commander in chief and didn't call public attention to his back problems.[21] (Among his other conditions, which he kept secret from the public, were gastrointestinal ailments and Addison's disease. He took many medications, including steroids and pain-killers, to feel better.[22])

* * *

TRETICK'S MOST FAMOUS picture was one of John F. Kennedy Jr. as a toddler playing under his father's desk in the Oval Office, while his dad pretended not to notice. The story behind that photograph revealed much about how the Kennedy White House operated and what Kennedy was like as a person, especially his strong desire to enhance his favorable image with the public.

In 1963, Kennedy's third year in office, Tretick was pushing hard to do a photo spread on Kennedy and his young son, but the first lady opposed the idea. She was concerned that the kids were being used too much for political purposes and they were in the spotlight too frequently.

President Kennedy didn't share her reluctance. Quite the contrary, he was eager to generate favorable publicity by using his kids. But there were several delays after President Kennedy informally approved the idea. One problem was that John Jr. was being difficult. Tretick recalled: "The first snag was 'Irving' [Tretick's nickname for John Jr.], who was two at the time and going through some kind of kid stage in which he didn't get along with his father. It was a little embarrassing for the President when he told me why we'd have to hold off for a while."[23] The photo session was also delayed by the president's trips to England, Germany, and Ireland.

But in October 1963, Kennedy and Tretick devised a plan to have Tretick take pictures of father and son while Jackie was on vacation with her sister Lee Radziwill and friends in Greece.

"Just as soon as Jackie left town I got a call that the coast was clear, and I hightailed it to the White House," Tretick recalled.[24]

At about 7:00 p.m. John Jr., dressed in pajamas and robe, appeared in the Oval Office with the children's nanny, Maud Shaw. It was supposed to be for pre-bedroom playtime with his dad. "I'm going to my secret house," the boy shouted as he ran to the president's historic desk, made from the oak timbers of the British ship H.M.S. *Resolute*, a gift from Queen Victoria to President Rutherford B. Hayes.

John Jr. crawled under the desk at the knees of his father and then pushed open a front panel and looked out at Tretick with mischievous delight. Tretick captured the moment with his camera, and then John Jr. popped out and began skipping around the Oval Office, after which he hid inside the desk again. Tretick got it all.[25]

The president noticed Cecil Stoughton, his official White House photographer (see Chapter Two) standing in a corner, and Kennedy considerately asked Tretick if he minded if Stoughton took a few frames of John Jr. in his secret house. Tretick obliged, but Tretick's images turned out to be superior.

After he developed the film, Tretick knew immediately that this would probably be his most remembered picture. It was.[26]

When Tretick showed the proofs to JFK later in the Cabinet Room, the PR-savvy Kennedy was immediately taken by the photos of the boy in the desk. Kennedy observed, "You can't miss with these, can you, Stan?"[27]

There was a sad postscript, however. President Kennedy was assassinated the following month during a trip to Dallas, and the pictures became poignant reminders of the young leader struck down in his prime.

*   *   *

TRETICK'S REPUTATION grew over the years to such an extent that Jimmy Carter offered him the job of personal photographer at the White House after Carter was elected in 1976. As noted in Chapter Two of this book, Tretick said "No" because he didn't think Carter would grant him the access he needed.[28]

Tretick's instinct was correct. Carter wasn't interested in granting access to photographers and he didn't leave behind a compelling visual history.

Tretick died of pneumonia in 1999 at age 77 after several strokes.[29]

*   *   *

SOMETIMES A NEWS PHOTOGRAPHER'S images don't become important until long after the pictures are taken.

Time magazine's Dirck Halstead's most famous picture was almost lost to history. The photo shows President Clinton from the back as a smiling Monica Lewinsky hugs him at a rope line in Washington, D.C., where supporters were greeting the president after a fund-raiser a few days before his reelection on November 6, 1996. She had heard about the event and positioned herself at the front of a crowd to greet him personally.

When the Clinton–Lewinsky story started to break, Halstead remembered Lewinsky's face and thought he might have some pictures of her among the thousands he had taken of Clinton over the years and he asked an assistant to find them. She did, and the photo was used endlessly in the media all through Clinton's impeachment by the House and acquittal by the Senate.[30]

Halstead, a bearded, dapper man with a wry sense of humor, prided himself on his cultural sophistication and commitment to the higher goals of journalism. "I never thought of myself as a great photographer," he said. "What I am is just a storyteller. My job as a photographer was never about what I saw, but about how I fulfilled my responsibility as a photojournalist to report history."[31]

Halstead was 17 when he had his first story published in *Life* magazine, but he eventually turned to photography as a career. He covered the Guatemalan Revolution in 1954 and in 1965 became UPI's first photo bureau chief in Saigon during the Vietnam War. He returned to the United States in 1966 and later started working for *Time* magazine, where he stayed from 1972 to 2001. He covered the fall of Saigon and the end of U.S. involvement there in the mid-1970s, President Richard Nixon's historic trip to China, and the assassination attempt on President Ronald Reagan in 1981.

He eventually became the senior White House photographer for *Time*, covering Presidents Ford, Carter, Reagan, George H.W. Bush, and Clinton. He had 51 photographs published on the magazine's cover. He then became a freelance photographer and documentary video-maker and ran *Digital Journalist*, an online photojournalism magazine.[32]

Halstead had no illusions about the kind of access he got at the White House, which was relatively little compared with the staff photographers, and he acknowledges that much of what he did was visually document public-relations events created by White House strategists. "On a daily basis," he says, "I was photographing events and images that had been carefully staged by White House staff. These are called 'photo ops.' They are open to a pool of photographers covering the White House. The 'truth' in this case is in the mind of the handlers, not the photographer."[33]

And he says the business, from which he is now retired, has changed dramatically: "In the glory days of photojournalism . . . stories were often assigned by major magazines and newspapers that had almost unlimited amounts of money to spend. That means travel around the world for the photographers and logistical support in far-flung areas. Photographers would travel with wads of cash in their pockets, thanks to advances. All of that is gone now. Today's photographers are like hobos. They somehow manage to get from place to place, but it is on very tight budgets. And there is rarely a payoff. Magazines and newspapers have no space to devote to in-depth stories. Even TV is hurting. The evolution of the backpack journalist takes place at the expense of a two- or three-person crew. News today on TV is told through talk shows. You don't have to send those people anywhere."[34]

*   *   *

BERNIE BOSTON showed the extent to which personal chemistry between a photographer and a president can result in rare access for a White House photojournalist. Boston was a long-time Washington-based cameraman for the *Los Angeles Times* and, before that, the *Washington Star*. He covered every president from Lyndon Johnson to Bill Clinton—seven in all.[35]

"A primary aim of his work was to distill and portray the intimate character of each president, not the well-honed persona specially designed for media consumption," wrote Therese Mulligan, professor and chair of the Rochester Institute of Technology School of Photographic Arts and Sciences, which published a catalog of Boston's work in 2006. (He had graduated from RIT's Department of Photographic Technology in 1955.[36])

He got especially close to President George H.W. Bush who, Boston recalled, "used to whisper things in my ear. I would know where he was going before anyone else did." Boston claimed he had more access to President Bush than anyone in Washington.[37]

He said he once walked without an official escort across the broad expanse of the South Lawn of the White House to the street, a security breach. A Secret Service agent later explained to him that the president's guards recognized Boston's trademark cowboy hat and let him proceed across the greensward.[38]

Boston was known for playing pranks. Once he and a few friends loaded a colleague's camera bag with lead weights, which the victim carried around with him for hours until he realized what had happened.[39]

Boston also captured Chelsea Clinton picking up her father Bill Clinton's notes after they dropped during his 1993 inauguration.[40]

Boston's most famous photograph was a picture taken on October 21, 1967 of an anti-Vietnam war protester placing carnations in the rifle barrels of soldiers guarding the Pentagon during a massive demonstration against the war. He worked for the *Washington Star* at the time. His editors weren't as impressed with the picture as he was and they buried it inside the paper. But others were very taken with the image, which Boston called "Flower Power," and it won second place for the Pulitzer Prize in news photography for 1967. It has been widely reproduced since then as a vivid example of the divisions and contradictions in America during the 1960s.

Boston experienced this turmoil personally in getting the photo. When he returned to his car after covering the protest, he found his tires slashed but noticed that someone had also placed a bouquet of flowers under his windshield wipers.[41]

Boston's parents gave him a Kodak Brownie camera when he was 7, and this sparked his interest in photography. Born in Washington, D.C., he served as the photographer for his high school newspaper and yearbook, worked as a freelance photographer as an adult and then took a job at the *Dayton Daily News*. He joined the *Washington Star* in June 1967 and eventually became the newspaper's director of photography, a remarkable achievement because African Americans such as Boston were rare in photojournalism at the time. He remained at the *Star* until it closed in 1981 and then he set up the photo department at the *Los Angeles Times* Washington Bureau. He retired from the *LA Times* in 1993.[42]

Boston died at age 74 in January 2008.

* * *

DIANA WALKER was another star on the White House beat. She worked as a *Time* White House photographer for 20 years, covering the presidency along with fellow *Time* photojournalist Dirck Halstead. One of her achievements was accumulating a photo archive of Hillary Clinton, initially as the spouse of Democratic presidential candidate Bill Clinton in his successful 1992 campaign, as the first lady for eight years, then as U.S. senator from New York, an unsuccessful presidential candidate in 2008, and President Barack Obama's secretary of state from 2009 to 2013.

"To have the opportunity to photograph somebody for 20 years is such a gift to a photographer," Walker once said. "Hillary Clinton, it seems to me, means a lot to women today. I think that she represents the opportunities for women in our country."[43]

One of her most famous pictures shows Clinton as secretary of state perusing her BlackBerry aboard a military plane headed for Tripoli, Libya, in 2011. Clinton is wearing sunglasses, making her stand out from aides and others bustling in the background. The sunglasses seem to be a mask of sorts that sets her apart, and she seems oblivious to everyone around her as she presumably scans her messages. "And I thought, wow, it's a strong picture," Walker said later.[44]

Working on a 2014 book of photographs about Clinton, *Hillary: The Photographs of Diana Walker*, she took the same approach she used in covering the White House day to day for *Time*. "I was trying to be as discreet as possible," she said. "I hardly ever spoke unless spoken to—I was not there for myself and I wanted them to ignore me." This was the same approach pioneered by Okamoto, Lyndon Johnson's chief photographer and emulated by the best White House photographers ever since. Walker added: "I used to rewind the film looking down and away from them so that I wouldn't catch their eye or make them think they had to speak to me."[45]

Walker was born in Washington, D.C., and grew up there, growing increasingly interested in the politics and government that dominated the capital. She attended Briarcliff College, majoring in drama, and worked for a decade at her mother's dress shop in the posh neighborhood of Georgetown in the 1970s before attempting to make photography, her hobby, into her occupation. While she and her husband raised two sons, Walker became a freelance photographer and opened a photography business with a friend which they called "I am a Camera," taking pictures at weddings and bar mitzvahs. "I always say if I lived in Cleveland I might have spent my life photographing horses and flowers and children and maybe the Chamber of Commerce," she said. But Walker was hired by the *Washington Monthly* magazine, which gave her entrée into the larger world of politicians, government officials, and journalists in the capital.[46]

She was hired as a contract photographer for *Time* in 1979 and was assigned to cover the White House in 1984, after covering Democratic presidential nominee Walter Mondale's unsuccessful campaign that year. During 20 years as a contract White House photographer for *Time*, she covered Ronald Reagan, George H.W. Bush, Bill Clinton, and George W. Bush.[47]

It wasn't easy for a woman as a White House photographer back then. Her male colleagues often ignored her, and she wasn't taken as seriously by White House staffers as she should have been. She remembers feeling "removed and irrelevant" in those early days on the beat. But through hard work, perseverance, and talent, she was accepted.[48]

She experienced the same fundamental highs and lows as any photojournalist assigned to the White House. She said that, most of the time, the job was very monotonous and tiresome (and it still is). "A normal day at the White House for someone who covers the White House is that you call the night before to a [press office] recording, and you find out what the president's plans are," Walker recalled. "So, you can kind of judge what your day is going to be like. And you have to be at the White House early and you sit there, and you wait for a photo op in the Oval Office. We go in, and we crouch down, and we take the picture of the two of them [the president and visitor] sitting in front of the fireplace that you've seen a million times. And if you're smart, you turn around and see who else is in the room, and snap that too, so you have something different with them and then you leave the room. It all lasts maybe 60 seconds. Then you might have a luncheon to photograph in the East Room or a speech the president's going to make on the South Lawn. That's what a normal day is like."[49]

Walker became one of Bill and Hillary Clinton's favored photographers. She got remarkable access. As she waited for the first family to leave the White House for Clinton's second inauguration in January 1997, she was on the State Floor of the Residence, and began snapping pictures of first daughter Chelsea walking up to her mother. Chelsea opened her coat and revealed that she was wearing a short skirt. Walker's photo captured the first lady's chagrin on seeing her daughter's outfit.[50]

"If you're doing behind-the-scenes work, you've put in a request to be with the president [or other senior official] at a certain day for a certain something," Walker recalled. "I'd go in quietly, shoot some pictures and leave. If I'm doing a cover shoot or something exciting like that, I would bring in an assistant, bring in lights and set it all up. The president would walk in. I would photograph him in a certain environment that I thought out and figured out. And I'd do it for as long as they'd let me do it, as many rolls as I could get off. And when I'd change my film, I'd look away 'cause I was always so afraid someone was going to tell me it was time to leave."[51]

She also refused to divulge what she heard on such occasions to *Time* reporters for their stories, or any other reporters for that matter, even when they pressed her for the information. This was actually common in recent years as photographers decided that their access was more important than passing along some tidbit overheard at an event. Walker's argument was that she had to keep what she heard confidential or her entire access would be restricted. Her decision to remain professionally "deaf" when working behind the scenes generated some arguments with her colleagues at *Time* but she continued to get special access at the White House.[52]

* * *

LARRY DOWNING, a long-time stalwart of the photographic press corps at the White House, started his White House career in 1978 when Jimmy Carter was president. He worked for United Press International, then *Newsweek*, and, starting in 1997, for Reuters, and provided an insight into the demands of covering the presidency. Asked what advice he had for aspiring photojournalists, he said: "That is answered with a simple question. . . . Are you willing to chase a dream at any cost? Photography is not a job or a career or even a fun hobby. Living with a camera is the product of a burning passion which flames hotter and brighter than anything else in your life. Thoughts of how much money you will make aren't even an issue. Realize that most successful photojournalists are not blessed with immediate talent, but are born with that uncontrolled desire to learn and challenge themselves before becoming a great photographer."[53]

Interviewed in 2015 after nearly four decades covering the White House, Downing said: "My responsibilities for Reuters now center on coverage of the White House and of the U.S. president. I started my Washington photojournalism career assigned to President Jimmy Carter 38 years ago and am now assigned to Barack Obama. That's a long time covering one beat and is artistically challenging but the physical demands get harder and harder with the passing of each year. My assignment requires that I accompany the current U.S president wherever he decides to go, both domestically and internationally. The rigorous precision of the schedule remains at an unforgiving high speed and the strenuous demands of six, seven, or eight days in a strange country are brutal. That wears everyone down. I'm 62 year old and still running with the young 'go fast' photographers and it hurts."[54]

He said one of the high points for him was being selected by White House officials to be part of a media "pool" to accompany President George W. Bush during a Thanksgiving holiday to leave the president's Texas ranch and secretly visit U.S. soldiers in Iraq. Downing said it was a great honor to have been chosen but added that he got some perspective on what really impressed the troops. Downing asked a soldier waiting in a mess hall who he was expecting, and the man replied with a smile, "The Dallas Cowboy cheerleaders are coming." That was apparently the rumor. It isn't known how disappointed the soldier was when the commander in chief walked in.[55]

In 1987, *Newsweek* editors were seeking a cover photo of retired Air Force Major General Richard Secord to illustrate a story about an arms-for-hostages deal, known as the Iran–Contra scandal, then erupting. *Newsweek* photographer Downing went to Secord's office in suburban Virginia, and began the waiting game. Suddenly, Secord arrived in a black Mercedes. As Secord began walking to his office, Downing was a few paces behind and called to the retired general. Secord didn't respond and kept walking. Just as Secord reached the door, Downing said, "Sir, you dropped something." Secord felt in his pocket and turned to look around. He hadn't dropped anything at all. But at that point. Downing began shooting pictures and he got the *Newsweek* cover image.[56]

Downing was known for his irreverence and practical jokes. He liked to quiet a room of people waiting for the president with a loud "Shh-hhh" even when there was no reason for it, trying to throw the dignitaries off balance and confuse them. It generally worked. I can recall him amid foreign reporters and photographers—his competitors on international trips—shouting suddenly, "Here we go!" This prompted the other journalists to line up or rush toward a door they found to be locked. When they realized it was a false warning, his competitors would return to their seats, embarrassed, and perplexed, which is the way Downing wanted them.

On a serious note, Downing said: "A photojournalist's reputation for accuracy is more important than any image; once that trust is violated it evaporates and his or her career as a truth teller is over. Our readership deserves the truth."[57]

Downing adds: "I'll always remember seeing the first photograph that triggered my desire to be a photojournalist: the amazing picture of East German soldier Conrad Schumann leaping over the razor wire of the early Berlin Wall. The picture was shot by photographer Peter Leibing and seen around the world. It needed no caption; it spoke loudly enough. I knew, after studying that dramatic moment, I would one day be a news photographer."[58]

Notes

1. "George Tames, Washington Photographer for the New York Times," Oral History Interviews, Senate Historical Office, Washington, D.C., May 16, 1988, www.senate.gov/artandhistory/history/oral_history/George_Tames.htm.
2. Ibid.
3. Ibid.
4. Ibid.
5. David Binder, "George Tames, Photographer, Dies at 75," *New York Times*, Feb. 24, 1994, www.nytimes.com/1994/02/24/obituaries-george-tames-photographer-dies-at-75.html.
6. Ibid.; see also George Tames, *Eye on Washington: The Presidents Who've Known Me*, New York: HarperCollins Publishers, 1990.

7. "George Tames, Washington Photographer for the New York Times."

8. Ibid.

9. Ibid.

10. Ibid.

11. Ibid.

12. Binder, "George Tames."

13. Kitty Kelley, *Capturing Camelot: Stanley Tretick's Iconic Images of the Kennedys*, New York: Thomas Dunne Books, 2012, pp. 4, 12, 19.

14. Ibid., p. 102.

15. Ibid., p. 109.

16. Ibid., p. 179.

17. Ibid., pp. 24, 33.

18. Ibid., pp. 142, 162, 166.

19. Ibid., p. 73.

20. Ibid., p. 42.

21. Ibid., p. 73.

22. Robert Dallek, interview with author, Sept. 1, 2016.

23. Kelley, *Capturing Camelot*, p. 136.

24. Ibid., p. 141.

25. Ibid.

26. Nick Ravo, "Stanley Tretick, 77: Photographer of Kennedys at the White House," *New York Times*, July 20, 1999, www.nytimes.com/1999/07/20/us/Stanley-tretick-77-photographer-of-kennedys-at-the-white house.

27. Kelley, *Capturing Camelot*, p. 141.

28. Ravo, "Stanley Tretick"; see also Kelley, *Capturing Camelot*, p. 221.

29. Ibid.

30. Terry Sullivan, "How Film Saved an Infamous Photo", *Professional Artist Magazine*, July 30, 2015, www.professionalartistmag.com/2015/jul/30/how-film-saved-now-infamous-clintonlewinsky-photo; see also "Bill and Monica," *Famous Picture Collection*, June 1, 2013, www.famouspictures.org/bill-and-monica.

31. Dirck Halstead, interview with Svetlana Bachevanova, *FotoEvidence*, July 6, 2016, www.fotoevidence.com/interview-dirck-halstead.

32. "Dirck Halstead: Biography," Briscoe Center for American History, *Photojournalism and the American Presidency: Reading America's Photos*, www.cah.utexas.edu/photojournalism/photojournalist_info.php?nickname=halstead.

33. Halstead, interview with Svetlana Bachevanova.

34. Ibid.

35. Therese Mulligan, "A Tribute to Photojournalist and Alumnus Bernie Boston," *News & Events* (Rochester Institute of Technology), Feb. 7, 2008, www.rit.edu/news/newsevents/2008/Feb01/story.php?file=v.

36. Scott Bureau, "Exhibit Shows 'Everyday with the President' through Lens of RIT Alumnus Bernie Boston," *University News* (Rochester Institute of Technology), Nov. 2, 2016, www.rit.edu/news/story.php?id=57869.

37. Alice Ashe, "Bernie Boston: View Finder," *Curio Magazine* (James Madison University), 2005, p. 13, https://web.archive.org/web/20090920062711/http://www.curiomagazine.com:80/archives/2005/images/boston.pdf.

38. Ibid.

39. Adam Bernstein, "Bernie Boston, 74: Took Iconic 1967 Photograph," *Washington Post*, Jan. 24, 2008, www.washingtonpost.com/wp-dyn/content/article/2008/01/23/AR2008012303713.html

40. Ibid.

41. Ibid.

42. Ibid.

43. Brianna Keilar and Rachel Streitfeld, "Meet the Woman who Took this Photo, Captured Private Clinton Moments," *CNN*, Apr. 10, 2015.

44. Ibid.

45. "LightBox: On Our Radar: An Intimate Portrait of Hillary Clinton in Photographs," *Time*, Oct. 23, 2014, www.time.com/3590171/an-intimate-portrait-of-Hillary-Clinton-in-photographs.

46. Frank Van Riper, "The Public and Private Diana Walker," *Washington Post*, www.washingtonpost.com/wp-srv/photo/essays/vanRiper/030306.htm

47. Keilar and Streitfeld, "Meet the Woman who Took this Photo."

48. Van Riper, "The Public and Private Diana Walker."

49. Diana Walker, "A Photojournalist's Normal Day at the White House: Transcript," Briscoe Center for American History, *Photojournalism and the American Presidency: Reading America's Photos*, www.cah.utexas.edu/photojournalism/transcript.php?media_id=3.

50. Dennis Brack, *Presidential Picture Stories: Behind the Cameras at the White House*, Washington, D.C.: Dennis Brack, Inc., 2013, p. 137.

51. Walker, "A Photojournalist's Normal Day at the White House."

52. Van Riper, "The Public and Private Diana Walker.".

53. "Larry Downing, WHNPA's 2015 Lifetime Achievement Award Recipient, on Career as Photographer," *Reuters Best: Journalist Spotlight*, Feb. 18, 2015, www.reutersbest.com/articles/view/3948/journalist-spotlight-larry-downing-whnpas-2015-lifetime-achievement-award-recipient-on-career-as-photographer.

54. Ibid.

55. Ibid.

56. Brack, *Presidential Picture Stories*, pp. 191–192.

57. "Larry Downing," *Reuters: The Wider Image*, July 6, 2016, https://widerimage.reuters.com/photographer/larry-downing

58. Ibid.

CHAPTER FIFTEEN
THE ULTIMATE INSIDERS' EVOLVING TOOLS
OF THE TRADE

Technology has vastly transformed White House photography over the years, making images of the president more accessible than ever. This has contributed to the celebrity of the presidents and made them extremely familiar to Americans and people around the world.

The success of photojournalism has always depended on technological improvements. News photography was greatly enhanced in the 1920s, for example, by the introduction of highly portable cameras containing film that held negative images that could be enlarged. "Photography is driven by technology, always has been," writes photo historian Ross Collins, "because, more than any other visual art, photography is built around machines and, at least until recently, chemistry. By the 1990s photojournalists were already shooting mostly color, and seldom making actual prints, but used computer technology to scan film directly into the design. And by the beginning of the new millennium, photojournalists were no longer using film; digital photography had become universal, both faster and cheaper in an industry preoccupied with both speed and profit."[1]

Daguerreotypes, introduced in the 1830s, were visually clear and focused, but not reproducible for news purposes. The wet plate collodion process in 1851 made photographic images with clarity, reproducibility, and relative speed. This technique was used to report the Crimean War, and later the American Civil War. Dry plates followed in 1871, making the equipment for developing pictures more portable and efficient. Roll film came into use in 1888 with George Eastman's Kodak camera, making multiple exposures easier than ever. The first snapshots on roll film were 2½-inch circular images.

Flash powder was used for the lighting necessary starting in 1880; stop-motion shutters in the early 1900s; the flash bulb came along in 1920, followed by portable 35mm Leica-type cameras in 1924. Harold Edgerton developed the flash strobe in the 1930s. But all these pre-digital processes required silver—tons of it. In 1936, 5 tons of 42-pound silver bars were shipped to Eastman Kodak's plant in Rochester, N.Y.[2]

* * *

IN THE mid-1800s, the wet-plate collodion process began to catch on as a way to make pictures. This involved a complicated procedure involving toxic chemicals to process images one at a time. It was also tedious for the subject of the pictures, including presidents. They had to sit still while the photographic plates, placed in a primitive form of camera, were exposed to the light, sometimes for 20 seconds or more. Clamps were used to steady a subject's head for the long exposures.[3]

During the 1860s, photographs were becoming popular across the country. Americans en masse started buying pocket-sized albumen prints, called "cartes de visite," which contained images of family members or public figures. Thousands of them were reproduced of President Abraham Lincoln, and this added to his renown.[4]

Technology improved in the succeeding decades, including the invention of more effective and convenient portable cameras, use of the flash-powder gun, a wide variety of flash bulbs for cameras, and photo transmissions by wire.[5]

In 1912, the 4×5 Speed Graphic camera was introduced. This device used sheet film, placed in a holder in the back of the camera after every exposure. The camera contained a cloth curtain focal plane shutter and rail-based bellows on a carriage that could be folded into a compact box. Over the years, a front leaf shutter improved the original design, as did other improvements. Says photojournalist Dennis Brack: "The 4×5 Speed Graphic was the sweetheart of press photographers for sixty years. At one time sixteen of the twenty Pulitzer Prize-winning photographs were made with this bulky but durable picture-making machine.

The Speed Graphic became the identifying symbol of the news photographer." Eventually, Rolliflexs, Nikons, and Leicas replaced the Speed Graphic with the news photographers.[6]

These cameras delivered negatives of excellent quality, making it easy for an operator to take good pictures without constantly worrying about exposure and focusing. But fully automatic exposure systems and automatic-focus cameras didn't become commonplace until the 1980s.[7]

In 1925, the invention of the Leica, the first 35mm camera, in Germany, began the era of modern photojournalism, according to Ross Collins of North Dakota State University in Fargo. "Before this," Collins says, "a photo of professional quality required bulky equipment; after this, photographers could go just about anywhere and take photos unobtrusively, without bulky lights or tripods. The difference was dramatic, [from] primarily posed photos, with people aware of the photographer's presence, to new, natural photos of people as they really lived."[8]

Today's photographers owe a big debt to an obscure German immigrant named Erich Salomon

In 1928, when news photography was still in its infancy and newspaper editors were beginning to add photo staffs, Salomon changed the direction of photojournalism forever. Salomon, a 60-ish former lawyer and banker and aficionado of the growing photography fad, acquired one of the unobtrusive new Ermanox "detective" cameras and set out to become, essentially, the first paparazzo. His camera did not require special lighting and could function effectively in the illumination available at public events and ceremonies. Under the nom de plume "Cyclops," Salomon's "candid" shots of the good and the great at ease were published in the London *Graphic* illustrated weekly, causing a sensation and inspiring news photographers across the Atlantic in America.[9]

Fortune magazine in 1931 imported the courtly, ingratiating Salomon to the U.S., to take "candids" at an international conference. President Hoover was not amused, and an aide complained that the "King of the Indiscreets" had "slopped one over on the boss."[10] The candid technique was adopted by other influential photographers of the time, including Alfred Eisenstadt and Lucien Aigner, and by news photographers around the world.[11] Salomon died at the Auschwitz concentration camp in 1944.

The advent of digital cameras was another huge leap, making it possible to capture more spontaneous images and transmit them almost instantaneously through wireless internet connections. Digital chips can store a thousand images, freeing photographers from the limits imposed by limited exposures on every roll of film. These changes also allowed digital photographs to be taken and distributed by small media organizations and even individuals and bloggers, eroding the dominance of large news organizations.[12]

Photography and photojournalism have been democratized.[13] Anyone can be a photographer, or at least anyone can now take pictures easily and distribute them simply and cheaply. The ubiquity and popularity of "selfies" and other photos taken with smart phones proves the point.

"Digital did deliver pictures to newspapers fast," photojournalist Dennis Brack writes. "Ron Edmonds of the Associated Press used a Nikon QV-1010T to transmit images of George H.W. Bush taking the presidential oath on January 20, 1989, directly from the camera stand. The [news] competition used film, running it to a trailer on the Capitol grounds, developing the film, scanning, and transmitting. The QV-1010T allowed the AP to beat their competition by thirty minutes."

"By the second decade of the twenty-first century, transmitting images direct from the camera had become common," Brack adds. "Generally at the White House or when the president traveled, the news photographer would make a few frames of the president speaking, put the card with the digital images into a laptop, edit or select the best frame, then send it along with a prepared caption. While the photographer transmitted the images, he or she kept one eye on the president to make sure that a good picture was not missed.

"Doug Mills of the *New York Times* sent his images directly to his picture desk via an ftp [file transfer protocol] site [an early method of transmitting data directly to a network.]. When Mandel Ngan of AFP received the Nikon D4, he learned that each had its own ftp site, allowing him to send his images instantly to Agence France Press editors. 'Who knows what is coming tomorrow?' "[14]

Notes

1. Ross Collins, "A Brief History of Photography and Photojournalism," North Dakota State University, COMM 330, Basic Photography for Mass Media, Class Resources, www.ndsu.edu/pubweb/-rcollins/242photojournalism/historyofphoto graphy.html.

2. Gary Haynes, "History of Photo Technology Spans the Globe," *Chicago Tribune*, Nov. 4, 1983, p. ND29. For an extensive history, see Richard Maxwell, *Greening the Media*, Oxford: Oxford University Press, 2012.

3. Dennis Brack, *Presidential Picture Stories: Behind the Cameras at the White House*, Washington, D.C.: Dennis Brack, Inc., 2013, pp. 196–197.
4. Ibid., p. 199.
5. Ibid., pp. 204–207.
6. Ibid., pp. 210, 211.
7. Collins, "A Brief History of Photography and Photojournalism."
8. Ibid.
9. "The Press: Candid Camera," *Time*, Feb. 17, 1930.
10. "Democracy at its Contradictory Best," *Oshkosh Daily Northwestern*, Nov. 21, 1931; see also "International: Roi de Indiscrets," *Time*, Nov. 9, 1931.
11. Margaret Luke, "Lucien Aigner, 97: Pioneer in Candid News Photography," *New York Times*, Apr. 3, 1999.
12. "A Brief History of Photojournalism," *Photography Schools*, Feb. 24, 2016, www.photography-schools.com/photojournalismhistory.htm
13. "Photojournalism"—the combination of photography and journalism—was a term coined by historian Frank Luther Mott, former dean of the University of Missouri School of Journalism (Collins, "A Brief History of Photography and Photojournalism").
14. Brack, *Presidential Picture Stories*, pp. 221–222.

Epilogue
The Future of White House Photography

Unfortunately, it likely will be more difficult than ever for photographers to provide fresh insights into the president and the first family during the Trump administration. The trend is toward more propaganda by the White House, more hostility toward the Fourth Estate, and more limitations on the role of the news media in disseminating information and images.

An important shift toward public relations came under President Barack Obama and his chief photographer Pete Souza. This was attempted under other regimes such as those of John F. Kennedy, Richard Nixon, and Ronald Reagan, but it reached new levels under Obama.

Souza seemed eager to become the nation's alpha White House photographer—the most prominent image maker in the history of the presidency. As pointed out earlier in this book, he was an excellent photographer with extensive experience. Adding to his impact, he served at a time when technological advances, such as digital photography and the internet, gave him many new options for making and conveying images of the president and his family. Using Facebook, Twitter, Instagram, Flickr, and other social media, Souza could easily disseminate huge numbers of White House images directly to the public without having to go through the mainstream media. He did this very effectively with Obama's full approval. My prediction is that President Trump will eventually do the same.

Souza also substantially limited the access of news photographers to presidential events, leaving news organizations with the choice of using Souza's handouts or no photos at all. This caused outrage in the news world. It wasn't a question of whether Souza's pictures were of high quality—they were. It was a matter of whether the White House photo office was turning into an ever-more-influential public-relations enterprise—it was. I expect Trump to shut out the news photographers in the same way.

Souza also pioneered the use of the White House website to disseminate his pictures. He sent out a stream of images day after day, reaching millions of Americans, often with his own personal explanation of what each photo showed and how he got the shot. I expect this is another area where Trump will imitate Obama and bypass the media.

"No one doubted Souza's integrity, but his photographs were being edited and released by the White House press office," wrote news photographer Dennis Brack. "The conflict had two parts: first, most were public relations photographs showing the Obamas at work, at play, and so on. The photographs were excellent. Perhaps it was the beautiful family. But the released pictures looked like the photographs used in banks or in soft drink advertisements. Second, by having official photographers take the pictures, the press office denied access to events that the press photographers would normally have covered."[1]

Olivier Knox, chief Washington correspondent for Yahoo! News and incoming president of the White House Correspondents' Association in 2018–2019, expressed concern about the Executive Branch's push for excessive government control over official information, including visual history. Knox expressed fear that the First Amendment's guarantee of a free and unfettered press was eroding. "I don't want the first draft of history to be a photograph by the official White House photographer whose job it is to make the president look good," Knox said. "I want news photographers to be at that event."[2]

Sharon Farmer, former chief photographer for President Bill Clinton during his second term, agreed that Souza shouldn't have limited the news photographers' access so severely. "There's more than one way of thinking, visually included," she told me, and other photographers could have added diversity to the images coming out of the White House—and this would have benefited everyone. There would have been "a more rounded view with different sets of eyes, different perspectives," Farmer said.[3]

Farmer added that in an austere era of cuts in news budgets, Souza might have actually cost jobs for some photographers who didn't get White House assignments because of Souza's restrictive policies.

Souza also broke the mold in another way—by entering the partisan battlefield after he left his White House job. As Trump's presidency began in 2017, one of the counterweights to his brash approach to governing was Souza's photography from the previous eight years. Obama's former image maker continued to circulate his pictures on social media even after exiting the White House with Obama. His goal was to draw a contrast between what Trump was doing and the way Obama handled similar situations, and Obama always looked better in Sousa's photos. After news reports emerged of President Trump's combative phone conversations with foreign leaders, including Australian Prime Minister Malcolm Turnbull, Souza posted a photo on Instagram of Obama talking pleasantly with Turnbull and New Zealand Prime Minister John Key at an international conference in Laos during September 2016. The picture illustrated Obama's commitment to conciliation and contrasted with Trump's emphasis on confrontation.[4]

As Michael Shaw noted in the *Columbia Journalism Review*, "Souza's commentary is an example of photography rising to new heights as an editorial form. The photos . . . are designed to draw blood without uttering a word. As visual 'one-liners,' we instantly know what they mean. In many of his other Instagram posts, I sense Souza aims to illuminate a deeper shift in attitude or mood between Obama's leadership and what is shaping up under Trump. Many of these images put a larger frame around what has been lost."[5]

* * *

ALL THIS was part of the overall erosion of the mainstream media's influence at the White House. I have covered the presidency since 1986, and it has been a gradual downward path for the media during those three decades, as one president after another narrowed the access, questioned the fairness of the media, undermined the Fourth Estate's credibility, and attempted, with increasing success, to bypass the White House press corps.

More important, the public has lost faith in mainstream journalism. We are considered out of touch with everyday America, according to a number of opinion polls. A Gallup survey found in September 2015 that only 40 percent of the public trusted the media "to report the news fully, accurately and fairly." This was the lowest rating since at least the 1990s.[6]

The 2016 presidential campaign hastened the decline of the media because the Fourth Estate's legitimacy was under constant attack. Both

Trump, the Republican nominee, and Hillary Clinton, the Democratic candidate, shared a deep cynicism about journalism. Neither of them saw the mainstream media as a straightforward conduit of information to the public, but rather a hostile force, a special interest to be manipulated, circumvented, and criticized. Clearly, the animosity toward the media was bipartisan.

Ed Kashi, an independent photographer writing in *Time* in November 2016, observed that photojournalists needed to ponder why their work didn't have as much impact on the public as it had in past years. It certainly didn't have the influence of social media, which was used effectively by Trump to dominate coverage and shape voter perceptions. "I'm increasingly wondering how and why some of the best photographic work doesn't seem to move the needle on public understanding, with none of it rising to the surface in the way it has in the past," Kashi wrote. "Perhaps Trump was just too loud and the media too tone deaf."[7]

Referring to photojournalists as "visual storytellers," Kashi added: "Never in my lifetime has there been such a vastly different interpretation of the facts. The blame does not lie squarely on our shoulders— what with social media algorithms that send us into echo chambers of our own beliefs—but now that we know the extent of the damage, we have a responsibility to act and change. It is alarming that even though we live in a time where access to information is easier than it has ever been before, so many people live within a closed loop of falsehoods."[8]

During the campaign Clinton wasn't as hostile to the media as Trump, at least overtly, but she had felt antagonistic toward mainstream journalists for many years. She believed that reporters and photographers were forever playing "gotcha" to force errors and embarrass her. This dated back to her husband Bill Clinton's 1992 run for president, her eight years as first lady from 1993 to 2001, and her unsuccessful bid for the White House in 2008. During her 2016 presidential campaign, she held few news conferences (although she did grant a modest number of interviews to selected journalists), and she reduced media access, including access for news photographers. This hurt her campaign by making it appear she had something to hide, and this in turn intensified public mistrust of her.

Trump was one of the worst media bashers in the history of presidential campaigns, exceeding the vitriol of Republican Vice President Spiro

Agnew during Richard Nixon's administration. Not content with attacking journalists as dishonest and despicable, sometimes by name, Trump banned a dozen news organizations, including the *Washington Post* and Politico, so they could no longer cover his rallies and other events in a normal fashion. The reporters found ways around this edict, such as by entering Trump events along with the general public rather than through press entrances. Sometimes this worked; sometimes it didn't. But the bans intensified the bitter relationship between Trump and the Fourth Estate, including photographers. Trump made matters worse by directly and regularly blasting what he called the "corrupt media" and stirring up fury among conservatives who had long harbored resentment toward mainstream journalists. For their part, media outlets including the *New York Times* said Trump was spreading falsehoods and lying. Leading journalists pledged to serve as truth squads to expose Trump's distortions.

When Trump became president, the hostility intensified. Trump attacked news organizations as "the enemy of the American people." This included photojournalists, who felt distrusted and were excluded from important presidential moments. And journalists pushed back with a series of stories and photos that embarrassed the new administration, inflaming Trump even more.

This animosity is likely to continue throughout Trump's presidency, and will probably get worse as each side tries to delegitimize the other. Sadly, millions of Americans won't know what or whom to believe. And this brave new world won't be good for anyone.

Notes

1. Dennis Brack, *Presidential Picture Stories: Behind the Cameras at the White House*, Washington, D.C.: Dennis Brack, Inc., 2013, pp. 146–147.
2. "Olivier Knox on Ben Rhodes, Foreign Policy, and White House Correspondents' Dinner," *The Federalist*, May 9, 2016, www.thefederalist.com/2016/05/09/olivier-knox-on-ben-rhodes-foreign-policy-and-white-house-correspondents-dinner.
3. Sharon Farmer, interview with author, Aug. 18, 2016.
4. "Former WH Photog Pete Souza Trolls Trump with Contrasting Obama Pics," *CBS News*, Feb. 15, 2017, www.cbsnews.com/news/pete-souzas-instagram-photo-commentary-on-trump.
5. Michael Shaw, "Former White House Photographer Grabs Headlines with Instagram Sass," *Columbia Journalism Review*, Feb. 15, 2017, www.cjr.org/analysis/pete-souza-obama-trump.php.

6. Emily Bazelon, "Stop the Presses," *New York Times Magazine*, Nov. 27, 2016, p. 52.

7. Ed Kashi with Gabriel Ellison-Scowcroft, "Lightbox Opinion: What Trump's Win Says about the State of Photography in America," *Time*, Nov 21, 2016, www.time.com/4578752/trump-America-photojournalism.

8. Ibid.

SELECTED READINGS

Atkins, Ollie, *The White House Years: Triumph and Tragedy*, Chicago: Playboy Press, 1977.

—— and Charles Baptie, *Camera . . . : On Assignment*, Fairfax, Va.: Fairfax Publishing Society, 1957.

Blumenthal, Sidney, and Thomas Byrne Edsall, eds., *The Reagan Legacy*, New York: Pantheon Books, 1988.

Boller, Paul F., Jr., *Presidential Diversions: Presidents at Play from George Washington to George W. Bush*, Orlando, Fla.: Harcourt Books, 2007.

Brack, Dennis, *Presidential Picture Stories: Behind the Cameras at the White House*, Washington, D.C.: Dennis Brack, Inc., 2013.

Bredar, John, *The President's Photographer: Fifty Years Inside the Oval Office*, Washington, D.C.: National Geographic Society, 2010.

Brinkley, Douglas, ed., *The Reagan Diaries*, New York: HarperCollins Publisher, 2007.

Broder, David S., *Behind the Front Page*, New York: Simon & Schuster, 1987.

Bush, George, *All the Best, George Bush: My Life in Letters and Other Writings*, New York: Scribner, 1999.

Cannon, Lou, *President Reagan: The Role of a Lifetime*, New York, Public Affairs, 1991.

Carter, Jimmy, *Keeping Faith: Memoirs of a President*, Fayetteville: University of Arkansas Press 1995.

—— *White House Diary*, New York: Farrar, Straus and Giroux, 2010.

Clinton, Bill, *My Life*, New York: Alfred A. Knopf, 2004.

Cooper, Andrew F., *Celebrity Diplomacy*, Boulder, Colo.: Paradigm Publishers, 2008.

Cronin, Thomas, *On the Presidency: Teacher, Soldier, Shaman, Pol*, Boulder, Colo.: Paradigm Publishers, 2009.

Dallek, Robert, *Flawed Giant: Lyndon Johnson and his Times, 1961–1973*, New York: Oxford University Press, 1998.

Deakin, James, *Straight Stuff*, New York: Morrow, 1984.

Deaver, Michael K., *Nancy: A Portrait of my Years with Nancy Reagan*, New York: William Morrow, 2004.

Dickson, Paul, *Words From the White House: Words and Phrases Coined or Popularized by America's Presidents*, New York: Walker & Company, 2013.

Draper, Eric, *Front Row Seat: A Photographic Portrait of the Presidency of George W. Bush*, Austin: University of Texas Press, 2013.

Drury, Allen, and Fred Maroon, *Courage and Hesitation: Notes and Photographs of the Nixon Administration*, Garden City, N.Y.: Doubleday & Company, 1971.

Duffy, Michael, and Dan Goodgame, *Marching in Place: The Status Quo Presidency of George Bush*, New York: Simon & Schuster, 1992.

Eisenhower, Julie Nixon, ed., *Eye on Nixon: A Photographic Study of the President and the Man*, New York: Hawthorn Books, 1972.

Faber, John, *Great News Photos and the Stories Behind Them*, New York: Dover Publications, Inc., 1978.

Feeney, Mark, *Nixon at the Movies*, Chicago: University of Chicago Press, 2004.

Fitzwater, Marlin, *Call the Briefing! Reagan and Bush, Sam and Helen: A Decade with Presidents and the Press*, New York: Times Books, 1995.

Fleischer, Ari, *Taking Heat: The President, the Press, and my Years in the White House*, New York: William Morrow, 2005.

Germond, Jack W., and Jules Witcover, *Whose Broad Stripes and Bright Stars? The Trivial Pursuit of the Presidency 1988*, New York: Warner, 1989.

Goldberg, Vicki, with the White House Historical Association, *The White House: The President's Home in Photographs and History*, New York: Little, Brown & Co., 2011.

Goldman, Peter, and Tom Mathews, *The Quest for the Presidency 1988*, New York: Simon & Schuster/Touchstone, 1989.

Goodwin, Doris Kearns, *No Ordinary Time: Franklin and Eleanor Roosevelt: The Home Front in World War II*, New York: Simon & Schuster, 1994.

Greenberg, David. *Republic of Spin: An Inside History of the American Presidency*, New York: W.W. Norton & Co., 2016.

Healy, Gene, *The Cult of the Presidency: America's Dangerous Devotion to Executive Power*, Washington. D.C.: Cato Institute, 2008.

Heilemann, John, and Mark Halperin, *Game Change: Obama and the Clintons, McCain and Palin, and the Race of a Lifetime*, New York: HarperCollins, 2010.

Holzer, Harold, *Lincoln at Cooper Union: The Speech that made Abraham Lincoln President*, New York: Simon & Schuster Paperbacks, 2004.

Inglis, Fred, *A Short History of Celebrity*, Princeton, N.J.: Princeton University Press, 2010.

Jamieson, Kathleen Hall, *Packaging the Presidency: A History and Criticism of Presidential Campaign Advertising*, New York: Oxford University Press, 1992.

Jeffries, Ona Griffin, *In and Out of the White House: From Washington to the Eisenhowers*, New York: Wilfred Funk, Inc., 1960.

Kantor, Jodi, *The Obamas*, New York: Little Brown, 2012.

Kelley, Kitty, *Capturing Camelot: Stanley Tretick's Iconic Images of the Kennedys*, New York: Thomas Dunne/St. Martin's Press, 2012.

Kennerly, David Hume, *Extraordinary Circumstances: The Presidency of Gerald R. Ford*, Austin: Briscoe Center for American History, 2007.

Klein, Edward, *Blood Feud: The Clintons vs. the Obamas*, Washington, D.C.: Regnery Publishing, 2014.

Kuhn, Jim, *Ronald Reagan in Private: A Memoir of My Years in the White House*, New York: Sentinel, 2004.

Kumar, Martha Joynt, *Managing the President's Message: The White House Communications Operation*, Baltimore, Md.: Johns Hopkins University Press, 2007.

Lederer, Richard, *Presidential Trivia*, Salt Lake City, Utah: Gibbs Smith, 2007.

Lindlop, Edmund, and Joseph Jares, *White House Sportsmen*, Boston: Houghton Mifflin Company, 1964.

Lowe, Jacques, *The Kennedy Years: A Memoir*, New York: Rizzoli, 2013.

Luntz, Frank, *Words that Work: It's not What You Say, It's What People Hear*, New York: Hyperion, 2007.

Lynes, Russell, *The Tastemakers: The Shaping of American Popular Taste*, New York: Dover Publications, Inc., 1980.

McCullough, David, *Truman*, New York: Simon & Schuster, 1992.

McNeely, Robert, *The Clinton Years: The Photographs of Robert McNeely*, New York: Callaway, 2000.

Maraniss, David, *First in His Class: A Biography of Bill Clinton*, New York: Simon & Schuster, 1995.

Maroon, Fred J., with Tom Wicker, *The Nixon Years 1969–1974: White House to Watergate*, New York: Abbeville Press, 1999.

Matviko, John W., ed., *The American President in Popular Culture*, Westport, Conn.: Greenwood Press, 2005.

Monkman, Betty C., *The White House: Its Historic Furnishings and First Families*, New York: Abbeville Press, 2014.

Morris, Dick, *Behind the Oval Office: Winning the Presidency in the Nineties*, New York: Random House, 1997.

Mundy, Liza, *Michelle: A Biography*, New York: Simon & Schuster, 2008.

Nardo, Don, *Assassination and Its Aftermath: How a Photograph Reassured a Shocked Nation*, North Mankato, Minn., Compass Point Books, 2014.

Nixon, Richard, *In the Arena: A Memoir of Victory, Defeat, and Renewal*, New York: Simon & Schuster, 1990.

Obama, Barack, *Dreams from My Father: A Story of Race and Inheritance*, New York: Crown, 2007.

Patterson, Thomas E., *Out of Order*, New York: Knopf, 1993.

Perlstein, Rick, *Nixonland: The Rise of a President and the Fracturing of America*, New York: Scribner, 2008.

Perry, Barbara A., *Jacqueline Kennedy: First Lady of the New Frontier*, Lawrence: University of Kansas Press, 2004.

Pollard, James E., *The Presidents and the Press*, New York: Macmillan, 1947.

Popadiuk, Roman, *The Leadership of George Bush: An Insider's View of the Forty-First President*, College Station: Texas A&M University Press, 2009.

Reagan, Nancy, with William Novak, *My Turn: The Memoirs of Nancy Reagan*, New York: Random House, 1989.

Reagan, Ronald, *Ronald Reagan: An American Life*, New York: Simon & Schuster, 1990.

Reedy, George E., *The Twilight of the Presidency*, Cleveland, Ohio, and New York: New American Library/World Publishing Company, 1970.

Reeves, Richard, *Portrait of Camelot: A Thousand Days in the Kennedy White House*, New York: Abrams, 2010.

—— *President Kennedy: Profile of Power*, New York: Touchstone/Simon & Schuster, 1993.

Rhodan, Maya, ed., *Time, Inside the White House: The History, Secrets and Style of the World's Most Famous Home*, New York: Time Books, 2016.

Rollins, Peter C., and John E. O'Connor, eds., *Hollywood's White House: The American Presidency in Film and History*, Lexington: University Press of Kentucky, 2003.

Rowell, Charles Henry, "Sharon Farmer", *Callaloo: A Journal of African Diaspora Arts and Letters*, vol. 38, no 4 (2016), p. 823.

Sabato, Larry, *Feeding Frenzy: How Attack Journalism has Transformed American Politics*, New York: Free Press/Macmillan, 1991.

Schroeder, Alan, *Celebrity-in-Chief: How Show Business Took Over the White House*, Boulder, Colo: Westview Press, 2004.

Schweizer, Peter, and Rochelle Schweizer, *The Bushes: Portrait of a Dynasty*, New York: Doubleday, 2004.

Skinner, Kiron K., Annelise Anderson, and Martin Anderson, *Reagan: In his Own Hand*, New York: Free Press, 2001.

Smith, Hedrick, *The Power Game*, New York: Ballantine, 1988.

Sorensen, Theodore C., *Kennedy*, New York: Harper & Row, 1965.

Souza, Pete, *Images of Greatness: An Intimate Look at the Presidency of Ronald Reagan*, Chicago: Triumph Books, 2004.

Stephanopoulos, George, *All Too Human: A Political Education*, Boston: Little, Brown, 1999.

Stoughton, Cecil, and Chester V. Clifton, *The Memories: JFK, 1961–1963*, New York: W.W. Norton & Company, 1973.

Tames, George, *Eye on Washington: The Presidents Who've Known Me*, New York: HarperCollins Publishers, 1990.

Taylor, Tim, *The Book of Presidents*, New York: Arno Press, 1972.

Tebbel, John, and Sarah Miles Watts, *The Press and the Presidency, from George Washington to Ronald Reagan*, New York: Oxford University Press, 1985.

Troy, Tevi, *What Jefferson Read, Ike Watched, and Obama Tweeted: 200 Years of Popular Culture in the White House*, Washington, D.C.: Regnery Publishing, 2013.

Truman, Margaret, *Harry S. Truman*, New York: William Morrow & Company, 1973.

Valdez, David, *George Herbert Walker Bush: A Photographic Profile*, College Station: Texas A&M University Press, 1997.

Van Natta, Don, Jr., *First off the Tee: Presidential Hackers, Duffers, and Cheaters from Taft to Bush*, New York: Public Affairs, 2003.

Walsh, Kenneth T., *Celebrity in Chief: A History of the Presidents and the Culture of Stardom*, New York: Routledge, 2016.

—— *Family of Freedom: Presidents and African Americans in the White House*, New York: Routledge, 2011.

—— *Feeding the Beast: The White House Versus the Press*, New York: Random House, 1996.

—— *From Mount Vernon to Crawford: A History of the Presidents and Their Retreats*. New York: Hyperion, 2005.

—— *Prisoners of the White House: The Isolation of America's Presidents and the Crisis of Leadership*, Boulder, Colo.: Paradigm, 2013; New York: Routledge, 2016.

—— *Ronald Reagan: Biography*, New York: Park Lane Press, 1997.

Watterson, John Sayle, *The Games Presidents Play: Sports and the Presidency*, Baltimore, Md.: Johns Hopkins University Press, 2006.

Winfield, Betty Houchin, *FDR and the News Media*, New York: Columbia University Press, 1994.

Woodward, Bob, *The Agenda*, New York: Simon & Schuster, 1994.

—— *The Choice*, New York: Simon & Schuster, 1996.

INDEX